PRAISE

KISS ME, SWAMI

"*Kiss Me, Swami* is an eye-opening, heart-warming and mind-blowing memoir by a gifted writer whose exotic life story sometimes reads like a novel but is always full of wisdom, humor, and surprise."

—JONATHAN KIRSCH, book critic and author of *The Short, Strange Life of Herschel Grynszpan: A Boy Avenger, a Nazi Diplomat and a Murder in Paris* (W. W. Norton/Liveright)

"Engaging, brutally honest, and laugh-out-loud hilarious! Kathalynn Turner Davis' *Kiss Me, Swami* takes us through some of the most exciting events of the latter half of the twentieth century with raw candor, razor sharp wit and mind-blowing insights. A unique story of a woman's quest for genuine fulfillment, Kathalynn opens up about the challenges she faced and shares with us the spiritual tools that got her through them all. A must read."

—HALE DWOSKIN, International Speaker, Author, and Co-founder of Sedona Training Associates

"Kathalynn Turner Davis' book, *Kiss Me, Swami*, should be on the top of every reading list for anyone who has ever had a difficult journey, which pretty much covers everyone on the planet! It's a joyous but reflective tale that shows how getting in touch with introspection and self-knowledge can alter your life in positive ways you have only been able to dream about.

"I loved every minute of reading it, and found her humor on her spiritual adventures to be unmatched by any book I have read in the last ten years. Run don't walk to buy a copy!"

—EMILY WACHTEL, Producer, Writer

KISS ME, SWAMI

KISS ME, SWAMI

THE SPIRITUAL EDUCATION
OF A BEAUTY QUEEN

Kathalynn Turner Davis

with

Genevieve Joy

SILVER FALCON PRESS

Silver Falcon Press
311 N. Robertson Blvd., #135
Beverly Hills, CA 90211
www.silverfalconpress.com

Kiss Me, Swami: The Spiritual Education of a Beauty Queen is a trademark of the author and is used by the publisher with permission.

Ordering Information
Quantity sales. Special discounts are available on quantity purchases by corporations, associations, and others. For details, contact the "Special Sales Department" at the address above.

Printed in the United States of America

Cataloging-in-Publication Data

ISBN: 978-1-7338407-0-5 (pb)
        978-1-7338407-1-2 (ebook)

First Edition

23 22 21 20 19   10 9 8 7 6 5 4 3 2 1

Cover design: Michi Turner
Back cover photo: Peter Hurley
Frontispiece: Barbara Mendes

To my past generation,
present family,
and future generations

Author's Note

· ·

All incidents and dialogue in this book are described to the best of my recollection, although neither my mind nor my recall is perfect. Still, I feel strongly that I owe the reader the truth as much as I owe it to myself, and the experiences I share are real. Self-examination is not always easy, but the truth, as we have learned, can set us free. That said, the names Mac Harris, Brad England, Bob Edwards, and Jas Madison are fictional.

Our job is not to deny the story, but to defy the ending—to rise strong, recognize our story, and rumble with the truth until we get to a place where we think, Yes. This is what happened. This is my truth. And I will choose how the story ends.

—BRENÉ BROWN, *Rising Strong*

Contents

....

Part III I'll Take Manhattan

Part IV Greenwich: A World Apart

Destiny or Choice?

....

*E*arly in life I made wishes upon stars, setting the course for what would become my destiny. Every night before I fell asleep, my ritual began with *Star light, star bright, first star I see tonight,* and I'd wish upon the first star I saw. On cloudy, starless nights I'd close my eyes and imagine a single bright, twinkling star. I'd lie back and transport myself to an elegant, exciting world where I was surrounded by everything missing in my present one. I saw myself living in a large, finely decorated home with an adoring husband and beautiful children. I was an actress in Hollywood, acting in movies and television and traveling the world. I even saw myself kissing Elvis Presley (I kissed Elvis a lot in those dreams). There were no limits on these flights of imagination.

I couldn't have put my finger on it at the time, but there was always something eerily undreamlike about these transports; they often felt more real to me than my current, more tangible world did. I started to see them as little windows into my future rather than unlikely fantasies. Of course, not everyone agreed.

In third grade, I was given an assignment to write a few sentences on how I saw my future. *I will be an actress in Hollywood,* I wrote, *and one day have a million dollars. I will drive a convertible, and I will have five children.* I didn't even put in the part about Elvis, and I still got a check minus (which equaled an F), with the comment, "Come back to reality and we can make real plans." I brought my failing grade home to my mother. She framed it.

I am as susceptible to fear and doubt as the next person. My belief in myself and my potential was continually at war with my many insecurities, and those insecurities won their share of battles. But overall, my life

1

has turned out to uncannily reflect those early, persistent wishes. Every night, as I left behind the world of limitation and turned my focus to the vast, boundless sky, I seemed to be sealing a kind of resolve with the universe. Because of the certainty behind those wishes, they stayed lodged in my subconscious and became the intentions behind my actions.

Like those of typical Anglo-Saxon Americans, my home was culturally Christian. But, before I was old enough to grasp the significance of spiritual images, I became enamored with a picture of Buddha, a jovial religious figure who was surrounded by laughing children, in contrast to the familiar sad and somber countenance of Jesus dying on the cross. There seemed to be a lack of joy in Christian religious imagery—not that Jesus had much to laugh about. I quickly lost interest in church, and later, as I plunged into my theological education, it was no surprise that I was immediately drawn to the bliss and simplicity of Eastern philosophies.

I never planned on going to India. I had no desire to live in an ashram or surrender myself to a guru or step away from the comforts and pleasures of the material world. Yet I always had a strong feeling that I'd find myself there someday. I imagined India to be a mystic paradise, full of magic. And India did not disappoint.

One ordinary summer morning in 2010, I woke up to a nagging feeling that would not let go. Being a double Scorpio, I think best in water, so I jumped into the pool for a swim, and as I came up for air a voice within said, *Go to India; it's time.*

I have learned from experience that when intuition speaks, it's best to listen; what comes from the gut outreaches what the limited mind can see or plan. I abandoned my swim, showered, and ate some breakfast, and by 9:00 a.m. I was on the phone with a travel agent arranging the adventure of a lifetime.

I arrived in Delhi a month later. When the plane touched ground and the captain said, "Welcome to India, and for many of you, welcome home," I felt as if he was talking directly to me, as though I was coming home, but for the first time. Because this trip was to be focused on spiritual discovery, I opted to avoid the hustle-bustle tours and hired a private guide, who greeted me as soon as I disembarked and led me to baggage claim, and after retrieving my (far too many) bags, we made our way to the car awaiting nearby.

Excited to be in this magical land, I immediately loved everything— even the heat others described as sweltering felt to me like a loving embrace. I didn't see one road sign or traffic light on the ride from the airport to the hotel, and my God, if there was a speed limit, our driver was over it. I said a quiet prayer, affirmed that I was divinely protected, and thanked God I had reviewed my will before I left.

Out of the window I saw swarms of people rushing this way and that, moving aside only if one of their sacred cows needed to pass. (The Indian people's reverence for cows would so affect me on this trip that I would never eat steak again.) Miraculously, we arrived at the hotel in one piece. I checked in, thinking I'd nap or at least lie down, but my body was tingling with too much excitement to submit to jet lag, I arranged to have an extra tour of that astonishing city, which successfully combines the ancient and modern world in a way that only India can.

Unlike what I'd brought to my other adventures abroad, I had no expectation or plan, I kept myself open and I trusted the universe to guide me. I soon set out for the northern parts of the country, finding particular enchantment in ancient Varanasi on the banks of the Ganges River, through which flows India's sacred water. Dating from the 11th century BC, Varanasi is one of the world's oldest inhabited cities and considered one of the holiest in India. Right on the outskirts of Varanasi, in Deer Park, is where the Buddha delivered his first sermon, circa 538 BC.

After walking around for a while, I was compelled to sit down on the grass outside of the square and meditate, a compulsion I do not get very often. I opened my eyes and discovered that a group of young monks in orange robes with beads hanging from their necks had gathered around and joined me.

Varanasi is a carnival for the senses. Ladies bustled around the marketplace in colorful saris, one more vibrant than the next. The trinkets in each little shop glittered like exotic treasures. As I meandered through the crowds, I breathed in a cocktail of sandalwood, curry, body odor, and cow dung, all enhanced by the oppressive heat, which was somehow not the least bit as terrible as it should have been.

At one point I ambled into a shop and was confronted by a bull—an actual bull—who had, I guessed, taken it upon himself to wander in from the heat and plop on the floor. No one seemed to notice but me; everyone else just stepped around him and carried on with shopping. I always thought "bull in a china shop" was just an expression. Well, not in India.

The peaceful attitudes of those people living in abject poverty filled me with mixed emotions. Little children without shoes and dressed in dirty rags who looked up at me with soulful brown eyes and stretched out their tiny hands for money, and still had smiles on their faces. Elderly people literally dying on the street provoked no concern or aid from passersby. A group of men walking single file, arms over their heads, carried bodies wrapped in rags, corpses en route to cremation. My guide explained that the old and infirm flocked to Varanasi because to die there would enrich their karma next time around.

It was easy to get distracted by the rich and varied buffet of life before me. There was so much to see, touch, and inhale. Without realizing it, I'd separated from my guide and come upon a staircase of fractured white marble steps that didn't look as though they led anywhere significant. I ascended the steps and when I reached the top, a man slight in stature and dressed in a loincloth stopped me and, sensing that I was American, summoned a translator who commanded in broken English that I state my business. I had wandered into a private ashram. Oops.

"I'm Kathalynn," I said. "I'd like to see your guru."

The man stared at me as though I'd said, "I'm Dorothy, here to meet the great wizard of Oz."

His eyes widened and a scowl creased his forehead. He turned away and consulted with a colleague.

"People don't just walk in here and see the Master," he said. "But my friend thinks he likes you. I will speak to the Master. Come back at eight o'clock."

I was so excited that I was going to meet the wizard—oops, I mean the Master—that I almost tripped down the broken marble staircase. There at the bottom, I caught sight of my guide, who had been losing his mind trying to find me. Noting where I was coming from, he became apoplectic. "You can't go up there!" he shouted, urging me to get back before anyone caught me.

I told him we would have to hang around for a while because I had an appointment with the wizard—uh, Master—at eight.

When eight finally rolled around, my new friend, the little guy in the loincloth, met me at the entrance and escorted me into his master's home.

The Master resembled a storybook image of God, the only difference being that he was seated on the floor and not a cloud. He had a long white beard, a gentle smile, and eyes full of wisdom as though they saw all.

I looked about the space, and except for a small shrine in the center the room was bare of decor. I joined the guru on the floor, and a man whose forehead was painted bright yellow with a red dot between his eyebrows served us a series of unidentifiable, delicious dishes. After the meal, the Master turned to me and asked why I had come to him.

On the spot, I asked the first question that came to mind: "In this life, is there destiny, or do we have choice?"

He looked at me closely as I prepared myself for the profound response sure to issue from his holy lips.

"It depends!" he said.

"What?"

"It depends!" he repeated.

And suddenly we burst simultaneously into fits of laughter. Our laughter spread through the group, breaking the language barrier. When I finally calmed down and could breathe again, the significance of that seemingly silly answer took hold. My entire life began to make sense in those two words: *It depends*. I started to see where my life had consisted of clusters of moments both painful and blissful and how it did in fact all *depend*—sometimes on my choices, sometimes on the force of a power that placed me in the right places at the most perfect times.

PART I

How It Begins:
Pageants and Parents

· ·

There is a great deal of truth, I dare say, in what
you said, and you looked very pretty while you said it, which is
much more important.

—OSCAR WILDE, *A Woman of No Importance*

CHAPTER 1

Girl on Her Way

....

As an excited and ambitious youth, I left my home in Maryland and set out for the foreign climes of Los Angeles. It was the morning of April 6, 1968. Winter had just edged away from Maryland and the leaves were not yet on the trees. I was twenty years old. My mother and father drove me to the airport in their copper-colored Oldsmobile. I would be boarding a plane for the very first time.

There I was, sitting in the backseat in my fashionable black-and-white suit and black pumps. My hair was long and very dark, my eyes a deep blue, and at five-feet-four I weighed 102 pounds. I carried a vinyl pocketbook and next to me was stowed the Samsonite luggage Dad had given me for my trip.

At one point during the drive, Dad turned to me and, breaking his typical silence, said, "You know, Katie, you'll never be back here to live. You're going to get discovered in Hollywood."

I caught my mother's eye and the two of us broke into fits of laughter.

I had no plan for California, as it wasn't a real place to me then. California was merely a sound in my mind, the song "Sealed with a Kiss," and the singer Brian Hyland.

My radical move was prompted by my crazy teenage crush on Brian, who'd shown up in my life for a moment and then was gone like the mist of a dream. In my naïveté, I imagined myself the princess in some fairy tale, and he my teen-idol Prince Charming. I assumed if I found my way to California he'd fall in love with me, marry me, and drive me off to our home in the Hollywood Hills, where we would live happily ever after.

And so I left home to go to L.A. Why? Because that's where Brian was. Love may have been what drove me there, but it was magic and mayhem that awaited.

CHAPTER 2

Flimsy Family Foundation

....

I wanted to be my cousin Marie. She was perfect: blond hair, blue eyes, dimples, like one of those expensive dolls you aren't supposed to take out of the case. Her sister, Sharon, was a close second. I would have settled for being either of them. When we all grew up I imagined Marie would look just like Cinderella and Sharon would be Sleeping Beauty—after the prince wakes her up, of course. As for me? Maybe I could be Snow White. Oh wait, no; Snow White wasn't chubby, was she? If I ever got into a fairytale, it was going to be in a supporting role (if only one of the dwarfs was a girl). I imagined the kids at school made fun of me behind my back, pointing and chanting, "Fatty, fatty, two by four," because that's the way I saw myself. And as if that weren't enough, I was also sickly.

There are few places more depressing than the children's ward at Bethesda Naval Hospital. I was a frequent visitor there due to a chronic bronchial condition that plagued me for much of my childhood.

One night when I was about six, my fever spiked to 105 and my parents rushed me to the ER where I was immediately hospitalized and submerged in a tub full of ice then confined to an oxygen tent. This medical issue eventually resolved itself, but I attribute much of what's motivated me in my adult life to what I experienced in that hospital.

Late one night during one of my longer stays, I was awakened by the sound of a child crying in agony. This girl, my new roommate, had just come from intensive care, where she was being treated for third-degree burns. She'd been playing with matches and her dress caught on fire. Fortunately, her face wasn't destroyed in the accident, but her body would be scarred for life.

The horror of her situation elicited a great deal of sympathy, which came in the form of toys and gifts that she was kind enough to share with me. She never complained; only occasionally at night did I hear her groan in her sleep from what must have been excruciating pain. On the day I was released, she said goodbye and gave me the paper doll set we had played with together.

On another visit I was entertaining myself by running wildly through the hospital corridors when I was stopped in my tracks by a sight that would sear itself in my mind forever: There was a woman cradling her very thin, nearly bald child in her arms. As she stroked the white fuzz barely covering the child's head, the mother repeated over and over, "My beautiful baby, my beautiful baby with beautiful blond hair and big blue eyes."

It was clear to me, even at six, that this child was dying. I had never seen such love or such suffering in the face of another human. I hardly knew what to make of it.

People have often asked why, later in life, I became a social worker and a psychotherapist. They expect me to tell them it was because of my family, but truly it was from the sight of this mother and her child. I wanted to help those who suffered mentally and emotionally as would this woman, no doubt, for the rest of her life.

It was hard going back to school after seeing such tragedy. I was no longer carefree like other children my age, having glimpsed what they hadn't, and now knowing something they didn't. It made me feel separate. My time in the hospital set me back in my schoolwork, and I was lost academically as well as socially. On my first day back, two girls who used to be my friends came through the door hand-in-hand, bursting right past me to show off their matching dresses, shouting, "Mrs. Brett! Mrs. Brett! We're twins."

Of course, Mrs. Brett, our teacher, adored them.

"Oh, girls! Spin around!"

Even if I had had a dress like that it probably would have looked awful on me. Moreover, although I was well enough to be out of the hospital and back in the classroom, my lungs still clogged up regularly, necessitating constant runs to the bathroom so I could cough something up. Since the bathroom was adjacent to the classroom, every cough could be heard loud and clear. Humiliated, I'd return to my seat as silently as possible, feeling disgusting, like an infected monster. Then I would stare out the window, not daring to make eye contact with anyone, and I'd let my daydreams take me somewhere else.

I also felt I was not smart enough. Falling behind in school from being absent so much due to illness only made matters worse. I wasn't stupid, but I'd sit there in class after weeks out of school with the lessons flying over my head. I became frustrated and lost interest. Only in my forties would I muster the courage to go back to school and reclaim the education I'd denied myself out of sheer insecurity.

It wasn't until one night in 1957, the night Mary Ann Mobley was crowned Miss America, that I began to wonder if perhaps I was wrong about myself.

I was on my way into the kitchen for an after-dinner snack that my chubby self probably shouldn't have been having. My father was lying in his usual spot on the floor (his preferred place, for reasons we'll never know). Focused on my mission, I was about to step right over him when he said, "Hey, sit down and watch this with me."

Always eager to hang out with my dad, I forgot about my appetite and plopped down in the cozy recliner to watch on our little black-and-white RCA Victor television, as Miss Mobley took her victory walk down the runway to the strains of *"There she is . . . Miss America."* She was mesmerizing—the whole thing was mesmerizing.

After the program ended, my father looked up at me from the floor. "What do you think? Do you want to be Miss America?" He said it so casually, as though he was asking if I wanted a sandwich for lunch.

"Of course I want to be Miss America, but those girls are beautiful."

"Katie, you're beautiful too! If you want to be in a pageant, you will, and you'll win."

"No, no, no." I shook my head. "Daddy! I'm ugly and fat!"

"You are certainly not ugly or fat. You're a little small, so drink your milk and you can have it."

Drink my milk and I can be Miss America? It seemed a little far-fetched, but what did I know? Besides, this was coming from my father, who I'd never known to be wrong. "Okay then," I agreed, "I'll drink my milk." And just like that, the course of my life changed forever. I didn't go on to become Miss America, but I got close. Of course, that was later.

It wasn't just my cousins' perfect hair and faces that I envied, it was pretty much everything else too. Their home felt like the set of a wholesome '50s romantic comedy, starring Aunt Margie and Uncle Bob as Doris Day and Rock Hudson. Like Doris and Rock, their dysfunction was well concealed.

Uncle Bob paraded Marie and Sharon around town in a pristine white Chrysler convertible, while my daddy shuffled us from point A to point B in an Oldsmobile the color of dirty pennies. If Joe Turner had been a car, he would have been that Oldsmobile. Durable, reliable, and plain.

My father's given name was Edward, but to call him Edward would be like naming a Rottweiler Fluffy. He was Joe, through and through: an officer in the United States Navy and all that implies. He had been the lightweight champion boxer of the navy, and my mother told me he could never get into a fistfight because his hands were registered and considered a weapon. Every Friday night he would make me a salami sandwich and sit me down in front of our television to watch the Friday night fights. He'd nurse a beer and I'd drink as many Cokes as I wanted.

Joe was neither sentimental nor romantic. He approached everything—from the way he ate to the way he slept to the way he loved—with military precision. He didn't subscribe to any spiritual practice, but he was good at living in the moment, day to day. He was a simple and straightforward man, who never took advantage of anyone.

My father had problems expressing his feelings; he rarely laughed or smiled and never once said to me, "I love you," but he was as devoted to me as a father can be to a child, and I adored him. During his fighting years his nose had been broken several times, but he was still gorgeous. With his blue eyes and sandy blond hair, he looked like a cross between Paul Newman and Spencer Tracy. He dressed sharply and maintained the same weight his entire life. People used to say, "The man never ages." He'd won the lottery in the genetics department.

My mother was the opposite of my father, except for looks. And though she was beautiful and statuesque, a true Irish beauty, between the pills, cigarettes, booze, and excessive sunbathing, she lost her looks early. To quote my granddaughter Kylie's favorite pop star, Taylor Swift, my mother, Louise, was "a nightmare dressed as a daydream." She had a beautiful voice and would sing to me all the time, anything from Irish lullabies to Mario Lanza songs (she had a thing for Mario Lanza).

She was often drunk from the time I was about five until I was eleven. That was the year she fell into the Christmas tree in full view of our entire extended family, including Margie and Bob. Eventually she did stop drinking and switched out booze for prescription drugs. They helped alleviate the inner turmoil with side effects that made her problem a little less obvious but certainly no less damaging in the long run.

One morning when I was in kindergarten, I woke up and saw my mother standing over my tiny bed, still drunk from the night before. Holding a filthy and wrinkled dress, she told me to put it on. "Mommy," I said, "I can't wear that! It's not clean or ironed."

My mother looked at me as though she didn't understand. "It's not that dirty."

Not *that* dirty? I wouldn't go to school until the dress was put to rights. Even at the age of five, I did not want other kids knowing I had a mother who couldn't keep it together enough to wash and iron her child's clothes. But that was more than she could manage at the time, and it conveyed to me that when it came to the kind of mom other kids had, I was out of luck. It's no wonder when I wished upon a star I imagined myself in beautiful clothing.

Children with alcoholics for parents cannot help being affected, and I was no exception. I felt devastated by my mother's erratic behavior, completely unable to comprehend why, for example, she would rather be drunk than come see me in the hospital when I was ill.

When I picture my mother, I still imagine her flaming red hair and huge breasts that I sadly did not inherit. She always had a cup of coffee in one hand and a Salem cigarette in the other (especially when my father wasn't around), laughing wildly at something inappropriate while quipping as she smoked, "Don't inhale 'em, Salem."

I loved and idolized my mother but simultaneously resented her for her drinking, and this shifted something in me. As I lost respect for her, she in turn lost any power or real authority she had over me, and this persisted even after she stopped drinking, when I was eleven. By then my attitude toward her had become fixed, and it would take many years and a great deal of spiritual growth before I could see her more compassionately as a loving if complicated human being.

Being so young, I was confused, as any child would be. Back in those days, alcoholism was not considered a disease but rather a weakness and a choice. I became Daddy's girl. At the same time, Daddy couldn't be there all the time; he had to work.

I learned to take care of myself, to dress myself and get my own meals. I shut down my emotions as a survival mechanism to protect my hypersensitive heart, and though this served me well at the time, it would take years to get back in touch with those emotions and open up to allow myself to become vulnerable. I managed, but I did it feeling worthless, filled with guilt and shame. And the beliefs I formed, based on faulty concepts of myself, would cripple me to some degree for years to come.

In all this, I felt a great responsibility to make up for my mother's lapses and promised myself to never disappoint my father. This was a huge responsibility for a child, but I was determined to fulfill that promise.

Later I came to understand that my mother was the real victim, not me.

The eldest of eight in a Depression-era Irish family, she had no education and few options. Her father had been on the vaudeville circuit, and I am told that he had a beautiful voice and was a fabulous dancer. Gone most of the time, he never provided much income for my grandmother, who divorced him when my mother was around three years old, claiming he was just a no-good actor and dancer who would never get a real job. Later my grandmother married John Page (who was not all that much more reliable) and had seven children with him. She died tragically at the age of forty-two, when gauze left inside her after routine gall bladder surgery became infected. All eight children were suddenly motherless, the youngest only two years old, with the older children left to take care of the younger ones.

My mother had no real self-confidence, despite the fact that she was quite beautiful. My father, then a navy officer, fell for her the moment he laid eyes on her. He wined and dined her and helped out a little financially with her siblings. She became dependent on him and felt he was the best she could do. So she married him.

One day I overheard her telling my aunt that she was terribly lonely and unhappy. She felt abandoned by my father's lack of affection and sexual interest in her. I don't remember him ever kissing her or showing any kind of affection toward her. I could never understand their complex dynamic, though through the years he was clearly loyal and devoted to her, and as far as I know he never pursued other women.

There was something in my father that seemed to reject pleasure of any kind. It was as though laughter stirred up something deep inside him that he didn't want disturbed, the way pouring fresh water into a stagnant puddle stirs up settled mire.

Despite her drinking, mother was tolerant, loving, and kind. She clearly was suffering alone. Even if professional help had been available, I don't think it would have occurred to her to seek it. And so, to quiet those "blue devils,"' as Tennessee Williams would call them in *The Night of the Iguana,* she sedated herself.

My one sibling, Donald, was eight years older than I was. I hardly saw him, much less knew him. Handsome, funny, nice—there was nothing not to like about Donald, except for the fact that he was a liar and a criminal. My first real memory of Donald is the time my mother had to go to court because he'd been caught stealing hubcaps. He also stole from us.

After the Miss America conversation that night with my father, I took up baton twirling and began entering local, state, and national competitions, along with talent events and beauty contests. When I won, I'd bring home trophies, or sometimes a radio, tape recorder, or even a TV.

One day I came home from school and found them all missing from my room. I ran to ask my mother where my things were. She didn't have to say anything—that "Donald's been at it again" look was all over her face. My mother was constantly making excuses and allowances for him, while my father took the opposite tack, which only exacerbated the tension between them. Donald, meanwhile, adored my mother, who always insisted he wasn't bad, merely "troubled."

Genuinely hating to see her upset, Donald reluctantly agreed to submit to a psychiatric evaluation. My father refused to take him, so my Uncle Pike, my mother's brother, who lived down the street, volunteered. When the nurse came into the waiting room and called out, "Donald Turner?" My brother jumped up and pointed at Pike. "Here he is! This is Donald!"

My uncle, horrified, stood up and asserted, "I am not Donald! This is Donald!" Slightly shaken, Pike then reached into his pocket for identification, and to his mortification discovered that Donald, at some point in that waiting room, had switched their wallets.

"He is very upset at having to be here," Donald explained to the nurses reasonably. "He gets this way—you may need to give him a sedative."

With that, Uncle Pike was whisked away and locked in a ward overnight, while Donald drove Pike's car to a hotel and charged hundreds of dollars in room service on his credit card. When the whole mess was finally sorted out, Pike stormed into our house and told my mother what her son had done. She erupted into gales of laughter. "Well, that's Donald!" Uncle Pike, for some reason, failed to see the humor.

Donald disappeared later in life, and none of us ever knew what happened to him. The one great thing he did do was leave behind a beautiful, smart, loving, and kind daughter, Michi Louise. She is one of the joys of my life and is now a mother of two adorable children.

As I mentioned before, my mother stopped drinking when I was eleven. There was no giant event or dramatization around it; she just stopped. From that day on, everything changed. Free of that addiction, she threw herself into being my mother one-hundred percent and did everything she could to make up for lost time. Years later, I asked how she was able to quit like that without help. She told me that one night, after an especially bad day of being sick from drinking, she was feeling disgusted with herself and afraid for her life. She got on her knees and asked God to help her stop drinking. The next morning, when she woke up, all desire was gone. Though she continued to abuse her body with tranquilizers and cigarettes, she never touched a drop of liquor again for the rest of her life.

CHAPTER 3

Pageant Prep

. . . .

*I*n hindsight, it makes perfect sense that from the moment I experienced the Miss America pageant with my father that September evening when I was eleven years old, my course was set. But if I was going to be Miss America, I was going to have to make some adjustments.

First and foremost, I needed to develop some sort of talent. A playmate down the block had just taken up baton lessons. Inspired, I ran home to my father and begged him to let me take lessons too. He agreed, and the following week I accompanied my friend to Miss Mary Lou Brookbank's baton class at the local ballet studio.

I knew nothing about the art of twirling, but once that baton was in my hand, it felt like an extension of my body. I worked tirelessly at baton twirling and quickly started qualifying for competitions. At one of my first events I took home three first-place trophies and two second-place medals.

My father looked at the second-place medals and said, "What happened here?"

As far as my dad, Joe Turner, was concerned, second place equaled first loser. He encouraged me to be my best, and the harder he was to please, the harder I would try. As I mentioned, the rest of my family seemed to disappoint my father so much, I felt it was on me to make him proud. If that meant taking first place every time, I'd do my best to make that happen.

A double message began to form. I felt hopeful and hopeless at the same time, creating a kind of jam-up that impeded progress. Fortunately, something was beginning to drive me besides the need to win and please my father, and that was the part that just wanted to twirl and perform. I got lost in twirling, my mind focusing on one thing and one thing only. The routines, difficult and demanding, forced me to concentrate and be in the moment, out of my head and away from my problems. And those times when I was simply in the flow were blissful.

I would practice three or four evenings a week with my team, and then on weekends when we were not competing, we practiced some more. There was no room to be a normal teenager, no time for parties or studies or dating. But I didn't much care; my interest in performing and ambition to be the best and to win far outweighed getting great grades and dating boys.

There was a satisfaction in winning competitions, but only on one occasion do I ever remember it filling me with real joy. In the state championship I had finished my routine in what was referred to as Fancy Strutting, a combination of baton twirling and dance. I was competing against more contestants than I ever had before.

When I finished my routine for the judges, I was exhausted and sat on the bleachers to watch the other girls compete. Most of them were excellent, which made the competition that much more intense. Noting how good each one was, I felt proud just be part of the line up. I let go of my need to beat them all out and felt oddly at peace. I didn't care if I won or not. I knew I'd done my best. At the end of the day, when they called out the runners-up, I thought I hadn't even placed.

Then I heard, "First place goes to Kathalynn Turner, our new Maryland state champion!"

As I walked to the stage to receive my trophy, I cried sudden, unexpected tears of joy. Along with the trophy they gave me my score sheet: "Excellent!" "Very striking appearance!" "Very talented young girl!" I kept that score sheet for years.

I performed for retirement centers (which we called old folks' homes) and hospitals. The patients would clap and smile; it was thrilling for them when I tossed my baton. I didn't need to be a gold medalist to make people happy. We also made the rounds of mental hospitals, where the patients constantly tried to touch me. I didn't mind. I understood that these people were not well and felt compassion for them, as well as gratitude for the opportunity to lighten their experience, even if it was just for a little while. That was enough reward.

To further refine myself, I enrolled in the Patricia Stevens Finishing School in Washington, DC. There, the beautiful Miss McKay oversaw grooming young ladies for participation in beauty pageants. We learned the pageant walk—one foot in front of the other, feet slightly turned out, arms moving slowly back and forth in unison. We learned to sit with ankles (never legs) crossed demurely, poised slightly left. We were drilled on table etiquette: of the two forks in the setting, the outer for salad, the inner for the main course. Also, a lady never puts her elbows on the table and, after cutting her food, she is to rest her left hand lightly in her lap while she eats.

Miss McKay, like my father, seemed to believe I could pull this off. I was grateful for her support even if I was too full of doubt to entirely believe her.

My father drove me to and from those classes. One evening, a girl from class asked if my dad would mind dropping her off at work, since her car was in the shop. He said yes, of course, but the address we pulled up to looked like an abandoned warehouse. She thanked my father for the ride and invited us in for a drink. To my surprise, my father gladly accepted.

As we walked in, the combination smell of beer, cologne, body odor, and cigarette smoke hit my nostrils. I wanted to gag. My classmate excused herself to change, and a scantily clad hostess escorted us to a table near a stage with two poles and a strobe light. A waitress, dressed in a G-string with pasties covering her nipples, brought my father a beer. The music started and two girls, one of them my classmate, took their places at the poles. I had no idea what I was even looking at—this was before the days of strip-club scenes on TV and pole-dancing classes at the Y.

I watched in half amazement, half horror as the girl I'd just spent all afternoon with learning how to properly hold a dinner fork performed half-naked acrobatics on a pole and then seductively crawled downstage until her abnormally large breasts were less than an inch from our faces. Her pasties had sparkling tassels, and as my father watched them spin, he looked like a kid on Christmas morning, smiling literally ear to ear.

I almost choked on my cherry Coke when I saw him reach into his wallet and tuck cash into her rhinestone-studded G-string (which could not have been comfortable) as though it was the most natural thing in the world.

"Daddy!" I shrieked, "What are you doing?"

My father, for maybe the only time I could remember, burst into a fit of laughter. "Oh, relax! Have another Coke?"

I thought he'd never want to leave. On our way home, he said, "What a nice girl. You really should bring her around sometime."

I expected my mother to be outraged when I told her where we'd been, but she seemed to love it. The more upset I got, describing how ridiculously he'd behaved, smiling over the stripper like a cock of the walk, the more she laughed. I suppose she was relieved that after all those years of his being the staunch, remote model soldier and citizen, her husband had loosened up for once.

CHAPTER 4

Music, Magic, a Promise,
and a Prayer

·····························

When I was sixteen, my parents and I road-tripped to Palisades Park, New Jersey, where I would participate in the Miss American Teenager pageant as Miss Washington, DC, Teenager. This was my first televised event, and I was nervous but ready. As I stood by the outdoor stage waiting for the competition to begin, I almost didn't notice the sweet-faced young man standing at the microphone in a navy-blue blazer and Beatles-style haircut. But once he started to sing "Sealed with a Kiss," the whole world disappeared.

The romantic lyrics and wistful melody of this haunting new song sailed straight from Brian Hyland's lips into my heart. And for every moment he was singing, there was no competition, there was only him.

He exited the stage to thunderous applause and was immediately swarmed by giddy contestants clamoring for autographs. I hung back but was still unable to keep my eyes off him. At one point our eyes locked, and when the groupies finally dispersed, he made his way over to where I was standing.

"Hi," he said casually, "I'm Brian. I noticed you when I first came in."

"Hi," I replied. "I'm Kathalynn."

There was just something about him; he was right on the line between smooth rock 'n' roll star and sweet, gentle boy next door.

"You're the prettiest girl here. You're going to win!"

And with that, he turned to greet another horde of crazed contestants wanting his attention. Within a few minutes they called the contestants to line up backstage. I took a deep breath and a long look up at the lights, the cameras, and the audience. But my head wasn't filled with thoughts of winning this time—it was filled with Brian. *He thought I was pretty. He thought I should win!*

While I was standing behind the stage, looking out over the water, one of the girls standing next to me pointed out Long Island, with Manhattan in the far distance. I had a strong, unmistakable feeling that I would live in New York City one day, as if the place was calling me. And then a voice within me foretold, "You're going to marry a boy from that city."

Where did that come from? I didn't know, didn't care. The future would take care of itself.

When the judges announced the name of the winner and it wasn't mine, I should have felt disappointed, and normally I would have, but in that moment the strangest thing happened: I felt a hand squeeze my shoulder, gently and reassuringly. When I turned to see who it was, no one was there. A chill ran through my body, after which I was completely at peace, knowing this night was about so much more than winning or losing that particular competition.

My life indeed did change because of that evening.

As I exited the stage, Brian stopped me. "That wasn't right," he said, shaking his head sympathetically. "You should have won."

"Thank you." It seemed the only thing to say.

Smiling, Brian took my hand. "Hey, I have to go, but we should keep in touch."

He didn't give me his phone number or ask for mine, but I wasn't worried because I knew our paths would cross again. I just knew it.

Although I wasn't too disappointed that I'd lost, letting my father down was difficult for me. The car ride home was a long one. My mother napped in the backseat while I sat up front with Dad.

Neither of us said a word, but his silence spoke volumes. Letting my insecurity get the best of me, I took his stillness as tacit confirmation that I just wasn't good enough, I didn't have what it took to be a winner. He very possibly may not have felt that way, but I had already gone too far down the rabbit hole of self-doubt to consider any other interpretation.

One freezing night the following winter, in my senior year, Brian Hyland came to Maryland and performed at my high school. It had been several months since I'd seen him at the pageant.

I was struck, as before, by his eyes and the clean-cut rocker style that defined the era. We held hands for a few minutes backstage (and by backstage, I mean the locker room of the high school gymnasium). I felt like the luckiest, most important person in the world.

After the show, I rode home with Brian in the back of his manager's car. The song "Do You Want to Know a Secret" came on the radio, and he talked to me about The Beatles and how much he loved them. The song ended just as we were pulling up to my house, at which point Brian leaned over and planted on me my first *real* kiss.

Why did my school have to be so close to my house! He stepped out of the car first, held the door for me, and then walked with me up the short path to my front door. He told me how much he liked seeing me and once again said that we would see each other in the future. He gave me another sweet kiss and said good night. My heart sank as he turned and made his way back to the car. I just had to see him again—but how?

Life moved on. I continued going to school and competing on weekends. The summer after graduation, I started dating the popular local DJ Marvelous Marv, and by dating I mean we had dinner together a handful of times and saw a few movies. It never got serious, as my heart belonged to one boy, and that was Brian. As far as I knew, Marv was fine with me being the Virgin Mary, because truthfully, I think he was more interested in my mother than he was in me! Not in a creepy way, of course, but whenever he'd come by the house, they'd talk and laugh so that I often felt like a third wheel. Mother just adored him, and I was grateful she had a friend. Marv was a fan of Brian's too, and he'd play his hits at night and dedicate them to me live on air. I was the envy of a lot of girls that summer, thanks to Marv and his radio show.

As I continued competing, my eye was fixed on the Miss America prize that had glimmered and beckoned ever since that night I'd watched my first pageant with my father. All pageants for me were merely preparation for the big one. By 1967 I'd won Miss Southern Maryland and was on my way to the state competition, the one that would send me to Atlantic City for the main, televised Miss America event.

Primed and experienced as I was by then, I pressed on further to improve and refine—I hired a coach at the Fred Astaire dancing school to develop my routine, which included a comedy skit, dancing, and baton twirling; I kept going to Miss McKay to polish my comportment and overall presentation. I carefully chose the most appropriate and becoming evening gown, bathing suit, and day outfit, part of my recent prize winnings, all to use for the Miss Maryland pageant. Between my father ferrying me to and from lessons, rehearsals, and competitions, and covering most of my expenses and local sponsorship, who generously underwrote the pageant and some of the clothes, I was enthusiastically supported and more than prepared.

The pageant went spectacularly well for me. I won the bathing suit and evening gown competitions, much to my surprise. Then I won the talent. My scores were up. It looked like a shoo-in. When I walked onstage, I was greeted with resounding applause.

Earlier, I had noticed a tall girl enter while the rest of us were rehearsing an opening song. I had no memory of ever having seen this girl before; it was as if she turned up out of nowhere. At five feet, nine inches, however, she was impossible to miss. I watched her play a piece on the piano for the judges and, marveling at how good she was, wished I knew how to play piano. When the winner was announced, it was she who strolled off with the Miss Maryland title and became the state's delegate.

I was devastated. I'd lost before, but this was so much more important, something I'd envisioned for years, and I had come close enough to touch it. Winning the title had been more than a goal to me; I saw it as my way out of Maryland and all it represented.

The next morning, as I returned from breakfast to the hotel to pack up, I spotted a few contestants gathered around one of the judges and overheard him raving about the winner. "Five foot nine, and without heels! They won't be able to miss her in Atlantic City!" Then he noticed me, said, "You look good in a swimsuit," and continued crowing about her.

I wholly hated that man in that moment, but even more I hated the injustice of it, and how something as impossible to control as my height could have tipped the scales. I flashed back to my father telling me I was too short and how I had to drink more milk to grow, but I would never top five-four, and there was nothing I could do about that.

Many pageant officials encouraged me to return to compete the next year, but there was no way that was going to happen. That was it. I was done. I would never compete in another pageant or contest from that day forth.

But what would come next? I'd been taking some classes and was considering applying to Maryland University for the following fall, never really intending to go since I was counting on winning Miss Maryland. I'd done well enough at school, despite having no real interest in it. My father, a huge believer in education, loved the idea of me going to college. However, something within told me this was not the time to do it. School would always be there to return to, but I would never, ever be this young or pretty again. I considered becoming an airline hostess but fell a half-inch short of the requirement. So I worked in a dress shop to pick up some cash while I contemplated my next move.

One day I read in a magazine that Brian Hyland had moved from New York to Los Angeles, and I immediately thought, *I've got to get there*. I knew nothing about L.A., but I resolved that one way or another I would find a way to go there to see Brian.

In keeping with my previous practice of wishing on stars, I set my intention and counted on the universe to show me the way. Sure enough, within days I received a letter from the popular TV show *The Dating Game*. Several weeks before, on a whim, I had mailed in my picture, and now they were telling me I'd been invited to audition! Immediately I called Marv, with whom I'd stayed in touch, and wonderful guy that he was, he used his connections in music to get me Brian's telephone number.

At first, I was terrified to call. What if he didn't remember me? But he did. And not only that, he offered to pick me up at the airport and help me get settled. I hung up that phone and screamed inside my head, *It's happening! It's happening!*

Now all I needed to do was concoct a scenario for my parents. I told them my old modeling coach, Mrs. Rowley, had moved to L.A. and was inviting some students to visit her. I reasoned that I could interview for *The Dating Game* and visit her all in one trip! They bought my story and, thank God, never called Mrs. Rowley to check it out.

It may seem strange that my parents let me go, but the truth is my father wanted me to leave Maryland just as badly as I myself did. His dream was to see me grow into a well traveled, educated woman who never had to rely on anyone for her survival, least of all a man. My mother, on the other hand, would have been happy for me to stay put, marry a local boy, and start popping out kids right away. She went along with the plan, however, because ultimately she wanted the best for me too.

The decision, which I believe was guided by an unseen force, to abandon my home of Maryland for Los Angeles, caused a ripple effect of things to come, bigger and more exciting than I ever could have imagined.

PART II

Hollywood: All I Had to Do Was Show Up

· ·

You have escaped the cage. Your wings
are stretched out. Now fly.

—RUMI

CHAPTER 5

Fools Rush In

....

As the plane touched down at Los Angeles International Airport the butterflies in my stomach began working overtime. Giddy with excitement, I nervously gathered up my pocketbook and little Samsonite makeup bag and headed for baggage claim, where Brian had agreed to meet me.

My bags arrived, but Brian didn't. I watched the last passenger from my flight pull the last bag off the conveyer belt and started to get the feeling maybe he wasn't coming. Frustrated and scared, I made my way to the nearest phone booth to give him a call. The phone rang a few times before an unfamiliar man's voice picked up on the other end.

"Hi," I said. "I'm looking for Brian Hyland, is he in?"

"Who's this?"

"Oh, this is Kathalynn. I'm a friend of Brian's. He was supposed to meet me at the airport and, well, I'm here. Who am I speaking with?"

"I'm Del," he said.

There was an awkward pause. I guess he expected me to know who Del was. "Del *Shannon*," he clarified. "I'm Brian's friend."

Oh yes, right; Del Shannon, as in "Run-run-run-run-runaway." Who didn't know that song?

"Brian did say something about meeting someone at the airport, but I'm pretty sure he thinks you're coming tomorrow."

"Oh no!" I panicked. "It's today!"

"Well, sorry," he replied coolly. "I'll tell him you called when I see him." Click.

Jerk! I was about to start crying when someone tapped on the phone booth. I looked up and saw two handsome young men with mod-top hair in very cool mandarin-style shirts. They were smiling.

31

"Oh, I'm sorry! You can use the phone now," I told them.

"Oh, no," one of them said, stopping me. "We don't need the phone. I wasn't meaning to eavesdrop, but did you just tell someone you were supposed to meet Brian Hyland? Because we might be able to help you."

"What? I mean, yes! Wait—how?" I was utterly confused. *What could this guy possibly be talking about?*

"My name's Jack Keller, I'm a songwriter. Have you seen the show *Gidget*?" he asked with a confident smile.

Had I seen Gidget!? I loved Gidget!

"Yes, of course!" I replied.

"I wrote the theme song."

"Great song!" I said, trying to somehow keep my cool.

"You look like a cute little Gidget yourself. Listen, we're on our way to a birthday party for our friend Tony Orlando. You may know who he is, he's a singer."

Was he joking? Tony Orlando. Yes, I knew who Tony Orlando was—the man had countless hit songs. My favorite of course was "Halfway to Paradise"

"Yes, of course!"

"Why don't you come with us? We can call Brian from there. He's a friend of Tony's, and he may even be coming to the party. Either way, it will be more fun than spending all night in the airport!"

While I have never been inclined to jump in a car with two perfect strangers, I figured, how dangerous could the composer for *Gidget* really be? Plus, going to Tony Orlando's party did sound like a much better way to spend an evening than crying in the airport. I told them yes, thank you, I'd go.

Jack carried my luggage from the terminal and helped me into the backseat of his sexy white convertible, and next thing I knew we were flying down the freeway with the radio blaring Dionne Warwick's "Do You Know the Way to San Jose?"

As we drove, I felt the effects of jet lag setting in, it being after 10 p.m. eastern time, but the prospect of seeing Brian kept me wide awake, as did the splendor of my first California sunset. I sat back as we exited into a lush residential neighborhood and marveled at the sight of that massive desert sun, melting like butterscotch over the stunning homes, cars, and endless rows of palm trees.

Jack's convertible wound through the Hollywood Hills until we reached Tony Orlando's house, where the party was in full swing. Never had I seen a more hip-looking crowd—throw a rock, hit a rock star. I recognized members of the Monkees and the American Breed and could only imagine who the others were whom I did not recognize.

British mod style was very much the rage. Almost every guy wore a bright Nehru jacket, while the girls were clad in either bell-bottoms or miniskirts with go-go boots. I took a seat on a couch and noticed a colossal white Christmas tree trimmed in pink ornaments in the corner. I guessed they'd missed the memo that Christmas had been over for months. But then again, what did I know? Maybe people just left their trees up all year in California.

I was loving this place already. Despite the celebrities around me and the fact that I did not know a soul there, I somehow—don't ask me how—didn't feel out of place. I sat calmly with my Newport Lights and black coffee, watching the partyers.

The only people missing were Tony Orlando himself and Brian. Tony would be arriving late because this was a surprise party. But what could be keeping Brian?

To the other people there who were drinking, smoking grass, and snorting some white power, I am sure I couldn't have seemed less cool, sitting there on the couch, chain-smoking and sipping the coffee that had been offered to me only after I'd turned down every alcoholic option. I wasn't being deliberately prissy; I just didn't drink.

My father and I had had only one conversation about drugs and alcohol. "Be careful," he'd told me. "If you get into trouble with drugs or alcohol, I won't be able to help you."

And having had a front-row seat to his repeated failure at helping my mother, I knew better than to drink or risk losing control. I kept my distance from inebriants in general.

"Surprise!!!" The room erupted in cheers as the guest of honor finally arrived.

Only that morning I'd never even been on a plane, and now I was joining my voice with the Monkees in a birthday serenade to Mr. Tony Orlando. Unable to keep my thoughts off Brian, I compulsively checked the door—and finally in he walked! We locked eyes and he made his way toward me. I felt my heart jump into my throat.

"I'm so sorry I didn't meet you at the airport. I thought you were coming in tomorrow. When Del told me you were here, I felt awful. But when I got a call from Jack and he told me he found you at the airport and brought you to the party, I got here as soon as I could."

"It's okay, Brian, I probably gave you the wrong day."

With a sweet and adoring look on his face he said, "Well, it's great to see you. Aren't you exhausted? It's after midnight East Coast time!"

"No!" I lied, "I'm fine. Not tired at all, actually!"

Brian excused himself for a moment to say a quick hello to a few people and promised to be right back. I found Jack and his friend and thanked him for everything. With a smile and a wink, he wished me luck.

Finally, Brian took my hand and led me to Jack's convertible to pick up my bags, which he carried as he escorted me into his own car, also a convertible.

Did everyone in California drive convertibles? I wondered. In any case, there I was, in beautiful California with the prince of my dreams, driving to his castle in the hills.

There was a battle going on in my body, the jet lag versus caffeine from the coffee, and the jet lag was starting to win, but I wasn't about to blow my first night with Brian by doing anything as lame as passing out.

When we arrived at his place, we were greeted by a man with a square jaw and wavy hair.

"Kathalynn," Brian announced, "this is Del, Del Shannon." (As in the jerk who hung up on me when I was stranded at the airport several hours ago. How could I forget?)

"Yes," I said, "we've sort of met. I was the one who called."

"Right, of course! Well, glad you found him. Welcome to L.A."

Yeah, I thought, *no thanks to you, dickhead.*

I had never been in a man's bedroom before. I guess I'd been holding out for a special guy—and there he was. He put my bags down in the corner and came over to where I was standing, nervously clutching my pocketbook. Gently, he took my purse and put it on the table. He slipped an arm around me and pulled me so close I could feel every part of his body. *Every* part.

"You have bedroom eyes," he said, looking through them and straight into my soul.

Bedroom eyes? I'd never heard that term before, but it sounded like the most wonderful compliment. Of course, as far I was concerned, every word he uttered was poetry.

"Beautiful, cat-like eyes," he continued.

Wow. I didn't see where my eyes looked especially cat-like, but I'd take it. The thank-you on my lips was silenced with a kiss that made my head spin and conscious thought vanish. At last, my prince had come. (Okay, technically, I'd come to him.)

As his hands started moving down my back, I finally understood how Eve must have felt, standing there in the Garden of Eden after the proverbial fall. I felt naked and self-conscious as hell, despite the fact that I was still fully clothed!

In my mind, I morphed into that chubby preteen with no chest and stomach that pooched out a mile. When his hand went for my bra, I felt myself breaking out into a sweat; I'd forgotten to take out my falsies! Well, I couldn't very well do it now, so I guided his hand away from the area.

He took off his shirt; I took off nothing. He took off his pants; I took off nothing. Then we fell onto the bed. Oh shit—this was a disaster, all happening so fast!

Suddenly, I started getting the feeling I was being watched. I looked up over Brian's shoulder, and there was Del, standing by the door with his eyes locked on the two of us and an intense, predatory grin on his face.

I shrieked. Brian looked over, saw Del, and ran to the door, slamming it shut. Del bolted away. Brian apologized for Del's behavior and hoped I wasn't too offended. What confused me, however, was that he didn't seem at all freaked out himself. I couldn't help wondering for a moment if maybe that was just what people did in California. Brian tried to pick up where we'd left off, but I couldn't relax.

"Kathalynn, what's the matter?"

By that time I was shaking and told him nothing, but he could see that I was frightened to death.

He looked at me and said, "It's all right, everything is okay. You must be very tired, and I think you should go to sleep."

I returned his gaze and, still shaking, meekly told him that yes, I was very tired and wanted to sleep.

Naïve as this may sound, I hadn't gone there that night to sleep with Brian. My fantasy of romance, the kind that inspired music and poetry, didn't include a one-night stand with a creepy roommate spying on us from a doorway.

Sweet as Brian was, he and I were definitely not on the same page. Finally, there was nothing left but to go to sleep. So still in my black-and-white travel suit, I lay down beside the now completely nude man of my dreams, closed my eyes, and dropped off.

When I woke up the next morning, I was alone in an unfamiliar room. Anxious to put this embarrassing event behind me, I dashed into the bathroom and attempted to freshen up. I desperately needed a shower but dared not take one after the Del Shannon episode.

Brian and Del, having breakfast in the living room, greeted me with casual politeness. They avoided awkwardness by filling the conversation with small talk about L.A. and the weather. Last night I had been an honored guest, but this morning I felt like an outsider, intruding on their morning ritual.

Since I didn't have anywhere to stay, Brian recommended a motel in Hollywood and offered to drive me there. He was attentive and sweet on the drive over, repeating how courageous he thought I was to come out all alone. He walked me inside, wished me good luck, and told me to call him anytime.

I checked into the motel in a daze.

Physically exhausted and emotionally drained, I lay down on the cheap twin-sized mattress and replayed the events of the night before about a hundred times.

I let every emotion take over, and none of them felt anything like bravery.

What had I gotten myself into? Aside from Brian and my old modeling teacher, whom I hadn't seen in years and who, it turned out, didn't even live in L.A., but rather some place called Laguna Beach, I didn't know anyone in California.

I waited a couple of days before reaching out to Brian again.

When I did, the phone rang a few times before a familiar (and not in a good way), voice came on.

"Hello?"

"Oh, hi, Del."

"Is this Kathalynn?"

"Yes. Is Brian home?"

"No, but I am. Come on over, we can play!"

Did he just say play? Yes, he did.

"Play what?" I responded, as if I didn't understand.

"You know, play. I dig you a lot."

"I don't know what you mean," I replied, knowing exactly what he meant.

"I dig you. I want to have sex with you."

Wow, thanks for spelling it out, creep.

I guess he assumed I wasn't catching on fast enough and that something more straightforward was required.

"You think I'm going to have sex for the first time with *you?*" I asked, horrified at his boldness.

"You're a virgin? Oh my God, I had no idea! That's great! You should definitely come over!"

Brian's best friend or not, this jerk had to be put in his place.

"I don't think so, baby," I said as scornfully as possible and hung up on him.

The triumphant feeling didn't last long. Thinking of Brian, my heart sank down into my stomach. Del was a pig, that much I knew, but he was also Brian's best friend, and even the sleaziest guy wouldn't go for a girl if his friend liked her. Somehow, he'd gotten the impression I was fair game. If Brian gave him the go-ahead, it could only mean one thing: this love-affair was one-hundred percent fabricated and only being experienced by me.

For the first time it occurred to me that all those months I'd been dreaming about Brian, planning our lives together, I hadn't known the first thing about him! For all I knew, he had a serious girlfriend . . . or six!

Suddenly it all seemed hilarious. I had moved three thousand miles across the country with no job, no plan, no nothing, over a crush! I had done something so ridiculous I felt right on the edge of either collapsing into sobs or laughing hysterically. I opted for the latter, and it went on for a good long while.

Eventually, I came up for air, and saw that through the window of that cheap ugly room was Sunset Boulevard. All anybody back home knew of Sunset Boulevard was that creepy old movie with Gloria Swanson, but there I was, actually there. All right, so my romance hadn't turned out to be a love that would inspire songs and poetry, but this was the place that inspired dreams! So I decided I'd tough it out and give it a shot. Isn't that what Hollywood is all about?

I called my father and told him I'd decided to stay here indefinitely. He wasn't at all surprised. He generously offered to send me the money he'd saved for my college. As soon as I accepted that money, my priority shifted.

My father had been investing in my future since the day I was born. He'd long given up on my brother, Donald, and I was all he had left to believe in. This time I was going to make him proud. I refocused my attention from Brian and set my mind to learn everything I could about Hollywood and how it all worked.

Later that afternoon, I was leaving the motel to look for an apartment when I passed a young man in the lobby with a handsome, familiar face. We exchanged smiles but I couldn't place him, and it drove me crazy all day.

On my way back in I saw him again, and this time he stopped me and introduced himself as Gary Loizzo of the American Breed. He'd recognized me from Tony Orlando's birthday party. His band had recently released their single "Bend Me, Shape Me," which was a massive hit.

Gary's looks were about as different from Brian Hyland's as possible, which was fine with me. Brian's eyes were bright and sweet, and Gary's were dark and enigmatic, but his smile was warm and it put me at ease. When he asked me if I'd like to come along with him to a recording session that night with his band, I was thrilled.

The first person we passed walking into the studio was the teen idol of teen idols, the man who made all the girls swoon, Frankie Avalon! Gary knew him, of course, so he stopped and causally introduced me.

"Kathalynn, this is Frankie."

"Oh my God," I blurted out before I could filter my gush, "I love you—I mean, I'm really happy to meet you."

They both broke out in laughter.

"Kathalynn, it's a pleasure to meet you too," Frankie said, rescuing me from further embarrassment.

After the session, Gary and I returned to the motel.

When we reached the place where I would go left to my room, he asked me if I'd like to join him for a while in his room. This time I had some idea of what he probably had in mind. I stopped and considered a minute, and then I said to myself, Well, if it can't be Brian, it may as well be him.

Gary opened the door, and before I could step through he scooped me into his arms and carried me like a new bride across the room to the bed. Then he climbed in beside me, but when he leaned in for a kiss I became very aware that I needed the bathroom. I awkwardly wriggled out of the romantic moment and excused myself.

Okay, I told myself, *this is it.* I slowly and mechanically removed everything but my underwear and assessed my reflection. As usual, I didn't like what I saw, an ungainly, flat-chested virgin in dorky cotton panties. I wrapped myself in one of those skimpy motel bath towels and cracked open the door.

Gary had taken this opportunity to make himself comfortable. He lay stark naked on top of the bed, looking completely calm, as if he did this sort of thing all the time. I dashed over to the bed and quickly dived under the covers.

Taking in Gary's nude body, I became anxious. I just didn't know where to put my eyes. At my request he turned off the lights and then slid up beside me and went in again for that kiss. My lips involuntarily seized into something like steel against his. Gary pulled away and looked at me intently.

"You're a virgin, am I right?" *Was it that obvious?*

"Yes," I admitted.

"Right," he said, moving away slowly. "I can't do this."

Relieved as I was not to have to go through with it, my familiar insecurities came flooding in. *Was there something wrong with me? Had I turned him off?*

Responding to the questions in my eyes he said gently, "Look, I like you. But I can't be your first. Can I show you something?" He pointed at his semi-erect penis. "See this? This means I'm turned on by you and could go inside you if we were going to do that, which we aren't."

I was speechless. A week ago I'd been home in Maryland with a head full of Disney-esque fantasies about romance. Today I was in a motel on Sunset Boulevard receiving a tutorial on sex from the lead singer of the American Breed.

Gary told me it was important I know all this so that when the time came with the person I loved, I would have some idea of what to do. He also warned me about men in general and those in Hollywood in particular, that often their intentions had more to do with adding a notch in their bedpost than anything else.

Once the sex talk was over, I relaxed a bit. He opened up to me about his goals. I was surprised to learn that he didn't plan on being a rock star forever and hoped to someday teach school. He asked me what my aspirations were, and for the sake of conversation I made some up. Truthfully, I didn't have a plan to speak of. All I knew was that I already loved this luminous, sunshine-filled land called California, and I was never going home to Maryland.

CHAPTER 6

Wheels, Digs, and a
Dance Class

....

One of the first things I did was visit a car dealer. I bought a new red
Fiat convertible with black interior right off the lot. My father sent
me the funds for a down payment, and every month he sent a money
order to cover my rent, car loan, food, plus a little extra. A car was a
necessity in L.A. Nobody walked anywhere. If you had a choice between
a car and an apartment, you would have to pick the car. You could always
sleep in your car, but you couldn't drive around in your apartment.

Eventually I found a modest one-bedroom furnished apartment on
Palm Avenue in West Hollywood between Sunset and Santa Monica
Boulevards. It had unsightly wall-to-wall brown shag carpeting with
orange and mustard yellow accents, but it was in a great location and an
affordable $150 a month.

The building was filled with twenty-something aspiring actors, musi-
cians, and writers who mostly waited on tables, hoping to be discovered.
Flower children seemed to dominate the scene around the Sunset Strip. In
that first blush, everything seemed magical.

With a roof over my head and a car to take me wherever I needed
to go, it was time to find a dance class. A girl I met at lunch recommended Steve Peck, a renowned dancer, choreographer, and character
actor who'd made his mark in the movie *Some Came Running* playing
Shirley MacLaine's boyfriend.

You couldn't just sign up for Steve Peck's dance class; you had to audition. I wasn't a fabulous dancer by any means, but I figured if I used a
little imagination I might have a chance. I had brought my baton with

me to L.A. so I decided to combine a familiar twirling routine with some dance moves.

Steve Peck, alarmingly masculine with a chiseled dancer's body and a full head of thick gray hair, stared at me after my audition, his arms folded and a curious look on his face.

"Kid, you need work, but my God, you really have something," he said.

"Does that mean I'm accepted, Mr. Peck?"

"It's Steve, kid, not Mr. Peck. And yes, you are. You'll start with intermediate jazz and beginner's ballet. I'll see you tomorrow."

My first day at class, I noticed a beautiful girl with long dark hair in front of me at the barre. She looked familiar but I couldn't place her, but when after class I heard someone call her Priscilla, it struck me: Priscilla Presley, Elvis's wife. Everything about her was beautiful—eyes, skin, hair, figure. I could certainly see how Elvis had gone for her.

A few days later I arrived early for a private lesson with Steve and saw Priscilla winding up her lesson with him. She was a wonderful dancer, and they were amazing together. I'd heard rumors about them, but rumors abounded in Hollywood, and I didn't think much of it. Besides, who among us wasn't a bit in love with Steve; it was almost impossible not to fall for him. But to my knowledge, he maintained a professional distance from us all.

I'd often note a Cadillac waiting outside for Priscilla. The other girls and I wondered if Elvis was in there waiting for her, but we never actually spotted him.

CHAPTER 7

As for You, Troy Donahue

·····························

From my new apartment I could walk to the Whisky A Go-Go nightclub and see dazzling movie stars mingling with regular people. Where else in the world could you find yourself sitting beside Jim Morrison and not even realize who it had been until hours later?

One night while I was with some friends at the Whisky I looked up and saw the most gorgeous man in the world staring me down from the other side of the room. I knew I recognized him but was too blinded by his beauty to make a conscious attempt to place him. I was only pulled out of the trance when my friend shrieked, "Oh, my God, Troy Donahue is staring right at you!"

After that I couldn't hear a thing because the theme from *A Summer Place* started blaring in my head. Then I saw him move in what looked like slow motion through the crowd toward our table. He came right over to me, introduced himself, and offered to buy me a drink.

I told him I'd have a cup of black coffee, and eventually my friends started finding excuses to leave us alone. He asked if he could sit down next to me, and naturally I said yes. He wasn't young like Brian; he had to be at least thirty-something, and that seemed ancient. Our conversation was effortless. We talked about my being new to Hollywood. I told him about my pageant life, which he seemed to find riveting.

Every now and then we'd take a break from talking to dance. When he put his arms around me I couldn't help thinking, *Oh my God, this is Troy Donahue!* And yet there was also something about him that felt comfortable and familiar, and not just because I'd seen him in movies.

When the time came to leave, Troy offered to drive me home. Not wanting the evening to end, I accepted his offer. As he pulled up in front of my apartment building, I turned to tell him good night and thanked him for the ride home. He said you're welcome, got out of the car, came over to my side, and opened the door for me. He took my hand and walked me to my door.

"Aren't you going to offer me a nightcap?"

"What's a nightcap?" (Could I have been more naïve?)

"A drink, to top off our night; night-cap, get it?" He laughed.

"I only have coffee and Diet Tab, but since it's after midnight I'm not sure you'll want that."

"I'd love a cup of coffee," he said.

He followed me into my apartment. I'd started for the kitchen to brew him some coffee when he grabbed me by the waist, pulled me close, and said, "I think I'll pass on the coffee, but I'd love a tour of your apartment."

As I removed his hand from my waist, I told him that a tour wasn't necessary, since there was only one more room, the bedroom. Putting his arms around me again and looking deep into my eyes, he replied that he very much wanted a tour of the bedroom.

"Okay," I said, "I would be happy to show it to you."

He didn't need a tour; the man seemed to know exactly where to go. Grabbing my hand, he sauntered into my bedroom as naturally as though he lived there. Then he casually slid down and into my bed and relaxed for a few moments.

Looking at me with that charming smile that had graced so many screens, he said, "Come in here with me."

I was surprised by his boldness but too excited to mind much. I climbed into my bed next to him and he kissed me passionately. There it was, the moment Gary Loizzo had prepared me for. This time I was ready.

"You're adorable," he said, as he pulled me close to him.

As if in slow motion, he removed my clothing one piece at a time.

Oh my God, I thought, I'm naked with a movie star in my bed. I guess this stuff happens in California! He gently cupped my breast and leaned over and kissed my nipples.

"You're beautiful," he told me.

Look who's talking, I wanted to say. I felt his hands between my legs, and then there was no going back. My body was on fire, and my mind shut down.

It was happening. I was going to give myself to this gorgeous man who looked as close to a Prince Charming (complete with blond hair and a suntan) as you could get. Sensing my inexperience, he was loving, kind, and very gentle with me. I was luckier in this respect than I knew.

Afterward, Troy was composed and playful. "I'm imagining us on the Riviera," he said, running his tongue along my shoulder.

"Where's the Riviera?" I said, teasingly pushing his tongue back in his mouth.

"The French Riviera."

"Right, of course; *that* Riviera!" It was all out of some script, lying there in a romantic afterglow with a matinee idol, making plans to be whisked away to exotic places.

The next morning, I bounced into the kitchen to make coffee and toast, attempting to behave naturally. I looked up at the tiny doorway and saw Troy with a guilty, apologetic look on his face. He told me he regretted what had happened between us the night before and hoped I wasn't too upset. He said he hadn't known until "the moment" that I was still a virgin.

I told him that it was okay, that I was happy and he should not be concerned. He smiled and took me into his arms and kissed me. I couldn't imagine any girl being upset about losing her virginity to Troy Donahue. We had an unromantic breakfast of black coffee and toast together and spent the morning laughing and talking.

Troy and I continued to see each other for about a year, but not exclusively. He knew his starlight was beginning to fade with the new revolution of actors. Newly divorced, out of work, nearly broke, and understandably a bit depressed, he was certainly in no shape to enter into any kind of committed relationship. I, meanwhile, was just beginning to experience my new found freedom, and the last thing I wanted was a serious boyfriend.

Troy too warned me about the pitfalls of Hollywood, along with the dangers of excessive hard drugs and alcohol. He opened up to me about his manager, his struggles, the various films he had made and the ones he'd lost out on.

He told me horror stories about the crazy things women did to stay thin in Hollywood, including a former costar who ate nothing but hard-boiled eggs and celery. He hoped I would never fall victim to that kind of neurosis.

I never went as far as some of the scenarios he described, but I still wrestled with the doubt demons inside my head that found my body unacceptable and persistently longed for it to be thinner, no matter how sweetly a movie-star lover claimed otherwise.

I appreciated Troy for his kindness and for going out of his way to make me feel beautiful. Most of our time together was spent lounging by the pool. I'd douse my body in baby oil and iodine; fortunately, I had a loathing for freckles, so I protected my face. Troy, on the other hand, used Coppertone, and to this day the aroma of that suntan lotion makes me think of him.

CHAPTER 8

Kissing the King

....

O
ne night, I was enjoying a cozy evening in my West Hollywood apartment, just me and my Elvis records. I had cracked the front door open to let in some fresh air, and a cute young man with sideburns poked his head in.

"Thank you for playing my boss's music!" he said in a charming Southern drawl while flashing a sweet smile.

"Excuse me?" I jumped, taken aback. "Who are you?"

"Oh! My name's Charlie Hodge. I sing backup for Elvis; he's one of my good friends. I live on the second floor, right upstairs from you."

In Hollywood, just about everyone introduced themselves as someone who knew someone famous or else rattled off their show business credits.

"Well, it's nice to meet you, Charlie Hodge," I said, not knowing exactly what to make of him.

"It's nice to meet you too, and your name?"

"Oh, it's Kathalynn Turner, from Maryland."

"Kathalynn, that's different. How did you get that name?"

"From my mother," I said, wondering how else in the hell he'd thought I gotten my name.

"Oh, I guess so." He laughed awkwardly.

Then he looked into my apartment and spotted my trophies from my baton and beauty competitions.

"Wow!" Charlie said. "Nice trophies! Elvis would love to see those!"

What on earth was this man getting at?

I loved my trophies so much I'd had my parents ship them from Maryland, hoping they'd give me confidence in my quest for an acting career. But I couldn't for the life of me figure out why they would be of any interest to Elvis.

"You look a lot like Priscilla," Charlie continued. "Hey, would you be interested in meeting Elvis?"

Would I what?

"Sure, why not," I replied, trying to sound nonchalant while my heart was doing cartwheels in my throat.

"Great! I'll come and pick you up Saturday evening around six if that's okay."

"That works," I said with a shrug.

As soon as Charlie was out of sight I slammed the door and ran for the phone to call my mother.

When she answered, I screamed, "I'm going to meet Elvis!"

"That's wonderful, Kathalynn. Do you know what time it is on the East Coast? I'm going back to bed. Good night."

Oops. The time difference.

As promised, Charlie showed up at my door Saturday night. It wasn't until I saw the crowd of fans clamoring at the gate to Elvis and Priscilla's Bel Air mansion that it really hit me as to where I was and whom I was about to meet.

"Charlie," I whispered as we passed through the gate, "I'm not sure I can do this."

"Oh, gosh!" he exclaimed, "Don't be nervous! You're going to love Elvis, and he's just going to love you!"

As we pulled up to the entrance of the house, I panicked and started shaking uncontrollably. Charlie came around, opened the car door, took my hand, and pulled me out. He led me to the huge white doors and rang the bell.

A housekeeper let us in and offered to take my wrap. As I awkwardly handed her my six-dollar shawl, I turned to my right and saw this tall, magnificent figure with blue-black hair and long sideburns moving toward me, wearing a red shirt and black pants. Before I could catch my breath, he took my hand and said, "Hi, I'm Elvis Presley."

My stomach was double and triple knotting as I forced out, "Hello, I'm Kathalynn Turner, from Maryland." *Like he cares where you're from, idiot.*

"She's nervous," Charlie giggled.

I did not think it was funny at all. Elvis smiled and squeezed my hand. My stomach twisted into a quadruple knot. Desperately, my mind darted to and fro trying to come up with something to say.

"I've loved you since I was a kid."

"Really?"

"Oh yes! I remember watching teenage girls on a bus one day and thinking how jealous I was of them, being old enough to maybe have a chance with you. I was just way too young." In my efforts to be nonchalant, smart, and unruffled, I just felt stupid, embarrassed, and pathetic.

Elvis laughed as he took me by the hand and led me to the family room, where a large white sofa positioned itself along a stone wall. Two chairs flanked the sofa, with a huge coffee table in front of it. Elvis sat at the end of the couch and motioned for me to take the chair next to him.

Across from the couch a TV was on. A handicapped child appeared on the screen and Elvis became distracted. He pointed and said, "Oh, no! He's one of those retarded kids."

The words weren't exactly P.C., but his tone was sweet and held no judgment. I could feel genuine caring radiate from him, which was no doubt one of the secret ingredients in his performance that put his music above the rest.

Elvis was nice to me. Charlie had already briefed him about my trophies, so he asked about my history competing in pageants and what my Hollywood ambitions were.

"You'll make it out here; you have the right look, and clearly you're talented."

I tried to play it very cool, but inside I was shaking and daunted sitting so close to him.

"Can I get you a drink?" he asked politely.

"No, thank you," I stammered. "I don't drink."

Elvis smiled. "I didn't drink when I first came to Hollywood either. Now I drink Bloody Marys."

I reached into my purse and pulled out a cigarette. I was fumbling around for my matches when Elvis produced a silver lighter. As I leaned forward to join the tip of my cigarette with the flame, he looked into my eyes. "Do you still think you're too young?" he asked in a whisper.

My hand started shaking, and Elvis put his hand over it and repeated, "Are you still too young?"

"I don't know," I whispered.

"Maybe you've grown up a little," he said with a laugh.

At that moment Priscilla entered the room. We quickly covered the awkwardness with some chatter about dance class, their baby, and acting. Eventually it was time to go. At the door, Elvis kissed me on the cheek, gave me a wink, and said, "We'll meet again, I am sure."

A few days later, around eleven in the evening, there was a knock at my door. I opened it to find Charlie leaning against the doorframe, smiling.

"I have a friend who wants to see your trophies, if that's okay with you."

Then, out of the darkness, Elvis stepped forward and stood in my doorway.

"May I come in?"

I moved aside and let him through, too shocked to say a word. Charlie then excused himself "to make a phone call."

Elvis headed straight over to the shelf with all the trophies.

"I just heard so much about these trophies, I had to see them for myself. What's it like, winning all these?"

"Winning's fun," I said. "Losing, not so much."

"It doesn't look like you lost too often."

He continued to scan my awards with what appeared to be genuine fascination. In an effort to break the ice, I offered him a Tab.

"How about a Bloody Mary?" he asked.

"I don't have any liquor." *Sorry, Elvis.*

I sat down on the couch and forced myself to drink my Tab. Elvis, having had enough of the trophies, came over and sat beside me. My body became so tense I started squeezing the can. Before I crushed it completely, Elvis gently removed it from my hand and placed it on the table. Then he said, "You're just the kind of woman I've always liked."

I'd never been called a woman before. I wasn't sure how I liked it.

He slid his arm around me and started moving his hand up my back and through my hair. My body erupted into goose bumps, and suddenly I was freezing. He squeezed me tighter and went in for a kiss.

At first it felt warm and soft, but then our teeth clashed together, sort of killing the moment. I pulled my head back. He tried for a second time, and I literally froze. My lips involuntarily sealed themselves shut.

Sensing my terror, he whispered in my ear, "I really like you."

I wouldn't let my mouth open for fear "I love you" would slip out. My mind was reeling. Everything was happening so fast, yet it felt like slow motion.

He glided his warm hand down to the nape of my neck and began caressing it with his fingers. Goosebumps rose all over my body. At that point my anxiety turned to utter panic. I looked down at my black-and-white polka-dot pajamas. I was hardly dressed for a night with "The King." My thoughts then turned to my flabby stomach and small breasts. *This should not be happening!*

Gently Elvis turned my face toward his. He leaned over me slowly, looked into my eyes, and pressed his lips to mine. Desire took over, and I kissed him back.

Our lips played and our tongues danced for a blissful few seconds, until our teeth clashed again, snapping me back into reality.

I became awkward, uncomfortable, and self-conscious. I was just way too painfully aware of who he was to possibly relax in that way. Accepting that this was not going to happen, Elvis released his grip on me and sat back.

"I understand. You're a nice girl. Please don't hold this against me."

"Never," I said. "It's okay."

"Well," he said as he got up from the couch. "I'm glad I got to see your trophies, and I wish you all the best in Hollywood. You're a good girl, but be careful out here. A lot of guys will try to take advantage of you."

He flashed me that signature Elvis Presley smile, the one that cocked up one side of his mouth.

Elvis left and I stood by the door, letting everything sink in. At first I wanted to bang my head against the wall. *What the fuck is wrong with you?*

I went to the mirror and surveyed the childlike face staring back at me. I'd never considered myself beautiful, and, being petite, I was a far cry from the popular tall, waifish, stunning blond models like Twiggy, Jean Shrimpton, Pattie Boyd, and Lauren Hutton. I wondered what could possibly have attracted Elvis to me.

Maybe there really was something in me that intrigued people. From beauty pageant judges to Elvis Presley, they seemed to be drawn to me, despite my having, in my opinion, a mediocre appearance. Either that or maybe it was just a wish on a star coming true at last.

Over the following three years in Hollywood, plenty of men tried to take advantage of me, just as Elvis had cautioned. As I reflected on it all, I became aware that an intuitive voice had guided me that night with Elvis, as it had done on so many other occasions and would continue to do.

I saw Elvis only once after that. It was in Las Vegas, at Nancy Sinatra's show. He was with Priscilla, and I went over to say hello. Priscilla asked me to give her love to our friends at the dance studio when I got back to L.A.

Elvis smiled and winked at me as he said, "Please give my love to everyone too."

In the years that followed when I told this story, people would ask if I regretted not sleeping with him. My official answer, of course, was, "No, I don't regret it! He was a married man, and I didn't even know him!"

But in reality? Hell, yes, I regretted it! He was *Elvis!*

CHAPTER 9

Changes in Attitudes

· ·

*L*os Angeles in the late '60s was both magical and frightening; underneath its "good vibrations" seemed to lie an undertone of dark energy, that threatened to envelop the city.

The world was changing fast. The decade of love was a confusing time, wrought with mixed messages as the cultural turn toward peace and free love was constantly interrupted by images of war and news of our leaders being assassinated. Sex was everywhere, drugs were everywhere, music was everywhere. The mantra of sex, drugs, and rock 'n' roll defined that era. It both fascinated and scared the hell out of me.

Two trends dominated fashion: British mod and hippie bohemian. I liked them both and couldn't choose, so my outfits were a fusion. I'd wear go-go boots and a micro-mini and no bra (though with breasts as small as mine, I wasn't making much of a statement).

The introduction of the birth control pill, coupled with the general anti-establishment mentality of the time, created a culture of sex that was a far cry from the image of romance I had cultivated back home. True love and connection seemed far from anyone's mind as instant gratification became the norm.

While I technically came of age during the flower-child generation, I was too self-conscious and uneducated about the issues to really take part in any of the changes that my generation was credited with. I felt more spectator than participant.

I recently saw a play set in the '60s that plunged me back into those times. It featured two characters, one a free-spirited, uninhibited hippie—the embodiment of the girl I had badly wanted to be then but could not quite pull off with my own ambitions and inhibitions—and the other an uptight, constrained character with an edge. Unlikeable as she was, it hit me that much as I longed to be the golden flower child then, I identified more with this tightly wound, controlling antagonist.

Shortly after I came to L.A., a girl I met in dance class invited me to a house party near Melrose Place, not too far from where I lived. I accepted and raced home to get ready.

When I arrived at the address, a few people were out on the lawn, laughing wildly at nothing. Coming closer, I could see they were high. I felt some trepidation as I approached the door, where I was greeted by a naked couple.

"Hi, come on in! The bedroom at the top of the stairs is where everyone's putting their clothes!"

Oh my God. Everyone was naked. Some were talking and milling about, drinks in hand, as though this was a regular party. Others were coupled (or tripled) off, touching and kissing; one couple, I could have sworn, was fornicating in the corner.

This was not my scene. I bolted out of the house as fast as I could. While I was fumbling for my keys, two stark-naked men ran onto the street with another behind them screaming bloody murder—they were clearly tripping on something. Then I heard sirens. Terrific, I thought, now I'm going to be arrested and thrown into a jail full of nudists high on LSD. Fortunately, I made it out of there before the police arrived; that would have been one awkward phone call to my parents.

As soon as I got home I called Troy. At first, he said, "Thank God you got out of there! They were probably going to abduct you and sell you as a human sex slave."

"What?" I shrieked, horrified.

Then I heard him cracking up.

"That's not funny!"

"Okay, tell you what; why don't you come over here, and we can have our own party."

CHAPTER 10

Hollywood, the Dark Side

· ·

I once saw Sharon Tate at the Candy Store, an elite club for members and their guests that was typically wall-to-wall with celebrities. She was drop-dead gorgeous, with her long straight blond hair (not a strand out of place), dressed in all black with gold chains dangling around her tiny waist. She was sitting on a couch with Roman Polanski, and they could not have looked more in love. This must have been right around the time she became pregnant.

Sharon Tate was everything I wanted to be—beautiful, successful, and in a loving relationship. She was perfect, and it appeared she had the perfect life. A year later, she was murdered. I went into shock. I just couldn't understand how someone so beautiful could come to such a disgusting, and disturbing end.

Friends from home and L.A. called to check in on me and make sure I was locking my door day and night. I assured them I was and told them I was not a likely target for the murderers as I wasn't rich *or* famous.

Before the arrest of Charles Manson and his cult, the police questioned many people in regard to the murders, and Troy Donahue was one of them. I was at his apartment when the police showed up to talk to him.

He assured me he was not connected in any way, that they would be knocking on every celebrity's door until they found a lead. But for some reason the whole event still made me uneasy. Not that I suspected he had anything to do with the crime; I just couldn't imagine why the police would want to question him without a reason. It was no secret that Troy had a drug history—there were several times when I went to his apartment and met hippies who were smoking weed. Sure, hippies and weed were a part of the culture in L.A. in 1969, but there was no doubt in my mind that he was mixed up with some other bad people.

It may have been irrational of me, but I never felt completely safe with Troy after that. There were shadows within this warm and gorgeous man I was not privy to and did not necessarily want to know about. It is maybe ironic that two years later he would play a character based on Charles Manson in the movie *Sweet Savior*.

CHAPTER 11

The Dating Game

....

We were deep into the dog days of summer when my interview for *The Dating Game*—the reason I'd given my parents for coming out to L.A.—finally came through. Why it took so long I will never know, but when the day arrived I was ready.

If there's one thing beauty pageants prepare you for, it's interviews. The waiting room for potential *Dating Game* contestants was populated with the most ridiculous crop of fame-hungry wannabes I had ever seen. The girls were so full of artificial pep I thought one or two of them might levitate out an open window at any given moment. The men, if you can imagine, were even worse. Only a couple of them sat; the rest leaned casually on walls, practicing their James Dean pose. One thing was for certain: none of these people were looking for love.

Finally, it was my turn. When I entered the office of the man who'd be interviewing me, I looked up and noticed a picture of a girl I recognized from my pageant days who'd gone on to become Miss USA.

"How do you know that girl?" I asked, hoping she might provide some common ground on which to start the interview.

"From my dreams!" he replied.

Great. The last thing I needed at this moment was a pageant winner staring down at me, feeding into every insecurity I had. I could just hear her cooing, *Get over it, Kathie* (knowing how I hated nicknames); *you're too short, you have flimsy black hair, and you'll never look right in a gown. You just don't have what it takes.*

The rest of the interview was a blur. I have no idea what I said in there, but it must have been okay because I got on the show.

Excited, I walked out of the building, but the feeling soon evaporated; as I passed a newsstand on the way to my car, there they were: Jean Shrimpton, Lauren Hutton, and Twiggy, the holy trinity of Mod perfection, each thinner and prettier than the next.

Suffused with feelings of inadequacy, I stopped at a Ralph's grocery store and picked up some snacks to take home—a coconut cream pie, three bags of potato chips, a quart of ice cream, and a fistful of candy bars. But it was fine because I had a plan; I would eat until I felt myself start to turn sick, and then I'd flip my toothbrush around and poke at the back of my throat until it all came back up. Once finished, I would congratulate myself on having discovered this brilliant alternative to dieting.

The term bulimia didn't exist yet. Of course, deep down I knew there was something abnormal and deeply unhealthy about what I was doing. The whole process was both disgusting and painful. My stomach would hurt and my throat would burn. But I endured this because nothing, and I mean nothing, could be worse than being fat.

I called Troy and told him what I'd done. He was deeply concerned and made me promise never to do it again. I promised, but I lied. I continued this behavior every month or so, my vanity trumping my health and pretty much everything else.

This ritual of throwing up my food had begun back at the Miss Maryland pageant. Sis Sussman, an acquaintance of mine who'd been involved in the Miss USA pageant, called to wish me luck. He told me I had the face of the next Miss America, but that I was a little bit overweight.

His exact words were: "Hold your head up, your shoulders back, suck in that stomach." Then he added, "Just stop eating!" Great advice for an insecure eighteen-year-old.

I started compulsively examining my body in the mirror and began not only to hate what I saw but developed body dysmorphia, panicking because I didn't have a nineteen-inch waist. I became obsessed with stars like Mitzi Gaynor from *South Pacific* with teeny-tiny waists and felt ashamed for not looking like them. Because I had to look perfect or I was a loser, unlovable and unacceptable.

I felt weak and nervous living on black coffee and grapefruit and started smoking so it might keep me from eating. Meanwhile, the critically important pageant was coming up fast, and we had all kinds of lunches and dinners leading up to the big night. I'd soon be in a bathing suit, my body on full display, with no way to hide my chubby stomach.

One night after dinner I thought, *Why don't you just throw up your dinner and get it out of you?* I went into the bathroom of the motel where my chaperone and I were staying, put my fingers down my throat, and threw up my meal. The next day, I won both the bathing suit and evening gown competitions. It would be years before I got a handle on the bulimia and conquered it for good.

Now in Los Angeles, my day to appear on *The Dating Game* finally arrived. I cruised down Sunset Boulevard singing along to the Rascals's "It's a Beautiful Morning," checking my hair and makeup at every red light.

I marched onto that set in my go-go boots and boxy minidress with pink, orange, and white stripes and buttons on the front, looking as stylish as ever. Completely unaware of showbiz procedure, I hadn't realized there would be stylists waiting for me there.

As the beauticians were touching me up, I thought of my mother and how much fun it would be for her to finally have something to brag about: her daughter was going to be on television!

Suddenly I became hyperaware of my bladder (the need to pee right before important events has plagued me for most my life), but before I could dwell on that too much the music started. I was escorted onto the set, adrenaline took over, and my bladder kept its composure as they played "Whipped Cream" by Herb Albert & the Tijuana Brass. I got goosebumps taking in the huge, colorful, psychedelic daisies on the wall that I had seen so often on television in my living room. Now I was the one on television.

The questions were written out in advance on little index cards; the producers were taking no risks in having the bachelorette forget the questions. The questions I was supposed to ask Bachelors 1, 2, and 3 couldn't have been stupider.

Question 1: "How would you impress my parents?"

Question 2: "What's your idea of the perfect marriage proposal?"

Question 3: "What's your theme song?"

Really? What's your theme song? I prayed no one back home would think I came up with these!

The men's responses couldn't have been much more interesting than the questions because I can't remember what a single one of them said.

I do remember Bachelor No. 1 had a charming-sounding voice. On the commercial break Jim, the show's host, asked me who I was planning on choosing and what I was going to give for my reason. I told him I was planning on going with Bachelor No. 1 because I liked his accent. He looked at me askance and asked, "That's not really what you're planning to say, is it?" *What was wrong with that?* I wondered. Besides, I didn't have time to come up with anything better. Before I could answer his question, the music played and we were back on the air.

"Okay, Kathalynn! Which bachelor will it be?"

"I choose Bachelor No. 1!" The audience erupted in applause.

"Why Bachelor No. 1?" Jim asked.

"I like his accent!"

The audience laughed, Jim did not. Being a professional, he managed to crack a big, phony smile just in time as the camera swung around to his face.

"Wonderful!" he said, beaming. "It's time to meet your date, but first let's meet the two you didn't pick," and he shot me a look that no one else saw, one that plainly transmitted something like *Great, another dumb starlet.*

The first guy was drop-dead gorgeous, and the second one looked even better. As the camera moved to door No. 1, the suspense heightened, and from behind the door emerged the most average-looking guy imaginable. Disappointed, I pretended to be thrilled and on cue threw my arms around him. The audience roared once again.

For our date, we were sent to exotic Scottsdale, Arizona, to spend a day at the glamorous Executive House Inn. Our photographer/romance coordinator directed us to look happy and excited. We posed everywhere: by the pool, in the arcade, in the garden, lunching in the café, and eating dinner in the restaurant. I was bored to death but didn't show it, at least in the photographs, because our date had to look like a success for the sake of ratings. As Oscar Levant said, "Strip away the phony tinsel of Hollywood and you'll find the real tinsel underneath."

CHAPTER 12

A Real Audition

·······························

*L*eaving the set of *The Dating Game,* I had been approached by a stout man with dark hair and piercing blue eyes.

"Excuse me," he said, "they're casting over at Paramount Studios for a new sitcom, *Barefoot in the Park,* and I think you'd be just perfect as Corie!"

"Oh! Wow, that's quite a compliment," I said, thinking he must be insane to think I had any business playing Jane Fonda's role.

"Would you be interested in auditioning for the part?"

Was this guy for real?

He handed me a card with his phone number on it. "Call me tomorrow and I'll arrange a meeting with Garry Marshall and Jerry Belson, the writer-producers."

I raced home to call my mother with the good news. My Aunt Ruthie answered.

"Kathalynn! Your mother embarrassed me today!"

"Oh no, Aunt Ruthie!" I said, fearing the worst. "What did she do?"

"We went shopping earlier and ran into this woman. Your mother, you know, she can't help herself—she just must tell everybody 'My daughter, Kathalynn, she's out in Hollywood and she's going to be on *The Dating Game!*' Well, the woman says to her, all snotty, 'I would never want my daughter to be on television.' And, would you believe what your mother said? She said, 'Oh, you won't have to worry about that. I've seen your daughter.' Well I just about died!"

One thing I could say for my mother, she was funny and told it the way she saw it.

The next day I followed up with the man who had given me his card. He told me to come to Paramount Studios the following morning and bring my headshot.

"What's a headshot?" I asked.

"It's a picture of you, Kathalynn, from the neck up."

Oh, *headshot*. I get it now. I thanked him for the opportunity and told him I'd be there at 10:00 a.m. sharp. Strangely enough, I never saw or spoke to that man again. I can't even remember his name, but he changed my life.

CHAPTER 13

The Grasshopper

....

T he morning of my first-ever acting audition in Hollywood, I jumped
out of bed, put on the same orange, pink, and white box dress I'd
worn on *The Dating Game* (figuring it was now my lucky outfit), brushed
my hair, put on some lipstick, grabbed my little black vinyl pocketbook,
and off I went!

There are no words to describe how it feels to pass under the ornate
arched gate of Paramount Studios for the first time. There was pressure
in my throat and my chest as my heart attempted to leap right out of my
body. I pulled up and gave the security guard my name.

"Welcome to Paramount, Miss Turner. Do you know where you're
going once you're inside?"

"Err . . . not really," I said, suddenly feeling self-conscious. "I'm supposed to meet these guys Garry Marshall and Jerry Belson?"

He smiled and pointed me in the right direction.

When I reached the building, I parked and went in to reception. A
pleasant-looking woman handed me a script and instructed me to "prepare."

Prepare what? I wondered, feeling completely out of place. I had
never held a script before in my life. It didn't help that when I surveyed
the waiting room every girl there looked more blond and perfect than the
next. And from the way they handled their scripts, it was clear to me that
they were all more experienced than I was. Of course, that wasn't saying
much. I suppressed the instinct to bolt, deciding I was already there so
what the hell, why not give it a try.

When my name was called, I entered the office timidly, hoping the
whole ordeal would be over with quickly.

My mood changed immediately, though, when I met Jerry Belson. With his Afro hairdo, shaggy beard, and open shirt exposing a chest full of love beads, he looked about as offbeat and opposite a big Hollywood producer of that time as I could have imagined. I had thought I was also going to meet Garry Marshall, but as I scanned the office I didn't see anyone else. I guessed it was going to be just Jerry and me.

Jerry immediately told me I looked a little like his girlfriend, who had just starred in a major movie. He asked me if I was ready to read. I said I was, and then he called a young actor into the room to read with me.

The scene was an argument between Corie and her husband, Paul. The stage direction said yell, and I thought, *Oh, I can do that.* So that's what I did. I yelled.

When the scene finished, I looked over at Jerry for a response.

He started to open his mouth to say something when instead of Jerry's voice I heard a much deeper, raspier one coming from behind me.

"Hey! That was great!"

I turned, and a head popped up from behind the couch. Garry Marshall, having figured he'd seen enough actresses that day, was having a nap during my audition, but my yelling woke him up. Looking at those two guys, it was no wonder they would have so much success producing *The Odd Couple* a few years later. They practically *were* the odd couple.

"Really fantastic! Kathalynn, where did you study?" Garry asked.

"Suitland High School."

"No," Garry laughed, "I mean study acting?"

"Oh, well, I was in a couple of the musicals."

"You haven't studied acting at all?" he asked.

Embarrassed, I shook my head.

"Looks like the kid's a natural!" Jerry said, jumping in, and Garry smiled in agreement.

They thanked me, and I left feeling that maybe I hadn't blown my first audition after all.

A few days later, Jerry and Garry called me together.

They had decided to go ahead with the show using black actors, so unfortunately, I had been dropped from consideration, but they wanted to invite me to read for a role in their new movie, *The Grasshopper*, starring the glamorous Jacqueline Bisset and Jim Brown, the football player. I would be auditioning for the role of Ann Marie Dekker, the thirteen-year-old child bride of a mobster. I was twenty, but no one seemed to think that was a problem.

The audition went well, but as soon as it was over Jerry pulled me aside and let me know that his girlfriend was also up for the same role, so I shouldn't take it personally if the part went to her.

I was leaving the building feeling a little disappointed when Hoyt Bowers, head of Paramount casting, stopped me and introduced himself. I imagine, looking back, that Garry and Jerry had told him about me. At the time, however, I just thought it was one more lucky coincidence. Hoyt was wonderful; he offered to show me all around the studio and the commissary, and when I told him I wasn't studying anywhere entered me into an acting class at Paramount taught by Bob McAndrew.

I went home and waited to hear about *Grasshopper*. About a week later, as I was replaying my audition in the shower, I wiped away the fog on the inside of my shower door and looked straight across at my reflection in the mirror on the opposite wall.

I turned off the water just in time to hear the phone ring, then threw on a towel and rushed to answer it. Garry Marshall and Jerry Belson were again calling together, and this time it was to tell me that I'd gotten the part!

Jerry said, "I haven't told my girlfriend she didn't get the role yet. I'm gonna let Garry make that phone call."

I immediately called my parents with the news. My mother screamed with joy and wanted to get off of the phone so she could call all her siblings. My father was pleased but not over the moon because, after all, he expected nothing less.

Days before shooting began, Jim Brown, the star, had been arrested for throwing a girl off the balcony of his Hollywood apartment, and the producers had to bail him out. Because my apartment was between Jim Brown's place and the studio, the producer arranged for Jim's driver to pick me up each morning.

On our first ride together to the movie set, he looked me straight in the eyes and asked, "Are you afraid of me?"

"No. Of course not," I responded, lying through my teeth.

Jim ended up being a real friend to me on set. He was generous, kind, and went out of his way to make sure I was comfortable. He invited a group of us from the set to a party at his house. I was thrilled to be included and had a great time, although, I have to confess, I made a special point to steer clear of the balcony.

I enjoyed shooting *The Grasshopper,* but the moment I saw myself on screen, the fun was over. All throughout the shoot people had complimented me and told me how pretty I was and how well I was doing. I was beginning to believe them, getting it into my head that this was something I might actually be able to do, until late one Friday afternoon Jerry asked if I'd like to come and see the rushes, footage they'd shot that day of my scene with Jackie Bisset. Excited, I accepted.

When I saw the silly, chubby little girl on the big screen, I was mortified. *Oh God,* I thought, *that can't be me!* I pitted myself next to stunning Jackie Bisset, who moved and spoke with the confidence of a goddess. I was clearly the comic relief; I felt like a joke. Though I received tons of planned-for laughs, I took them the wrong way. I imagined people were laughing at me. When I received compliments to the effect of, "You were adorable," I became furious. Despite my round, cherubic face, petiteness of stature, and knack for comedic timing, I was still a seasoned beauty-pageant winner, and I wanted to be seen as such! I wanted to be elegant and sensual, not cute and funny!

I went back to my apartment, packed a bag, and decided to drive out to Palm Springs to hide from the world for a couple of days. When I told Troy what had happened and that I just needed to get away, he wanted to join me but I insisted on going alone and set out for the drive east.

He decided to follow me anyway and brought along my friend Alison, reasoning that I ought to have a girlfriend there to talk to. What I didn't know was that Alison had a mad crush on Troy and was thrilled to have his company for a long drive. That evening, when they couldn't track me down, they got their own room. Troy swore that she seduced him. Good thing I wasn't in love with him.

When the movie came out, the *Washington Post* review, which likened me to a young Judy Holliday, should have made me very happy. Being referred to as the Judy Holliday of the '70s was about as awesome a compliment as a new actress could receive. But accolades for charm, talent and humor were irrelevant, as far as I was concerned, unless counterbalanced with mention of my beauty, of which there was none.

The most important thing that came out of *The Grasshopper* was my lifelong bond with Garry Marshall. Garry was the big brother to me when I was a young girl in a strange land, always there for me.

Garry was a true artist and funnier than anyone I've ever known, but he was also straight as an arrow, a genuine family man who maintained a beautiful and lasting marriage, which is a rare thing in Hollywood. He was smart and knew himself well. He liked to say "I'm a hypochondriac, so I married a nurse! Smartest thing I ever did."

CHAPTER 14

Inaugural Ball: The President
Sees My Falsies

. . . .

A s part of the promotion for *The Grasshopper*, I did countless radio
spots, one of which was an interview with Johnny Grant. After the
program, he asked if I would be interested in joining the campaign for
Richard Nixon. The campaign managers were looking for Hollywood
starlets to glam up the campaign.

Truth be told, I didn't know a thing about Nixon or what he stood
for, but a campaign tour sounded exciting, and I wanted the experience
and the publicity. Fortunately, I didn't need to know much to stand on
the platform, look pretty, and wave.

I got to know Donald Nixon, the brother of the soon-to-be president.
While on the tour, and he asked me, should Nixon win the election, if
I would consider accompanying his son Ricky to the inaugural ball. I
loved the idea of going to the ball but not necessarily with a stranger. Mr.
Nixon understood that and assured me I'd be invited regardless.

He kept his word, and when Richard Nixon was elected thirty-seventh
president of the United States, I received an invitation to the inaugural ball.

My first impulse was to call Brian. I hadn't heard from him, of course,
since that uncomfortable phone interaction with his creepy friend Del,
but in my heart, he was still my ideal. If I was going to dance at the
inaugural ball with anyone, I still felt it should be with him. When I
called him, he sounded thrilled to be hearing from me. I filled him in on
the movie. "Wow," he said, "it takes most people years to book a movie.
Congratulations!" Finally, I brought up the ball and asked if he would
like to go. He hesitated and asked me the date.

"January twentieth," I told him.

"I have a gig," he replied quickly.

"Oh. Okay."

"Look, I'm sorry," he continued, sensing my disappointment. "I'm flattered you thought of me, but I just can't make it."

I hung up feeling embarrassed and stupid for even asking him. I had known deep down that Brian had no real interest in me, but deluded myself that if I impressed him enough, he may magically come to his senses and return my affections. What could possibly be more impressive than the inaugural ball? It was perfectly possible that he did in fact have a gig that night, but the casual way in which he dismissed the invitation told me all I needed to know. I wouldn't be hearing from Brian. In fact, it would be close to forty years before I saw him again.

The next call I made was to Donald Nixon, to tell him I'd be honored to be Ricky's date. My parents were delighted because since the event was in DC they'd have me back home for a few days. My father sent me money for a gown because I had nothing to wear. Clueless, I consulted a saleslady for help. She suggested a skimpy low-cut gown that couldn't have been less appropriate for the inaugural ball. Even after all those pageant years, I didn't have any idea how to dress for something like this, so I took her advice and bought it.

Because I was with the president's nephew, I was given the presidential treatment and invited to several pre-inaugural events, some of which turned out to be much more fun than the gala itself. At one such event, I was seated beside the president's two daughters, Julie and Tricia, Julie's husband David, who was former President Eisenhower's grandson, and Tricia's fiancé Ed Cox. I felt self-conscious and totally out of place. I imagined the four of them thought I was trash, but if they did, they never let on. In fact, they could not have been kinder.

The night of the ball, the Nixons sent a limousine to pick me up outside my mom and dad's house. The evening began with a reception, and wherever I turned I spotted a famous person, everyone from Colonel Sanders in the famous white suit he wore in those commercials to the current Miss America, who of course looked to-die-for in her perfect gown.

When Ricky and I got to the ball we were directed to the family section, where everyone stood except for the president's elderly aunt, who was easily the most charming person I met that night. Per protocol, we waited for the president and his immediate family to arrive.

I was wearing the brand-new high heels I had bought to go with the dress, and standing there for what seemed like forever, my feet were in so much pain I considered plopping down onto the floor. Finally, the big moment arrived; the doors burst open and President Nixon and Mrs. Nixon entered with Julie, David, Tricia, and Ed, and were met with thunderous applause and fanfare. When he got to our area, he shook my hand and not so subtly glanced down my dress. "Ricky," he said, "you've got good taste."

I suppose that was meant to be a compliment for me, but all I could think was *Oh God, the president just saw my falsies!*

The rest of the event was a letdown. It was crowded and stuffy, and they didn't serve anything to eat. People just milled about and tried not to complain about the lack of food or places to sit. When it was all over Ricky accompanied me back to my house, trying more than once to cop a feel in the limo. I couldn't have been less interested. The next day I was on a plane back to Los Angeles, and that was the last I heard from the Nixon family.

Attending such a historic event as the inaugural ball is an honor, for sure. However, the highlight of the whole experience for me was walking arm in arm with my father, the short distance from our door to the limo. My father's entire career was motivated by one thing: love of country. He beamed with pride as he walked me to the limo that would deliver me, his daughter, to the inaugural ball. He opened the door for me, and I climbed into the back seat. Before shutting it, he leaned down and whispered in my ear, "Go get em, Uga!" Uga was the nickname he'd come up with for me as a baby. It meant "little papoose."

The party was boring, I didn't care for my date, and the dress I showed up in was all wrong, but my dad was happy, and that meant more to me than everything else put together.

CHAPTER 15

Frank Sinatra Teaches Me
How to Eat Spaghetti

. . . .

One day Hoyt Bowers, Paramount's casting director, sent me to meet television producer Tony Owen, who was married to the hugely successful actress Donna Reed. The meeting was casual and general, meaning not for any particular role. We chatted about my acting class, *The Grasshopper,* and my career goals. At the end of the meeting, he asked for a picture and resume and exclaimed, "Wow! You photograph like a dream."

"Thanks," I replied, a little taken aback, but in a good way.

"Well," he said, "I have to show this to Frank."

"Frank?" I asked. "Who's Frank?"

"Frank Sinatra. Do you mind if I give him this picture and your telephone number? He'll love you."

My first thought was that my mother would love this one!

"Okay," I said, "sure." And I left, not for one minute believing he was serious.

The following Friday afternoon, having completely forgotten about the interview and the weird Frank Sinatra comment, I was returning from lunch with a girlfriend when I heard the phone ringing as I entered the apartment, and I ran to pick it up.

"Hello, I'm looking for Kathalynn."

"Speaking," I said.

"Hi, Kathalynn, this is Frank Sinatra."

71

"Frank! How're you doing, sexy?" I replied, laughing, convinced it was my friend Sam from acting class. He loved making prank calls and was the best at impressions.

"I'm well. How are you?" the voice replied after a long pause.

"Just terrific, Frankie. To what do I owe the pleasure of this call?"

"Well, I hope you don't mind, I got your number from Tony Owen. He seems to think we would get along. I'm going to be having dinner at Chasen's with some friends tomorrow and thought you might like to join us."

Tony Owen. Oh, my God! He was serious! And this was definitely not Sam on the phone. Mortified, I came up with the first lie I could think of.

"I'm terribly sorry, but I'll be in acting class Saturday night."

"Your acting class is on Saturday night?"

"Yup."

"What time does it end?"

"Around nine," I lied.

"Well, why don't you come to Chasen's after class? I'll still be there at nine, and you can join us for dessert. I would like to meet you."

"Sure," I said.

After I hung up the phone, I kicked myself for spitting out 'nine o'clock.' The whole point of pretending to have class was to get myself *out* of the date, not just push it till later! I realize, of course, that I sound nuts, talking about how I actively tried to avoid having dinner with Frank Sinatra. The truth was, however, that Frank Sinatra intimidated the crap out of me. I couldn't imagine sitting in his company and I was certain I'd make a fool of myself.

There was, of course, no acting class Saturday night, so I had to find something to do with myself until nine. I opted for a massage, hoping it would calm my nerves. It did not.

When the time came, I dressed in my usual going-out outfit, a black velvet skirt and matching vest over a white blouse, then slipped on my black pumps, got into the car, and headed for the corner of Beverly Boulevard and Doheny Drive. The valet at Chasen's took my keys, and I stepped onto a carpet under the green-and-white striped canopy.

The first thing I noticed was a glass showcase containing a coat, cane, top hat, and pair of gloves that had belonged to W. C. Fields. I was welcomed inside by a friendly maître d' who smiled broadly when I gave him my name.

"Yes, of course! Mr. Sinatra is waiting for you."

I scanned the room and there he was, at a table full of men, like a king surrounded by his adoring subjects. I froze when I saw him recognize me. Then, pulling myself together, I started to move toward the table. As I approached, he stood.

"My God, you are pretty! Tony was right!" he said, looking right into my eyes.

I had heard Frank Sinatra was charismatic, but this was a level of magnetism for which there could be no description. He offered me dinner, but I could barely speak in front of the man, let alone eat. With much difficulty, I managed to eke out, "Black coffee, please."

Frank Sinatra had an aura about him that was completely overpowering. It was a few minutes before I noticed that Sean Connery was also at the table. The conversation mostly consisted of yachts and boating, topics I knew nothing about. I sat for much of the time in silence, sipping my coffee and glancing back and forth between two of the sexiest men who had ever lived.

Every now and then Frank would catch my eye and give me a reassuring wink so I'd still feel included, even though it was clear I didn't belong. What can I say? The man knew how to make you feel good.

After dinner Frank invited me to the Daisy, a members-only nightclub in Beverly Hills. Showing up at a club with Frank Sinatra was like showing up in church with Jesus Christ himself, only cooler. He commanded the attention of literally everyone yet managed to stay completely attentive to me.

The place was crawling with Hollywood's crème de la crème. I spotted Jill St. John, Warren Beatty, and Ryan O'Neal, to name a few, but I was with the biggest star of all. At one point, Mort Viner, one of the biggest agents in Hollywood, approached our table, and Frank introduced us.

"Aren't you the girl from *The Grasshopper*?" he asked.

I nodded yes, surprised to be recognized.

"I've been hearing your name a lot lately. They're calling you the Judy Holliday of the '70s! I'd love to have you come by my office for a meeting. Shall we exchange numbers?"

We wrote our numbers down on cocktail napkins, and as we traded them I felt like a real starlet for the first time.

After Mort walked away, Frank asked, "Why didn't you tell me you were such a good actress?" Then he laughed and said, "Oh, I forgot! You don't talk."

After a couple of drinks for him and another black coffee for me, we moved on to the Candy Store, where as usual beautiful girls were everywhere, laughing freely and dancing with each other, looking so confident in their tight designer clothes. I felt lumpy and badly dressed and completely out of place, despite the man who'd brought me. Young women approached Frank and asked him to dance, but he told all of them, "No, thank you; I haven't danced with my date yet."

The girls would then cast looks at me and either walk away or flash big phony Hollywood smiles and even compliment my outfit, which of course was way below their pay grade.

When Frank and I finally danced, I was so nervous I must have stepped on his feet twenty times. I literally forgot how to do the simplest steps and bumbled like an uncoordinated child, praying for the song to end. Frank played it off like it was the greatest dance of his life. He looked at me like I was someone, and everyone else followed his lead. When I went to the ladies' room, girls stepped aside and offered me the front of the line. It was surreal.

Eventually it was time to go. Frank walked me out to the valet and stood with me, arm around my waist, while I waited for my car. In the awkward silence I finally turned to him and said, "Thank you for a lovely evening, Mr. Sinatra."

"Please don't call me Mr. Sinatra—that makes me feel old! Call me Frank."

"Yes, sir," I answered. He laughed.

"You're a sweet kid. I like you. I want you to call me if you ever need anything, and I do mean anything. Understand?"

I nodded, and he took out a pen and wrote down his private number. When my car pulled up he gave me a kiss on the cheek and said, "Remember what I said. If you need anything, call me."

As I drove away, the whole evening played back in my mind. Once home, I called my friend Vicky from Bob McAndrew's acting class. She jokingly referred to me as Alice in Wonderland, and that night that was exactly how I felt.

The next time I saw Frank Sinatra was a few months later when the comedian Pat Henry, whom I'd become friendly with, invited me to "a friend's house" for dinner. I didn't realize where we'd be going until we pulled up outside Sinatra's Bel Air mansion.

Frank greeted us at the door and seemed pleasantly surprised to see me. At dinner, he sat at the head of the table and insisted I sit beside him. I was given a plate of spaghetti that I had no idea what to do with. I tried to stab it with my fork, and when that didn't work, I tried to scoop it up with my spoon, but the slippery mass just kept sliding off and back onto the plate.

"Kathalynn," Frank finally asked, "do you not know how to eat spaghetti?"

"I don't!" I admitted, embarrassed. "I've never had it before!"

"Tell me you're kidding," Frank said, sitting back in his chair and eyeing me suspiciously.

"My mother never made it," I explained. "We're Irish, Mr. Sinatra, not Italian."

He burst out laughing, and the rest of the guests, following his lead, joined in.

"I'm not Mr. Sinatra, I'm Frank, remember?"

Then Frank picked up a fork with his right hand, scooped up a little spaghetti, twirled it against the spoon in his left, said, "Open your mouth," and fed me my first bite.

Then he told me to try it myself. My first few attempts were failures; my hands shook and he had to hold them while I scooped and twirled. Eventually I got the hang of it. When I finally finished my plate he said, "Now you're an honorary Italian!"

Everyone cheered and congratulated me. Frank then insisted that I stand up and take a bow.

After dinner, Frank took my hand and led me to his living room. I just sat there quietly. At one point he turned to me and asked if I could recite the ABCs backward. I was so intimidated I could not even remember them in order. I declined, and smiling, he took my hand again and gave me a reassuring wink.

Later in the evening, Frank made a point of mentioning that I hadn't called. "We have unfinished business," he admonished. "You never called me."

He was right. I hadn't, nor was I going to. When I told Vicky, she couldn't believe it. "How could you not call Frank Sinatra? Don't you know what he could do for you?!"

It wasn't that I didn't trust Frank; he was respectful and seemed wholly genuine; I never once got the vibe he was trying to use me. The reason I couldn't reach out was because, truthfully, I felt unworthy of whatever opportunity he could have made happen for me. I was also afraid that if he set me up on an audition, I would blow it and embarrass both myself and him.

During that time, I connected with many famous men, but Frank was different. There was something in his energy that I was just no match for. I couldn't connect with him, I couldn't engage with him; put bluntly, I felt out of my league around him. I think Rosamond Lehmann put it best when she wrote, "One can present people with opportunities. One cannot make them equal to them."

CHAPTER 16

Acting Class

· ·

After *The Grasshopper*, I got good feedback on my performance, but the truth is I didn't know the first thing about acting. I did well with my small part, and maybe that was enough to fool a few critics into thinking I could act, but I had no skill or training to speak of. All I had was beginner's luck—and I couldn't count on that to get me to the next level.

I loved actors and wanted to be one. However, I could not personally fathom ever being able to dig inside and reveal the kind of emotion I saw in the performances that inspired me. If I was ever going to make any kind of impression with my acting, I needed to find the right teacher to help me get serious.

Hollywood was then (and still is today) rumored to be a shallow town where the only things that mattered were looks and 'who you knew.' The fact is, that could not be further from the truth. Most people bust their asses for years before they make it 'overnight.' Yes, a pretty face could get you in the door—I won't argue that, especially considering it was largely my looks that secured me the role in *The Grasshopper* to begin with. However, there was no patience for ineptness on a set where money was on the line. Therefore, if there was no skill behind that 'pretty face,' the door wouldn't stay open for long.

In addition, things were changing in terms of what the new concept of 'good acting' was to become. Movies like *Midnight Cowboy, Easy Rider*, and *The Graduate* launched a standard that was more 'naturalistic.' Everyone was learning the Stanislavsky Method and if you weren't in class, well, you weren't serious.

I began researching different classes and teachers. I wasn't a hundred percent sure what I was even looking for—as there were so many different kinds of classes. Some teachers offered scene study, while others wanted their actors more to focus on exercises. One person would tell me 'repetition' was the only way, and then someone else would say, 'No, it's all about improvisation!' I had no idea what they were talking about.

Before I did *The Grasshopper*, my dance teacher, Steve Peck, began offering an acting class one evening a week, more for dancers than actresses, which I remember Priscilla Presley sitting in on, but after a few sessions I wasn't noticing that I was getting what I felt I needed. I had great respect for Steve, but this was not where I wanted to put the little money I had. Finally, Holt suggested a man named Bob McAndrew who taught a class at Paramount for professionals. From what he described, it was exactly what I was looking for.

McAndrew's class was strictly scene study. I would watch actors who had prepared scenes perform them for us, after which Bob would give feedback on their work before the next scene went up. Having never done a scene for class before and with very little knowledge of plays, I felt completely out of place and often had no idea what Bob was talking about. Many working actors and celebrities took this class—one in particular I remember was Tony Scotti, who'd been in *The Valley of the Dolls* with Sharon Tate. Too intimidated to do a scene, I mostly watched the other actors work and hoped I'd learn by osmosis.

One day I was invited to sit in and observe a class taught elsewhere by Jack Waltzer. I liked Jack right away. Warm and down to earth, he had no personal agenda but wanted only for his students to grow and reach their fullest potential.

My first day in Jack's class, I noticed that many of the faces were familiar to me from the big screen. It surprised me that so many actors who'd already "made it" so to speak, were still in class working to improve their skills. Among the most impressive of these working actors was a young woman named Susan Anspach, who had recently costarred with Jack Nicholson in *Five Easy Pieces*. Despite her enormous recent success, she was humble and sweet and I loved being in class with her.

Jack had such reverence for actors and for the craft, it was inspiring just to be there. He extracted much of what he taught from the Stanislavsky Method of Acting. Of course, I didn't know that at the time—being so new to the world acting class and acting in general. His style was probably most similar to that of Lee Strasberg, who I had the pleasure of meeting years later in New York.

The class was primarily comprised of relaxation and mood exercises, along with cold readings. Jack was interested in opening the actor up emotionally to be completely real and present onstage. He was more concerned with the subtext behind each line than with the words themselves—and emphasized the connection between the actors on stage (or on screen, it didn't really matter) as being the the element most essential to a truthful performance. When Jack gave us scripts, we had to look at our partner and take up one line at a time, delivering that line based on how we felt in that moment. He stressed the importance of really seeing and listening to one's partner; taking in his or her energy, *feeling* the affect, and then responding truthfully. The idea was to allow the relationship to inform how the words would come out—the way it would in real life. It was so simple—sometimes deceptively so—and completely brilliant. I felt free to explore my feelings as well as to simply be. There was no right or wrong, no chance of failing. Jack enabled me to experience a great freedom to explore onstage.

The exercises, simple as they seemed, could be challenging. We would be asked to stand and make sounds in front of the group in order to help us break out of our conditioning. His mantra was to relax; in relaxing our bodies, emotions would surface. We'd even be called upon to sing in front of the class, including those of us afflicted with inadequate voices, in order to stir emotions that way. He'd then ask us what we were feeling and why we were we feeling it. We might not always have the answer, he advised, but we needed to keep asking the questions.

The song exercise was especially hard for me, as I have always been extremely insecure when it came to my singing voice. One time, while struggling through it, I locked eyes with Susan across the room. She did not look away, but rather held my gaze the entire time with nothing but compassion in her eyes—making me feel completely supported and safe. That moment endeared me to her as a person and as an actress forever. A real master of the art of staying in the present, it was no wonder to me that she worked so much.

Stanley Beck, another classmate and a trained stage actor, became a good friend and for a short time, more. We were opposites in many ways, and I was never sure what he saw in me, serious actor that he was, but I suppose we reinforced the claim that opposites attract. Stanley, a New Yorker through and through (and a screener of scripts for Dustin Hoffman), was steeped in the theater world, and along with others in the class, including Jack, told countless stories of the great acting teachers of that era—Stella Adler, Lee Strasberg, Sanford Meisner—that made me long to go to that city to see for myself. If the classes in New York were anything like Jack's, challenging me to strengthen my imagination and concentration, urging me to go deeper and more organically and authentically, I wanted more. I knew I had a long way to go, but I also knew I was on a track that was as fulfilling as it was inspiring. I practically lived for Jack's class—it was my first real step toward becoming the actress I hoped to someday be.

CHAPTER 17

Steak for Four with Dean Martin

....

Mort Viner never became my agent, but he did briefly become my boyfriend. One night he invited me to dinner with Dean Martin—his client and good friend—and Dean's girlfriend, Cathy, at Mastro's steakhouse in Beverly Hills. Mort warned me before we left that Cathy probably wouldn't like me.

"Mort, if you don't want me to go . . ." I offered.

"Oh, no!" he interrupted, "Of course, I want you there, silly. Cathy doesn't like anyone, really. I just don't want you to be hurt if she's cold or rude to you."

I assured him I could handle it.

When Mort and I arrived at Mastro's, Dean and Cathy were waiting for us. As it turned out, the terrible, infamous Cathy who didn't like anyone was the same Cathy Hawn I had met and connected with at a party a year or so before that had been given by producer-director-documentarian Jack Haley Jr. (the son of Jack Haley, who had played the Tin Man in *The Wizard of Oz)*. Jack, known for his fabulous Hollywood parties, had thrown this one for Joe Namath, who had led the New York Jets to Super Bowl victory.

The party was crawling with movie stars and beautiful people. The girls all had long, flowing hair and wore expensive-looking sweaters and tight leather pants. Some had on darling baby-doll dresses with spaghetti straps. The men were equally sharp in their Nehru jackets or high-collared velour shirts and Italian loafers.

I was standing alone taking it all in when a girl came up to me and said, "Christ, can you believe some of the egos in this room? What a bunch of phonies! You look sane. I'm Cathy Hawn."

I thought she was fantastic. She warned me that Hollywood was full of insincere men who would use you for sex and even less-sincere girls who claimed to be your friend but would stab you in the back at the drop of a hat.

That evening at Mastro's, Cathy and I spent the entire meal laughing and carrying on, just as we had at the party. As for Dean Martin, he seemed shy and sweet and belied his star image by drinking hardly any alcohol. He talked a little about his son Dean Paul Martin, who was an up-and-coming star. Sadly, years later Dean Paul's life tragically ended in a plane accident. When I heard about it I couldn't help remembering how proud Dean was of him and how unbearably crushed he must have been to lose his son.

After dinner, we went on to the Candy Store, and even though this time I had to wait in line for the bathroom like everyone else, the evening was a blast. Cathy and Dean got married and then got divorced. Mort and I did not, but we did remain friends.

CHAPTER 18

Sitting on
Jack Nicholson's Lap

....

I began to seriously focus my attention on improving my acting skills and clearly it was paying off. One day my agent, Ted Witzer, called me with an audition for a movie starring Jack Nicholson.

When I arrived at the studio, I was told that the star himself would be reading with me. Jack greeted me with a smile when I came into the room. After a brief introduction, he told me that for this role I would have to appear in my underwear and asked me to strip down to my bra and panties. (In those days agents did not necessarily warn actresses about that kind of expectation at an audition, possibly because they themselves had not been told, but in any case it was not considered anywhere as unprofessional as it would be today.)

Caught off-guard, I was much too self-conscious to undress that far, and so I compromised by slipping off my skirt but leaving my blouse on—I felt confident about my legs but not so much about my chubby middle. After checking me out, Nicholson smiled and asked me to sit on his lap. There was another man in the room with us who never said a word and who I assumed was a casting director or producer. I looked at him as if to ask, *Is this normal?* He gave me a subtle nod, so I consented.

I felt horribly nervous as I balanced myself on Jack's leg. His face broke into that famous Jack Nicholson smile, and looking me dead in the eyes, he asked, "What is it you want more than anything else in the world?"

I started to feel like a kid sitting in Santa's lap. I totally froze at the question. My mind, for some bizarre reason went to this book I had just finished reading about a girl obsessed with a red Ferrari. I blurted out, "a red Ferrari!"

"That's what you want more than anything in the world?" he asked with a puzzled look.

"Yes," I said, trying to sound confident in my ridiculous choice.

"Well, that's a first!" he said, laughing.

I asked if there was anything to read for the audition and Jack said no, not at this time. I put my skirt back on, said thank you, and left.

I didn't get the part.

CHAPTER 19

Bob Hope . . . Hopes

....

A few weeks later, I booked a spot on a Bob Hope television special. My car broke down the morning of the taping and I took a cab to the set. Toward the end of the day I started asking around for a ride. Someone approached me and said, "Excuse me, Mr. Hope would like to drive you home himself."

Instantly, I started having flashbacks to the Jack Nicholson audition. Granted, I confess I didn't exactly mind sitting on Jack's lap, but if Bob Hope tried to pull the same maneuver it was going to be a very uncomfortable ride home.

"Are you ready to go?" I heard a voice say from behind me. I knew without looking who it was.

"Yes, Mr. Hope," I replied, turning around. "I'm ready!"

"Call me Bob, Blue Eyes," he shot back. *Oh God.*

"I hope you're hungry." *Wait, no one said anything about dinner!*

We entered a dimly lit restaurant somewhere in the Valley and were seated in a very private booth toward the back.

"What would you like to drink, wine, a margarita?" Mr. Hope asked.

"Black coffee."

"Oh, do you not drink?"

"Nope."

"I'm impressed. Not a lot of girls in Hollywood who don't drink."

"Yes, I've heard."

It was no secret that Bob Hope was an ardent supporter as well as a dear friend of President Nixon's, so to steer the conversation away from me and my not drinking, I brought up Ricky and the inaugural ball, making it sound as if Ricky and I were a couple. On the off-chance my host

85

was under the impression that this was some kind of date, it might help if he thought I was involved with someone he knew and respected. My plan worked.

"What a small world!" Mr. Hope finally said.

The rest of the dinner went by quickly. I don't think we even had dessert. When he dropped me off he gave me a quick peck on the cheek and wished me luck in whatever I did.

Once safely back in my apartment, I called Vicky and told her everything, to which she replied "And???"

"And what?" I asked. "He took me to dinner, I felt weird, I talked about Nixon the whole time, and he brought me home!"

"Wow did you blow it! Jesus, Kathalynn, Bob Hope! Imagine what he could do for your career!"

Vicky had a point, but what a man like Bob Hope *could* do and what he *would* do were two very different things. And even if he *had* had it in mind to open some doors, I got the vibe he would have expected me to open my legs in return. And *that* was not about to happen.

CHAPTER 20

The French Disconnection

....

One morning, my agent called with exciting news. He had secured me an audition for the famous French director Roger Vadim's next film, *Pretty Maids All in a Row*. This time, though—unlike when I auditioned for Nicholson, they let us know that we would need to appear in our underwear at the audition. The plan was to stand us all literally *in a row*, while the producers looked us over and cherry-picked their favorites. The tone with which my agent described what I'd be expected to do at that audition was so nonchalant, as though it didn't occur to him that I may be uncomfortable with it. I rolled the idea around in my head briefly, but deep down I knew I wouldn't go through with it. It wasn't that I didn't want the job, I would have loved to have been in that movie. But I'd never measure up to these picture-perfect bodies, at least that's what I believed; and couldn't justify putting myself through the humiliation. I loved acting, but the whole prospect of being judged for my body brought me right back to grade school—imagining the kids pointing and laughing and calling me 'fatty, fatty, two-by-four.' I called my agent back told him that due to a sudden onset of food poisoning, I wouldn't be making it to the audition. I hung up the phone and started to cry. For the first time it occurred to me that maybe I didn't belong in this business.

CHAPTER 21

Farming Out Fat
with the Stars

. . . .

One day, while waiting for Garry Marshall to finish a meeting so that we could have lunch, I started chatting with one of his secretaries about diet tricks, a popular subject. She told me all the stars saw a woman named Louise Long for weight loss. Louise was famous for her magical massage therapy technique that took the fat out of your body. (Yes, she actually said that.) Interested, I asked for Louise's phone number and called right way to set up an appointment.

When I arrived for my first appointment, Louise Long, weighing in at a minimum of three-hundred pounds, greeted me from behind a giant desk. The image of her, sitting there with her whale-like figure in a white, Hawaiian print muumuu, red rose sticking out of the right bun atop her head, is forever etched in my memory.

Louise showed me around a large, bright, sterile room with rows of massage tables occupied by women lying on white sheets. There was no privacy to speak of. Beside each table was a machine for "tightening up the muscles." Glancing around, I recognized many familiar faces from movies and television.

Louise introduced me to Winnie, a sweet-faced woman of about forty with short brown hair, who would be my body therapist. Winnie instructed me to strip down to my panties and lie face down on a table between Angie Dickinson and Suzanne Pleshette—at least I was in good company. Then Winnie began the treatment, which meant squeezing and pulling the skin on my body.

"*What are you doing?*" I squealed from the pain, trying not to attract too much attention.

"This is how we separate the fat from your body," she answered calmly. "Once it's all loosened up it will be absorbed back into your body and you'll pee it out."

When Winnie finished, she hooked me up to the machine, which would contract my muscles to make them "tight and strong." It was excruciating. Afterward, I was instructed to go home and drink plenty of water to encourage urination. The next morning I could hardly move. I didn't notice any fat in my pee, but I did notice bruises all over my body.

If I'd had any sense then, I'd have quit Louise Long's after that first day. But I didn't have any sense, so I returned.

During this time, my friend Stanley would occasionally ask me to dog-sit his adorable poodle-mix, Malibu. When he had to leave town for a week, I took Malibu everywhere with me, including Louise's. On the table next to me was Jane Fonda, who had her two-year-old daughter, Vanessa, with her.

Vanessa was playing with Malibu when suddenly there was a growl and then a cry. I jumped up, terrified Malibu had just bitten Jane Fonda's child. Jane hopped off the table, checked that Vanessa was okay, and then reprimanded her for pulling the dog's tail. She then apologized to *me*. Her composure and kindness was as unusual as her daughter's name was beautiful. I decided at that moment that if I should have a daughter, she'd be named Vanessa.

Another time at Louise's, while I was waiting to go in for treatment, Olivia Hussey, the beautiful young actress who'd just starred in Franco Zeffirelli's *Romeo and Juliet*, struck up a conversation with me. We hit it off, and she invited me to lunch at her house the next day.

I drove up Benedict Canyon, turned onto Cielo Drive, and pulled up to a gate manned by two security guards and their vicious-looking dogs. I remember thinking how strange it was that they had these ferocious, growling dogs at the gate to greet people. At the end of the cul-de-sac was a stunning French Country–style house.

Olivia met me at the front door and showed me around. Rudi Altobelli, her manager, who was working at a desk near the window, greeted me coolly when she introduced us, slightly irritated at the interruption. She brought me into her massive kitchen, where we made sandwiches we then took to her room, and we lounged on her bed for some girl talk.

We talked about her dating Dean Paul Martin, Dean Martin's son. He had flown to England to meet her after he saw her in *Romeo and Juliet*. We laughed about Louise Long and how nuts we were for going. I liked her a lot, and if not for something I read a few days later, we might have been good friends.

Perusing the magazine section at a drugstore, a headline caught my eye: ACTRESS OLIVIA HUSSEY LIVING IN SHARON TATE'S HOUSE. My stomach lurched, and I thought I was going to be sick. I picked up the magazine and immediately flipped through it to find the article.

There before me were photos of all the rooms I had been in, as well as a shot of Olivia's manager. Apparently, he owned the house and had been renting it to Roman Polanski and Sharon Tate when the murders occurred. Knowing I had been in the same rooms that had hosted that horrific event rattled me to the core. It was recent history and most of L.A. was still traumatized by what happened. This was emblematic of something deep and dark of which I wanted no part. I never accepted another invitation to that house, and Olivia and I eventually fell out of touch. I did hear that she went on to marry Dean Paul Martin, and I was very happy for her. I liked Olivia, but there was no way I was ever going back to that house.

CHAPTER 22

Lei-ing with Don Ho

....

L.A. may have been a film and television town, but not everyone was there for show business. My friend Joanne, a doctor whom I met at the Candy Store, had come to open a practice with her boyfriend, Omar. Joanne seemed to be everything I was not: brainy, self-sufficient, secure, and successful in her own right.

One night she called to say Omar had backed out of their Hawaii trip because he was too busy to get away. She was going to cancel the whole thing unless I wanted to come in his place, her treat. Naturally, I was in.

We stepped off the plane and walked straight into a postcard fantasy. Girls in hula skirts welcomed us with lavender orchid leis. Men in Hawaiian shirts serenaded us with ukuleles.

Among the first things Joanne and I did was make plans to see Don Ho, the Frank Sinatra of Hawaii, at the Waikiki Beachcomber Hotel. He was so well known that every place we went had his signature "Tiny Bubbles" playing on repeat.

Don Ho commanded the stage with a strength and vitality I've rarely seen before or since. When he sang "I'll Remember You," chills ran through my entire body. Like Sinatra, he was charisma on a stick.

Joanne and I were seated close to the stage, and every now and then Don would catch my eye and throw me a wink. At one point in the concert he invited me onto the stage, but I was too nervous to get up out of my chair.

After the show, a man approached our table to invite us backstage for a private party. Don was chatting with a group of people, but when he spotted me he excused himself and came right over. We chatted briefly about how nice Hawaii was, and he had a few suggestions as to what Joanne and I might do on our visit.

At one point I got into a conversation with an attractive blond girl and her friend, who was dressed as a boy and had short, somewhat unconventional hair. After a few minutes of small talk, the blond turned to her friend and asked if she could invite me to their picnic the next day.

The girl looked me up and down appraisingly. "Sure. Invite her."

I was just about to accept when Don came over and asked me to step away with him. Out of earshot, he asked me what was going on.

"Oh, your friends are so nice!" I said. "They invited me out to the Big Island tomorrow for a picnic."

"Did they mention that you'll be dessert?" he asked.

"Huh?"

Then he sweetly explained to me what lesbians were.

The following night we returned to the Waikiki Beachcomber to see the show again, this time as Don's special guests. Once more we were invited to the after party, but this time I didn't leave with Joanne.

Until I met and fell for Don Ho, I couldn't even conceive of having an affair with a married man, but there was something spellbinding about Don.

We spent our mornings together having leisurely breakfasts. Don shared his philosophy of life and opened up about some of the disappointments he'd suffered. Human experience, he believed, was a balance of happiness and suffering, that for every good there was bad. This philosophy did not sit well with me; it seemed a great way to avoid doing anything. What would be the point of seeking happiness if you knew that terrible despair was sure to follow? Why become rich and famous if it meant being doomed for a fall?

Don didn't want me to leave Waikiki. He offered to put me up in an apartment and pay my bills if I could forget about acting and stay in Hawaii. As much as I adored him, I wasn't about to throw my life away to live on an island and be anyone's mistress, and so our affair ended after a couple of weeks, and I returned to L.A.

CHAPTER 23

Star Magnet?

·····························

Often, when I tell people about my days living in Hollywood, they marvel at the amount of celebrities I interacted with. I've even been asked silly questions like "What do you think made you such a star magnet?" *Star magnet?* Hardly. The truth is, I didn't really think about it. Hollywood was a different town back then from what it is today—it was smaller and more intimate—and famous people were as much a part of the fabric of the community as anyone else. Yes, there were photographers and paparazzi types who caused their share of annoyance—but it was understood that you were supposed to leave them alone in public and most people—at least locals anyway—did respect those boundaries.

Living on Palm Avenue, right off of Sunset Boulevard, I'd often pop into Schwab's drugstore for my morning coffee (Schwab's is the spot where Lana Turner was rumored to have been 'discovered'). On one such morning, gazing to my left and then my right, I noticed I was sitting between Natalie Wood and Marlon Brando's son, Christian, who was little at the time and with his babysitter. I was a fan of Natalie Wood's (who wasn't?), but it wouldn't have occurred to me try to make an occasion out of the fact that we happened to be sharing the same counter space. And even if it had, I didn't live in Hollywood during an era of selfies and social media. We didn't have cameras that fit in our pockets or the means to instantly blast news of a celebrity sighting to everyone we knew—and I think that was for the best.

Today, with everyone essentially a photographer, a public figure can't just walk into an establishment without fear of his or her whereabouts being announced to the world by some trigger-happy Twitter enthusiast.

It's a fear they just kind of have to live with now, which is probably why you don't see them around so much anymore.

I would be lying if I said that it wasn't exciting to look up in line at the supermarket, for example, and see standing in front of me someone I just watched on TV the night before. However, to express such excitement would have been tacky and just plain 'uncool.' And if I was ever going to be seen as an *equal* to someone like Natalie Wood (as was my intention, since I was an actress), I had to be able to keep my composure. Nobody wants to hang out with a sycophant and they certainly aren't going to work with one.

CHAPTER 24

Confounded by Kazan

....

U pon my return from Hawaii, a well-connected actress I knew, Terry Moore, offered to introduce me to Elia Kazan, who was in town for a few days from New York. According to her, Kazan loved to work with little-known actors, which is exactly what I was.

I was familiar with Kazan's films and loved them all. I would never forget Troy's horror story about his audition for *Splendor in the Grass*. As he told it, for one scene they asked him to hide in some bushes, but its thorns went right through his pants and into his butt. Wincing with pain, he threw his performance and could not get back on track. Warren Beatty ended up getting the role.

Terry set up the interview at the Beverly Hills Hotel, where Kazan had a suite. When I arrived, Mr. Kazan opened the door and without saying a word gestured for me to have a seat on a comfortable-looking chair opposite a couch. Then he said, "Tell me about your childhood."

"It was wonderful," I said.

"Was it?" he asked skeptically.

"Of course it was," I answered, feeling a little defensive.

"Tell me about your mother."

"She's great. Just your usual stay-at-home mother."

"What's your father like?"

"Great."

"What are you angry at them for?"

"I'm not angry." This was starting to feel a tad invasive.

"So you have no anger at all? And your childhood was perfect?"

"Yes."

As he continued to stare at me, I felt my facial muscles harden. Watching him as he tried to analyze me, I would not budge.

He was digging for something. He wanted to know what made me tick. But even I didn't know what made me tick. I was guarded, determined to hide feelings about my past from myself and everyone else. Maybe if I'd revealed something, anything, he would have seen something he could work with. But I gave him nothing. After staring at me for maybe thirty more seconds that felt like an hour, he told me it was nice to have met me and excused himself.

I couldn't believe I'd been stupid enough to blow it with one of the greatest directors of my time. That day in Jack Nicholson's office I'd been asked to show him my body, and now this guy was poking around at my soul. It was too much for me. I wondered again if maybe I just wasn't cut out for this place.

CHAPTER 25

One Thing Leads to Another

·····························

*E*lia Kazan, in an indirect way, did end up having an impact on my life. About a month after meeting him, a friend told me a guy named Nicholas had seen me in acting class and asked her to set him up with me. When I asked her to tell me a little bit more about this fellow she said, "Okay, well . . . he's Elia Kazan's son, but he doesn't like people to know, so don't say anything."

I promised I wouldn't.

The date was arranged for me to meet Nicholas No-Last-Name for coffee, but I fell ill and couldn't make it. He was very understanding and suggested that if I was feeling better by the weekend I could join him at a party. I accepted, never letting on that I knew who he was.

Nicholas Kazan was sweet, charming, and polite. He never gave me the third degree about my childhood, my mother, or anything else. At the party, he introduced me to an older woman who I believe was his step-mother. She asked me to sit next to her, and we ended up talking most of the evening. She talked a good deal about her psychic, who sounded fabulous and who for a month or so was in town and working out of the Beverly Wilshire Hotel. Would I be interested in seeing her? Of course I would! The psychic was impossible to get an appointment with, but she could get me in if I promised to keep the appointment.

The next day, I called and was booked for that afternoon.

CHAPTER 26

In the Cards and in the Stars

....

As I walked into the lobby of the elegant Beverly Wilshire Hotel, I knew something significant was about to take place, and that whatever it was, I was ready for it.

Before I even knocked on the door of the suite it opened, and there stood a plump middle-aged woman with short, teased blond hair, heavy makeup, and flawless manicured nails. She was wearing a bubblegum pink suit with a white blouse. She looked normal, I thought, not at all like the gypsy fortune tellers in the movies.

Her psychic's lair, however, was right out of the movies. There were heavy velvet curtains over the windows, plush cushions all around, and an elegant chandelier hanging from the high ceiling. A small square card table in the middle of the room featured a crystal ball, a treasure chest full of strange-looking stones, and a stack of cards with pictures on them. Across the wall from us a sign read DON'T WORRY, EVERYTHING WILL BE OK.

She invited me to sit across from her and asked me to hold out my right hand. After studying the lines on my palm, she said, "You will be married more than once. I see four or five children."

"What about my acting career?" I asked. I couldn't have cared less about marriage or babies.

She asked for my other hand, considered it for a few moments, and said nothing. Looking intense, she picked up some beautifully illustrated cards and told me to draw a few from the pile.

"You'll be leaving Los Angeles soon, and you won't come back for a very long time, if ever."

She must have seen the worry on my face because she followed it with, "You'll find love! You will not want to come back!"

"But what about my career?"

She handed me the pile of cards and told me to pull out a few more.

"You're an actress," she said. *Well, she at least knew that.*

"You've been an actress in lifetimes before, but there is so much in the way this time; so much doubt. You will travel, you will grow, you will evolve."

"But will I act?" That's all I wanted to know.

"They aren't telling me."

"Who isn't telling you?"

"My guides. But whatever does happen, it will be for your highest good."

Well, great, I thought.

"You have no belief in yourself, you are drowning in doubt. The acting will fade from you unless you heal yourself spiritually."

I didn't like the way this reading was going at all. I had so many questions, but what she was telling me didn't address any of them. I asked her one more time.

"Will I act?"

"That will be up to you when the time comes and when you've let go of your doubt."

"How am I supposed to do that?"

"Angels and guides are all around. Two relatives also watch over you. You didn't meet them in this lifetime, but they know you. Do you understand?"

"I guess," I said, having no idea.

"All of life's challenges and limitations exist for you to break through. We are here to connect with the light within and perfect our souls. Your journey begins today."

At that point I just wanted to leave. "So what do I do?"

"The first thing you need to do is read *Power Through Constructive Thinking* by Emmet Fox. Get it right away. It will change your life."

That was it. That was her great advice. *Read a book.*

I had a lot to think about as I left the hotel. I wasn't so sure about the angels, guides, and past lives. But as I considered the other things she said, I had to admit she was right about one thing: I was practically drowning in feelings of doubt.

When I really thought about it, I didn't believe I was all that good as an actress and was already having serious reservations about staying in Los Angeles. Despite my getting small parts and making extra money with walk-ons and other work, and despite my rubbing shoulders (and more) with celebrities, I was not making the kind of professional progress that was leading me anywhere. I felt ready for a change.

I often heard actors who'd relocate from New York talk with so much pride about the training they'd received back home and all the work they'd done in theater. They'd throw around words like 'little black box' or 'off-off broadway.' I couldn't get enough of their stories about the bums and the noise and the subways. From the way they talked, it sounded magical. Apparently, in New York, theater was considered the actor's real medium, as opposed to just a stepping stone to getting on TV.

I wanted to act, but in the environment of Hollywood I couldn't let go of my insecurities long enough to allow whatever talent I had to develop and shine. I was terrified of becoming one of those out-of-work actors who would lie by the pool and then wake up twenty years later, a washed-up cliché. Like the line in "Do You Know the Way to San Jose?"—the song I'd heard in the car on my very first day in L.A.— would I too somehow end up being a star that never was, parking cars and pumping gas? Perhaps if I went to New York, surrounded by actors who cared about their craft and got the best training, I could one day be a good actress myself.

Returning home from the psychic, I turned onto my street and saw that my building was surrounded by police cars and a lot of commotion. I got out of my car and asked a police officer what was going on, explaining to him that I lived there and needed to get home. He said nothing but checked my ID and let me through. I saw one of my neighbors standing in the hallway and asked her what had happened.

"Did you know Carrie?" she asked, "the actress who lived at the end of the hall?"

"Yeah, not well, though. I've seen her around. Wait, what do you mean, *did* I?"

"She killed herself tonight. She once told me that if she didn't make it before she turned thirty that she wanted to die. I guess she was serious because today was her thirtieth birthday."

I moved to the doorway and looked out across the lawn as the paramedics loaded the body, covered by a sheet, into the back of the ambulance. A feeling of dread and desperation crept through my body.

In that moment I knew I had to get out of that town. Because one thing was for certain: I did not want to become another Carrie.

The next morning, I went to a book store in Beverly Hills and bought the book by Emmet Fox. It would be a little while before I actually read it.

CHAPTER 27

New York Beckons

....

The next day I got a call from Angels Dupine, an agent from Abrams-Rubaloff. She had received my picture and resumé and wanted to sign me, but she was leaving Los Angeles and her agency to move to New York and partner with Bill Cunningham, another top commercial agent. Together they were going to open Cunningham and Associates in New York. *New York*, I thought. *Perfect.*

"What a coincidence," I told her. "I'm moving to New York too!"

"You're kidding!" she said. "Well, that's wonderful. We have an office on 3rd Avenue and 55th Street. I'll see you there in a month!"

There it was, the sign that the psychic had predicted. That, and Carrie's suicide.

My final TV gig in L.A. was a second appearance on *The Dating Game*. This time I was of one of the three bachelorettes. I lost. One more sign that it was time to go.

While back home in Maryland for Christmas, I rode the metro up to New York for a visit and met a woman who told me she'd been a 'Gibson Girl' back in the day. I'm not sure how that was possible, because Toni was only roughly twenty years older than me, but I didn't dispute her claim because I liked her.

Toni was a voluptuous, raven-haired beauty with huge brown eyes and a smile that despite her advanced years, had men tripping over themselves when she passed. We liked each other right away and exchanged phone numbers. When I decided for certain that I was moving to New York, Toni was the first person I called. She asked me what my budget was for an apartment, and I told her about $150 a month.

As destiny would have it, Toni's neighbor at the Parc Vendome on West 57th Street had a room in her apartment for rent at exactly that amount, opening up in May. I got it. The only hitch was that I had to be out of my place in L.A. in just three weeks. No problem, Toni said; she knew of a cheap hotel, the Wellington, where I could stay until the room was ready.

I sold my candy-apple-red Fiat convertible for $500 to a neighbor who was going through a divorce. She got the deal of a lifetime, but I didn't care. I boxed up my apartment, threw out my trophies, and bought myself a one-way ticket to New York City. Then I said my goodbyes and left California with the same Samsonite luggage I'd brought with me three years earlier, almost to the date.

I loved the sunshine and the beach, and especially the Pacific coastline, but I longed for the change of seasons, the snow on my face and the crunch of autumn leaves beneath my feet. Fond as I was of the glorious Los Angeles palm trees, I didn't want to die under one of them.

PART III

I'll Take Manhattan

. . . .

The only way to make sense out of change is
to plunge into it, move with it, and join the dance.
—ALAN WATTS

CHAPTER 28

My World Expands

·····························

While the California I experienced in the late '60s was a hotbed of sexual revolution, my New York of the '70s and eighties was all about personal growth, and my drug of choice was motivational seminars. I was not always particularly selective; in fact, one could argue I was addicted. In one group I'd walk in circles, and when the instructor called, "Pause," I'd turn to the nearest stranger and say, "Hi. I used to be called Kathalynn." I told people I'd never met how gorgeous, brilliant, and powerful they were; the same people, who didn't know me, told me how beautiful, intelligent, and special I was. I met gurus and other enlightened ones who hit me with feathers and pressed their thumbs between my eyebrows to open my third eye. I aired my dirty laundry in front of strangers, who in appreciation of my bravery, flowed me vibes of love and support. I jumped up down and, flushed with enthusiasm, shouted, "I'm fabulous!" Weird? *Hell, yes.* I even stood naked before a mirror and told myself I was beautiful; that part I did alone, and only once because it freaked me out.

Where personal growth was concerned, I put my money where my mouth was. I worked one-on-one with The Sedona Method teachers and practitioners of the Science of Mind. I attended hundreds of lectures and went off on countless retreats, climbing mountains to push through my limits and jumping off cliffs to tackle my fears. I meditated, prayed, communed with nature, consulted psychic healers and aura readers, and sought blessings from sages. I tried every kind of body/energy work available, from acupuncture to Rolfing to ethereal body massages. I inhaled every self-help book I could find. I learned about accountability, personal responsibility, and possibility. I learned how my wanting to control and wanting to be controlled was dictating my decisions. I became addicted to working on myself. And Lord knows I needed to.

Enlightenment was big business and personal growth was for sale. A lot of the seminars I attended assured us that we were 'enough' while simultaneously convincing us that we needed to spring for advanced workshops. Many people, myself included, acquiesced with the hope that by the end of the next course or seminar we would have that magic bullet.

One afternoon in a shop in Greenwich Village, I saw a plain little box on display with the message "For Those Momentous Crossroads and Difficult Times in Life." It was made in China and contained a small book of affirmations, a small crystal, silk cloth, and a rock, and it cost $150. Customers lined up for it, including me. I was an easy mark.

I encountered many charlatans playing at being gurus, not always seeing through them before I'd spent too much time and money on them. Then again, there were also the success stories. Countless times I watched people move away from old, destructive concepts that had darkened their lives for years and step into a place of power and wholeness. I saw married couples go from the brink of divorce to madly in love. I even saw people heal physically. It was all there, the genuine, the fake, and everything in between.

In the name of personal growth and transformation I shuffled through the garbage, the craziness, and the nonsense to find the gems that were worth it all and that to this day inform my life and make it deeper, richer, and more meaningful.

I never looked for enlightenment per se, or to be self-realized—both concepts then seeming too "woo-woo" and out of reach. I just wanted to be the best actress I could be and get over whatever it was that was holding me back.

CHAPTER 29

Keeping Body Together

....

The best way to get to know Manhattan is to walk it. So the first thing I purchased on my arrival was a pair of comfortable shoes. Cabs were expensive, and at that time New York's subway system was considered unsafe, plus it was always breaking down. I tried taking it once when I was pressed for time. The doors opened, and I was violently shoved from the platform into the dirty tin capsule that lurched and rattled. I remember clinging to the pole for dear life. Forever after, "subway" would trigger visions of being pushed, shoved, and trampled. It would be more than thirty years before I'd give it another try.

L.A. may have been the land of the beautiful people, but New York was a hot and happening melting pot. It attracted literally every type—artists, intellectuals, beggars, aristocrats, and everything in between. When I first arrived, I was struck by the noise, and my neighborhood around 57th Street by Columbus Circle was especially loud. But within a short time I stopped noticing it altogether, the first sign that I was becoming a real New Yorker. I fell hard for the city's energy and rhythm and did not for one moment regret trading in California's coastline and perfect weather for New York's stifling humidity and stinking garbage.

My first address, the Wellington Hotel, on 7th Avenue and 55th Street, near Carnegie Hall, was close to where I was planning to live and would do until my room was ready. It was a short walk from Times Square, which in the '70s was rife with hookers and drugs—in other words, a no-go zone, unless of course you were headed for the theater. Thankfully, I had an innate ability to look out for myself. I instinctively skirted the unsavory blocks and always kept an ear out for danger. After all, this was New York.

One morning, while exploring my neighborhood, I noticed a sign across the street from the Wellington that read LUIGI'S DANCE STUDIO. I'd been missing my dance class in L.A., and how fortuitous to find a studio so nearby.

I was greeted by a handsome young man with an impeccable body who introduced himself as Ronnie. Ronnie turned out to be one of the instructors and Luigi's boyfriend. As Ronnie was showing me the class schedule, a dark-haired man with a twisted face and flawless physique came over to us; it was Luigi himself, and his sudden appearance caught me off guard. I would later learn that he had been left paralyzed by a car accident many years before, and though he had regained movement through an exercise regimen he created, his face remained partially frozen. After knowing him just a short time I ceased noticing the disfiguration. He was a lovable soul whose mission in life was to help dancers achieve feeling, elegance, and sophistication. To this day, I can still hear Luigi's mottos: "Feel it from the inside!" and "Never stop moving!"

I still had enough money from what my father had put away for my education to cover my basic expenses, which allowed me the freedom to take three classes a day at Luigi's. My morning routine would consist of rolling down to the Carnegie Deli for coffee and a macaroon and then working it off in class.

You never knew who would show up at Luigi's. Often I'd find myself dancing next to Bobby Morse (a Broadway star who made his mark in *How to Succeed in Business without Really Trying*). Bobby was a class regular. I still remember the gap between his two front teeth and how nice he was to everyone.

After getting settled in my small room at the Wellington, I called the Cunningham Agency. Angela picked up the phone and invited me in for a meeting at their new space off 3rd Avenue, behind the popular watering hole, P. J. Clarke's. After signing an exclusive contract with the agency, Angela gave me a list of top photographers. By now I knew what headshots were and went out to get new ones right away. I even got a large portfolio to include shots of different poses and a composite that showed me with different looks and hair styles that might be right for different commercials. I was ready to make the rounds! Angela started sending me out on go-sees, which were basically auditions. I got callbacks and good feedback but couldn't seem to book anything. One night, frustrated, I went home and picked up the book that the "bugga-bugga" psychic had told me to read.

CHAPTER 30

And What about the Soul?

....

*E*mmet Fox's *Power Through Constructive Thinking,* my first conscious step in a lifelong expedition into self-realization did, as the
psychic predicted, change my life. I was immediately drawn to the
concept of God as energy and light that exists within us, as opposed
to the old paradigm—a dictator-like figure, wagging his finger in judgment from his cozy perch on a cloud. "Right within your own mentality there lies a source of energy stronger than electricity, more potent
than high explosives; unlimited and inexhaustible." The teaching stirred
something deep within and seemed to be what I had been waiting for
all of my life. I brought the book everywhere, read it repeatedly, quoted
its passages to whoever would listen. I was hooked on the possibility
of turning my life into what I wanted it to be. I branched out to Ralph
Waldo Emerson: "Most of the shadows of this life are caused by our
standing in our own sunshine." The next day, feeling empowered by
the principles I was learning, I walked into a commercial audition for
Atlantic Airline School with this principle in mind. I asked myself, *What
do you want in this moment?* I answered that question by booking not
only that job but the following three as well. The energy and confidence
I brought to the auditions seemed to be the element I'd been missing.

After I booked my fourth commercial in a row, Angela told me that
Bill Cunningham wanted to meet for lunch at P. J. Clarke's the following
afternoon. I was thrilled to meet Bill Cunningham himself and surprised
he wanted to meet me. But of course, why wouldn't he? I was his client,
and I was making him money. Old concepts around self-worth die hard,

however effective a new approach might be in booking jobs. I clearly had more work to do on that front.

During this time, I often went to the Georgette Klinger salon on Madison Avenue for facials. Ms. Klinger was always around and keenly aware of her clientele. One day she asked me if I was a model. No, I said, I'd never thought about modeling; I was an actress. She told me she thought I had a fresh face and a great look and offered to arrange for some people from *Seventeen* magazine to meet me and added that a few agents might be there as well. I was interested in the prospect and flattered that Ms. Klinger thought I was pretty enough to represent her brand. The day of the meeting she had her top makeup artist do my face, and I sailed into the room with high hopes and a new confidence. It seemed to be going well, until someone raised the issue of my height—or rather, lack thereof. Ms. Klinger interrupted and suggested they could use only my face, for covers. No, they said, it didn't work that way; you had to be at least five-feet-seven to be considered, and I was just hitting five-feet-four. I think Ms. Klinger was more disappointed than I was. For my part, I'd been around that block before with the pageants. Thankfully, I wasn't too heartbroken over the prospect of not being a model. It wasn't something I was ever all that interested in, although I wouldn't have minded the extra money.

Bill Cunningham was drop-dead gorgeous, with a smile that lit up the room. He had a tan that never seemed to fade (kept up, I learned later, by lying on the roof of his Manhattan apartment building every day during optimal sun hours, whatever the temperature). Despite being in some indeterminate middle age, he was fit and trim and disciplined, confining himself to a single meal a day and playing tennis every chance he got. When he, unlike the psychic at the Beverly Wilshire, told me he saw great things ahead for my acting career, I decided he was my new best friend.

At lunch Bill told me he was impressed by my booking streak and asked to what I attributed this good luck. When I told him about Emmet Fox, a look of recognition came over his face. Was I free Sunday morning, he asked, to join him for church at Alice Tully Hall in Lincoln Center to hear Dr. Raymond Charles Barker?

The First Church of Religious Science was like no other church I had been to before. After the service we roamed the book table, and Bill bought me the Science of Mind textbook. Then we went on to brunch with some of Bill's friends, an outing that would become a Sunday ritual. He loved the camaraderie of these gatherings, and Bill was careful to put together the right mix of people. The conversations were always stimulating, engaging, and fun.

Bill was a charmer and people loved being around his positive energy. He and I enjoyed an easy rapport, but our friendship never veered into anything romantic. Whether it was the age difference that deterred Bill from making a move, or his professional scruples I do not know. It is also a possibility that he just simply wasn't attracted to me. Whatever his reasons were, the decision was for the best because I enjoyed Bill tremendously as a friend and would have hated for things to become messy between us. He took me to the best restaurants in town and introduced me to everyone who was anyone. Afterward we would take long strolls around the city, during which I got to know a variety of neighborhoods. He also acquainted me with New York's cultural scene and exposed me to Broadway and off-Broadway. Wanting to stay ahead of the curve by signing stage actors to do commercials, he'd take me to just about every show there was in this quest. And we had great fun sharing Hollywood gossip and exchanging stories of our adventures there. More than being an excellent agent, he became an invaluable friend.

Bill did a number of wonderful things for me, but the most important by far was introducing me to Science of Mind. Listening to Dr. Barker every Sunday communicate so effectively and in such a positive way was life changing; I had never heard anything like it. He stressed the notion of power residing in the use of your mind—a concept as deceptively simple as it was profoundly enlightening. One thing that jumped out at me as confusing was when he said, "The principle of life responds by corresponding; your life becomes the thing you have decided it shall be," I asked Bill to explain what exactly he'd meant.

"Kathalynn, it means that you can take control of your life by using your thoughts and create whatever you desire for yourself. You have the right to decide for yourself, not your parents or anyone else. It's all up to you."

I was captivated, having never heard anything like this in the mostly somber and depressing churches I'd attended as a child. This was the first spiritual practice I had ever encountered that I could imagine myself getting behind.

"It's mostly about your belief. You can claim something is yours—and if you really believe it, then it will be. If you want something to happen, but your inner self-talk negates the possibility, well—it can never be. That is why the quality of our thoughts and self-talk is so important."

I had never heard anyone speak this way before. I asked him where the ideas came from and he told me they dated back as early as humanity itself. Science of Mind was mostly ancient wisdom repackaged to fit a modern person's understanding. He also told me that it was this teaching that got him through the darkest period of his life—when he lost his only daughter, Lynn, to drugs.

I had known Bill a relatively short time, but when he opened up to me about his daughter and what had happened, I felt myself grow very close to him. He made me promise I would stay away from drugs—they terrified him (with good reason).

"I know her spirit is still with me. Spirit," he explained, "can never be destroyed—only the body. But still, I miss her so much."

Eventually, he left that topic and circled back to my questions about Science of Mind. He told me it was developed by a man named Ernest Holmes, who basically took the tenets of Christianity but eliminated the "hocus-pocus" to create a sort of *applied* religion—something that offered practical approaches to life's challenges, starting with the principle that human beings are the physical expression of the infinite power for good, or God. When fear and doubt interfere with our thinking, we separate ourselves from our God-like nature, which is all good, and our experience is affected. The object of Science of Mind is to reconnect to our true nature and the infinite intelligence within that will direct our mind toward all we desire.

I fell in love with Science of Mind, Dr. Barker, and the center itself which was alive with palpable, transformational energy. It was a wonderful place to hear inspiring speakers and ministers of the day, including one of my personal favorites, Louise Hay who wrote *Heal Your Body*.

Back home in Maryland, we were Presbyterians, I think. Or was it Baptists? I have vague memories of my father dropping me off at Sunday school at my mother's request, but I soon refused to return when I found out there'd be homework.

Some of my mother's siblings had married Catholics and converted. I was envious of the identity and community that came with being a

Catholic. I watched my cousins put on lovely white dresses for their Holy Communions and confirmations. They even got to pick out new middle names! I asked my mother when I was going to have a white dress and ice-cream cake, and she just laughed. When I'd spend occasional weekends with my Aunt Shirley and her family, they'd bring me along to Mass at their fancy Catholic church on Sundays. Our own Protestant church was a little shack in comparison.

I was painfully aware that I was a guest at Mass—I didn't understand what the priest was talking about or what any of the hand gestures meant; didn't know when to stand, when to kneel, when to sit back down again. I felt out of the loop where religion was concerned and reticent about church in general. But at the First Church of Religious Science, all that melted away. I felt for the first time, a God of love.

I bought all the Ernest Holmes books and tapes, and I studied hard. Something I read affected me in particular: "All the Power in the Universe is with you. Feel it, know it, and then act as though it were." I began to act as if I was already successful. I dressed better. I started to laugh more. Life was exciting! I felt I had some control over my destiny. I no longer felt like an outsider. I belonged to something.

There was a new language to acquaint myself with. I learned that Spiritual Mind Treatment, or Affirmative Prayer—sometimes just called "treatment"—was the technique used by those who practiced Science of Mind to clear away the blocks that interfered with goals. Eager to learn this technique for myself, I enrolled in a class at the center.

I soon found that when I applied myself and did the treatment, my mind would get clearer and I felt more centered and relaxed. I was slowly reprogramming old patterns and messages about being unworthy and deficient and replacing them with fresh approaches and beliefs. I had a new energy about me, I couldn't wait for class. I felt I had been given the key to a new life.

Treatment seemed to produce magical results. Knowing that things would work out for my highest best meant they did.

I started working privately with a practitioner every week, a minister under Dr. Barker who also taught classes at the center. I was immediately drawn to Eric Pace, a former dancer, a true New Yorker, warm and loving, and his great faith in treatment inspired me to go deeper into my own. I adored Eric and trusted him completely.

Eric charged five dollars for a half-hour visit, but he was worth at least $500. We would begin our sessions by acknowledging what wasn't working in my life. Then Eric would say, "Okay, we know what the issue is and that the solution is not in our minds, so let us now turn to spirit." I'd close my eyes and listen to his words. As I took them in, my body would relax, my mind would quiet down, and I could feel a shift inside, opening me to whatever the spirit or the higher mind knew. I was totally receptive. Perhaps it was my beginner's mind or my childlike trust that everything would work out, but treatment gave me more than hope; it gave me a way to change myself and attain the success that would make me feel valuable as a human being. I am conscious that this awareness and openness to something greater and deeper—this awareness that we can change the course of our lives and are deserving of it—can also be achieved by some through other means, be it psychotherapy, meditation, other practices and beliefs, or even conventional forms of religion, but for me this is what opened the door to a new way of viewing the world and my place in it.

Soon I found physical manifestations of the work around me. One time, for instance, I wanted to get away for a while and thought Mexico would be nice, but there was no internet back then, and I didn't know how to begin to put a trip like that together—I didn't even really know about travel agents. Eric listened and said we'd go into treatment, that spirit would know how to arrange this trip. Sure enough, as I was walking home from our session, I passed the window of a travel agency with a sign that read ALL-INCLUSIVE AFFORDABLE MEXICO VACATIONS. I went in and emerged with an airline ticket and my trip completely booked, and for even less money than I'd budgeted for. Was it the treatment at work? Coincidence? Magic? I had a feeling I knew, and I smiled all the way home.

Dr. Barker encouraged us to expand our prosperity consciousness by going shopping on Madison Avenue, not to buy something we couldn't afford, of course, but to get comfortable with the idea that anything we could want in this world was within our reach should we choose to have it. That prompted me to ask myself what I really wanted, and oddly, the first thing that came to mind was a ruby. Why I am not sure to this day, but I do remember thinking they were beautiful and that red represented power and passion, two traits I felt I could use more of. I imagined the ruby, saw it clearly in my mind, and within a few months I indeed was given one. Again, I could never know for sure how much was happenstance and how much the work I was doing; the fact was, I was slowly discovering a practice that made sense to me and seemed to work.

But I was still a beginner, and if I'm honest I must admit that while I was interested and committed to the spiritual and to addressing whatever it was that was standing in the way of my success as an actress, I often got impatient with the process, and caught up with the desire for faster and more tangible validation.

I had never been driven by a need to consume material things. In Hollywood, I had maybe five outfits hanging in the closet that came with me to New York. Knowing that they served me well, I was content with them. My apartment was furnished, I owned very little and I rarely felt compelled to shop. At some point, however, I started to judge my spiritual progress by the quality of what was appearing for me in the physical realm. Meaning, while I enjoyed the work—I lost sight a little bit of the real purpose, which was to bring myself up to a place, consciousness-wise, where I could achieve whatever I desired. I wanted instant gratification. I also couldn't get around the idea that I needed to be a famous actress in order to feel like *somebody*. Then again, I was young, and my perspective on life and what it's all about was limited.

CHAPTER 31

Love and Marriage

. . . .

During this busy time of going to the theater, dance classes, metaphysics classes, and commercial auditions, I never thought of having a boyfriend, let alone marriage and children. In fact, those first few months in New York, dating was the last thing on my mind. I didn't even have girlfriends, except for Toni, who was older and whom I'd meet only for the occasional lunch. I spent a lot of time with Bill and became a regular at his favorite hangout, P. J. Clarke's, where we'd talk about the theater, books, philosophy, and of course Science of Mind. He was still my agent, mentor, and best friend.

One evening as I was stepping out of a cab on the way in to meet up with Bill and some friends at P. J.'s, I turned to see a great-looking dark-haired man smiling at me. Not placing him, I stopped and smiled back as he walked toward me. And then I did a double take—sure enough, it was Warren Beatty. He caught my eye and reached to open the door, stepping aside as I gave him an awkward nod of thanks and passed through. Once at the bar, I felt a tap on my shoulder and turned around. Warren had followed me across the room. He introduced himself coolly and asked me my name. We chatted for a minute, and then I told him I needed to stop ignoring my friends. He laughed and said, "May I assault you with a call, Kathalynn?"

"Assault me?"

"Yes."

"No, thank you," I replied.

He looked shocked, turned around, and walked away. I'm sorry, but *assault me?* Yes, it was Warren Beatty, and yes, he was every bit as gorgeous in real life, but there was just something in the way he'd asked—an arrogance that turned me off. Besides, I was fully aware of his reputation, and I hadn't come all the way to New York to get toyed with by another Hollywood playboy. In fact, I really wasn't interested in dating at all—my life was full. Then one day, I received a phone call from a woman named Barbara.

I didn't know Barbara, but she was a friend of Toni's and needed a favor. Recently divorced, Barbara was living in New Jersey next door to another divorcee whose ex-husband, Mac, was a successful open-heart surgeon—just the kind of man Barbara was looking to meet. She and Mac hadn't hit it off, but she figured that maybe if she fixed him up, he'd return the favor and set her up in turn with a doctor acquaintance of his. I had zero interest in meeting this doctor, but Barbara was relentless, and I figured a friend of Toni's was a friend of mine, so I agreed to meet the two of them for lunch the following day.

It was October 6, 1971, when I walked into La Caravelle for what would turn out to be a blind date with destiny. A charming hostess escorted me through the main part of the restaurant toward the bar where I was to meet Mac and Barbara. Murals depicted Paris parks and street scenes. The clientele was exquisitely dressed. I loved this place already.

Barbara was waiting for me, seated at a leather-front bar. To her right was an odd but familiar-looking man with large round eyes and an impressively twisty mustache. *Wow,* I thought, *this guy Mac looks just like Salvador Dali! Oh wait, nevermind. That's Salvador Dali.* Just then, the man who'd been seated to her left stood up and smiled at me. He was dressed in a navy-blue blazer, crisp white shirt, dark tie, and gray pants and had no mustache. He held out his hand and said, "Hello, Kathie. I'm Mac."

Mac gestured for me to sit down and offered to buy a drink. I ordered my regular black coffee, and as we started to talk it seemed we clicked right away. We moved to a table for lunch and the two of us got so engrossed in conversation we all but forgot Barbara was there. After an hour or so of being ignored, Barbara excused herself for the bathroom and Mac invited me to join him for dinner that same night.

After he picked me up outside my apartment, he took me to a steak-house in Greenwich Village and told me about his days at Princeton University and Columbia Medical School. I had never talked at length with anyone that educated. I loved hearing about his life and how he became one of the top surgeons in the city. We sat getting to know each other until the restaurant closed. I didn't want the evening to end.

Mac Harris was thirty-nine and a father of three. When he told me about his kids, all I could think was that I couldn't wait to meet them. The sixteen-year age difference didn't throw me at all because for all his impressive statistics he was completely charming, personable, and down to earth.

Two weeks later, on a Saturday afternoon, Mac suggested we get out of the city for a day. As soon as I got into the car, he told me he was taking me to New Jersey to meet his mother. "Really? Already?" I asked, pleasantly surprised. Mac and I had been inseparable since the day we'd met, so while things were moving fast, it felt natural.

"I think it's time she meets my future wife."

"Are you sure?" I asked.

"As sure as I am when I take my scalpel and do this," and he pressed his finger into my knee and slid it straight to the top of my leg.

"When I cut open a patient, there is no hesitating. When you hesitate, your confidence fades. It's the same feeling I have right now. I want to marry you. Do you want to marry me or not?"

He was dead serious. I didn't want to lose him, and so I said, "Yes, I will marry you."

It made perfect sense that I would marry a doctor. As a frightened child in the hospital those years ago, doctors seemed like gods. The sight of a man in a white coat gave me a sense of emotional and physical safety that I yearned for. Despite my recent personal and professional growth and my developing independence, deep inside I still often felt like that sick little girl. I loved Mac, although it wasn't a fairytale or passion-filled kind of love. I was in awe of him and what he did. And concerned as I was with my career at that time, far more avidly than finding Prince Charming, Mac was the perfect fit for me, as I was for him.

Eric Pace married us at the Lotos Club in New York City on March 4, 1972, just five months after we met. Both our mothers and a best man were in attendance. Mac, though he was raised Jewish, embraced the Science of Mind inspired ceremony, feeling it was closer to his own religion than Christianity. He looked impeccable in his customary blue blazer, crisp white shirt, pink tie, and gray pants. I wore a white sequined poncho edged with fringe, white pants, and a headband, with my black hair hanging loose. My look leaned more toward Pocahontas than 'girl about to marry a doctor.' Mac's mother did a double take when I walked in, but did her best to cover it. She even managed to stammer out the words "You look . . . beautiful." After the ceremony and a quick Champagne toast, Mac, my mother, and I took the Metroliner to Washington, DC, and then drove to my parents' house for a small family reception. Our European honeymoon was postponed until the summer to accommodate Mac's hectic hospital schedule.

Mac and I found a comfortable two-bedroom penthouse apartment on West 57th Street that overlooked Columbus Circle, large enough for any of his children who came to visit and a five-minute walk to Roosevelt Hospital, where he was often on call at all hours of the day and night.

One night around midnight Mac was called in for an emergency surgery, a stab wound to the chest. The victim had been attacked in his room at the Plaza Hotel. A lady of the night he had with him had pulled a knife from the tall black boots she was wearing and stabbed him in the chest and eye. The hapless fellow, naked and with several drinks in him, couldn't defend himself. Fortunately, a housekeeper on her nightly rounds heard him screaming from the hall and called security. They apprehended the perpetrator and called 911.

The man, it turns out, was a top executive in the automobile industry. He and his wife were so grateful to Mac for saving his life they invited us to Detroit to be their guests at a black-tie affair held in honor of John DeLorean. My concept of formal at the time was a black knit skirt with suspenders and a high-collared white blouse off a department-store rack. Finding myself in a sea of exquisite designer gowns and blinding jewelry, I thought, *Shit. This will not happen again.* I did my best to steer clear of photographers, but the man who invited us insisted that our presence be documented. The next morning my fashion faux pas was all over the Detroit society pages. I was grateful those photos did not leave that city.

Even with a patch over one eye, our host was seriously handsome. I always wondered if his wife ever found out that the perp who attacked her husband was a cracked-out hooker he'd picked up for the night.

Another of Mac's patients was a close relative of Ian Schrager's, co-owner and founder of trendy Studio 54. When Mac arrived at the hospital to treat him the prognosis was grim, but after a grueling time in the operating room, the man pulled through. His family, and in particular Ian, were so grateful that we were granted VIP treatment at Studio 54 anytime we wanted to go. This was much more my speed—certainly more than a stuffy black-tie gala in Detroit. Mac, needless to say, had little interest in hanging out at the very cool and slightly disreputable hotspot, feeling quite rightly that he was too old for the scene. So I brought my friend Harold from dance class. He wore a ruffled white shirt, open down the front, black leather pants, and combat boots, with a large earring in his right ear and heavy eyeliner and mascara. He was clearly ready to party. Trembling with excitement at being in such close proximity to famous people, he kept muttering for me to be cool and act like I belonged, whatever that meant. When I gave the doorman my name, we were escorted past the line that extended to the end of the block. Inside, I felt like I was back in the Candy Store. A couple of tables over were Andy Warhol, Bianca Jagger, and Liza Minnelli. Liza, recognizing me from Luigi's dance class, waved, or at least that's what I told Harold; most likely she thought I was somebody else. At one point I reached into my purse and pulled out a lipstick and a small compact mirror to touch up my makeup. Harold snatched it out of my hand and screamed, "What are you doing?"

"What?" I asked.

"This is Maybelline!" He said in horror.

"I know."

"Are you crazy? Pulling out Maybelline in a place like this? What if someone saw? Here—for God's sakes, if you need to touch up your lipstick, use mine!" he urged, handing me a tube of Chanel. That was the last time I ever used Maybelline.

CHAPTER 32

Opportunity Knocks

....

Mac worked around the clock and I continued to study dance and audition. While shooting a commercial for Piels Beer at Jones Beach on Long Island, I met Alan Paul, who was starring in the mega-hit Broadway musical *Grease*. Alan and I hit it off right away, and he invited me to come to a rehearsal of his new jazz-fusion band at The Lambs Club in Manhattan. Listening to the unique sound, I got the feeling I was sitting in on history. I was right. Alan's band went on to become the Manhattan Transfer. After the rehearsal, Alan and I grabbed some coffee, and he mentioned that a few of the lead actors' contracts would be ending soon and the producers of *Grease* had already begun searching for replacements. He offered to set me up with an audition. As soon as I found out my audition date, I hired a voice coach and worked on those songs every day for a month.

As if the prospect of auditioning for a Broadway show wasn't intimidating enough, the auditions were held on the actual stage where the show was playing. Waiting in the wings for my turn, I felt dizzy and nervous, but as soon as I walked onto the stage, I felt confident and completely in control—very much as I had during my beauty pageants. I looked out at the rows of empty seats and I imagined them filled with people. The footlights were dim but I could see the director and producers out there.

I was not a professional singer by any stretch, but fortunately, the late '50s–themed pop/rock songs weren't too vocally challenging. I sang "Freddy My Love" and "There Are Worse Things I Could Do." Shockingly, I passed the singing part of the audition and moved on to the dancing portion, and then finally the acting, where I read for the parts of Frenchie and Rizzo.

On the morning of what would have been my final callback, I woke up feeling violently ill. I could barely stop vomiting long enough to call my agent and let her know I wouldn't make the audition. At first I suspected it was something I ate and assumed it would pass; when it didn't, I went to the doctor. I was pregnant.

"How did I get pregnant?"

"Well, dear, most likely it happened the old-fashioned way," he answered with a chuckle.

In the moments following the phone call, I experienced a gamut of emotions. The women's movement was in full swing and the traditional route to marriage and babies was not in vogue. Many women I knew had opted out of motherhood completely or at least put it on hold so they could concentrate fully on careers. Having a child so young was not part of my plan, but I couldn't bring myself to part with the little life that was growing inside me. I called my agent and told her I would not be available for *Grease*. My Broadway debut was on its way out, and a baby was on its way in.

The pregnancy brought my life to a screeching halt. I was too ill to do anything but lie around, vomit, and watch the Watergate trials on TV. From the moment I'd wake up until around three in the afternoon, the little stranger who'd taken over my body wouldn't let me keep anything down, including the medicine that was supposed to relieve my nausea. Once the vomiting subsided, I'd order a dry turkey sandwich and a piece of German chocolate cake from the deli around the corner. Thank God they delivered!

There was one advantage to this physical distress, however: I was finally able to quit smoking. I'd started when I was nineteen, thinking it made me look cool and would curb my appetite. It also gave me something to do with my hands when I was nervous. Few people around me seriously considered the health issues associated with smoking back in those days, except my father, who was convinced I had weak lungs and smoking would only weaken them further, so I never smoked them when he was around. During the pregnancy, the smell of smoke compounded my nausea. After nine months, the habit was broken.

Around December, when I was fit enough to leave the house again, I was having lunch with a friend who asked me why I wasn't in an acting class. I had been so caught up with dance, commercials, Science of Mind classes, and getting married that I had let that part of my life slip, even though it had been the fundamental reason I'd come to New York in the first place.

My friend was studying with Stella Adler, whom I had heard so much about in L.A., and said that Stella was interviewing for her winter-semester class. I called that afternoon and scheduled my meeting, even though I was seven months pregnant.

CHAPTER 33

The Stella Adler
Conservatory of Acting

....

On a freezing day in December, dressed in an oversized shirt, black wool pants with an elastic waistband to accommodate my growing belly, and a pair of boots, I made my way over to the Stella Adler conservatory of acting for my interview. Ms. Adler had a reputation for disliking women and favoring the guys in her classes, so I figured I had nothing to lose. Worst case scenario, she'd take one look at my stomach and throw me out for daring to show up pregnant.

I was greeted in the lobby by a tall, good-looking young man.

"I'm Kathalynn Turner," I said, "and I have an appointment to meet Ms. Adler."

"Yes, of course," he said, smiling. "Please have a seat, and Ms. Adler will be with you shortly."

I took a moment to survey the walls lined with photos of Stella and some of her famous students, including my favorite, Marlon Brando. I noticed a portrait of a man with a plaque beneath it that read JACOB ADLER: YIDDISH THEATER. The woman I was about to meet had come from a line of important figures in theater history, and my heart quickened at the prospect of studying with her. Just then the handsome fellow returned to say, "Ms. Adler will see you now."

I was escorted into a small black-box theater, a dark room with a stage and a few rows of chairs. Ms. Adler was seated to the left on a red velvet throne-like chair. She was the most elegant woman I'd ever seen. Stunningly beautiful—with piercing blue eyes, flawless posture, immaculately coiffed blond hair, and that famous cleavage accentuated by a low-cut yet classy white blouse—she was the embodiment of poise and charisma. After studying me for several beats, Stella gave me a beguiling smile. "Hello, darling. What a pretty thing you are. Tell me about yourself, other than the fact that you'll be having a baby soon."

"I'm Kathalynn, Ms. Adler," I said, pleasantly surprised by her kindness. Now at ease, I revealed why I was there and what my goals were. She applauded me for leaving Los Angeles, claiming that Hollywood was no place for artists, and told me I was welcome to join her class as soon as I had my baby. "And darling," she added, "please call me Stella."

I left that meeting feeling elated. Being accepted into Stella Adler's class was a solid step in the direction of being able to call myself a real actress. Unfortunately, my excitement was short-lived. The demons of doubt and insecurity flew to their familiar perches inside my head. Stella hadn't asked me to audition, and I wondered, had she admitted me solely on the basis of my looks? For a young woman living in a constant turmoil over not feeling pretty enough, one would think that would have made me feel great, but it didn't. It actually made me feel like a fraud. By conventional standards, I knew was a pretty girl, but somehow I always felt that I sort of missed. Some days it was my hair that I hated. Some days it was my inadequate breasts. Some days my belly just wouldn't stay flat. Some days I thought my eyes should be brown, not blue. No matter what, there was always something about my look that bothered me. Since I like cars, I think this car metaphor illustrates it best. It was as if *I* was a red Ferrari—just like the one I told Jack Nicholson I wanted more than anything else in the world—only with a great big dent in it. From certain angles sure, I could pass for a luxury car, but look a little closer and you'd see I was basically worthless. I dreaded returning to the studio for fear I'd be cast out and humiliated for my repulsive post-childbirth appearance, not to mention my non-existent acting skills.

CHAPTER 34

Birth and Rebirth

. . . .

That Christmas, most of the gifts I received from my family and friends were maternity themed. Baby clothes, baby toys, baby books, baby everything. Among the books was a hardcover copy of Margery Williams's *The Velveteen Rabbit,* which had been a favorite of mine as a child. I opened it up and started reading aloud to myself:

> "It doesn't happen all at once," said the Skin Horse. "You become. It takes a long time. That's why it doesn't happen often to people who break easily, or have sharp edges, or who have to be carefully kept. Generally, by the time you are Real, most of your hair has been loved off, and your eyes drop out and you get loose in the joints and very shabby. But these things don't matter at all, because once you are Real you can't be ugly, except to people who don't understand."

As the familiar lesson from this beloved book resonated, I was reminded why I'd loved it so much back then and why I now hungered so much for the Real, even with my twisted emphasis on appearances.

On February 26, 1974, one day after my due-date, I gave birth to an exquisite baby girl, Vanessa Paulette. I still remember the feeling of her little body exiting mine and the doctor shouting, "It's a girl!" When the nurses gave her to me, I understood love at first sight. She lay there calm in my arms, looking up at me with piercing blue eyes and with a full head of black hair. Gazing into her sweet face, I felt my life turn a corner. My years of supreme self-absorption were officially over, and the only thing that mattered was her. I'd been afraid at times throughout the pregnancy that I wasn't ready for motherhood, that once the excitement of a new baby wore off I would come to resent the responsibility and yearn for freedom. My experience, however, was the opposite; the responsibilities weren't a burden but a pleasure. And, among other things, becoming a mother put a stop to my bulimia once and for all.

CHAPTER 35

Back to Class

· ·

I joined Stella Adler's conservatory in the spring, shortly after Vanessa was born. The curriculum consisted of scene study, voice and speech, and script interpretation. It wasn't unusual to see Harvey Keitel or Robert De Niro and others of that level sitting in the back row for her famous script-interpretation class. Within a few moments in her class, it became clear that Stella Adler was possessed of a certain genius, with bottomless reverence and curiosity about the human condition. She never judged, she merely observed.

To illustrate the need to understand what motivates behavior, Stella used an example from her own acting career, when she played a woman who abused alcohol. She herself had never abused alcohol, but an important person in her life had. This woman confided to Stella that she didn't really like people and couldn't connect with them until she'd had a few drinks. Getting drunk at parties or gatherings was how she made those events bearable. Stella taught that to truthfully represent a character, an actor must to go past the given circumstance—in this case the drinking—and determine the underlying *cause* of it. Without understanding and empathizing with the cause behind the behavior, the actor's performance would be little more than a shallow parody.

I saw Stella bring actors to levels I hadn't known existed, but she also did not suffer fools. To her, the theater was the most sacred place on Earth. She believed actors had the power to transform lives and that there was no responsibility greater. "You must be better than what you are! You must build yourselves, your bodies, your voices, your minds because you are part of a two-thousand-year-old tradition! You are an actor and therefore you are an artist, and because you are an artist, you have a responsibility and obligation to make yourself better. You are American aristocracy."

Stella was known for stopping actors midscene and shouting, "Get off my stage!" if she deemed the work subpar. It was not uncommon for students to leave in tears. Like Goethe, she wished the stage were "as narrow as the wire of a tightrope dancer, so that no incompetent would step upon it." I was both terrified and awestruck.

One of the first principles of Stella Adler's technique is that your talent is in your choice, meaning that the impact of the dialogue is completely contingent on how the actor conveys the importance of the circumstance, as well as the use of behavior and even the selection of a prop. As an example, she read a scene in which two people were having an apparent argument. The first time around, she raised her voice and did all the usual things people do in an argument; we got the gist of it, but we weren't especially moved. The second time around, however, she walked onstage with a gun behind her back. Her scene partner couldn't see it but the audience could. The scene took on a whole new level of intensity, and we were riveted. A choice, the addition of a single prop, was the difference between our passive understanding and deep emotional investment.

My first presentation for Stella was a scene from Tennessee Williams's *The Glass Menagerie*. Determined to do my best and employ everything I'd already absorbed, I took extra care to avoid all the "actor mistakes" I'd seen send Stella into her rages. I started with step one, "Who Am I?" and created the character of Laura piece by piece, from the outside in. Keeping in mind the lesson of the gun, I made sure each choice was a strong one. My voice still had a slight southern lilt, a carryover from my childhood, so a mild St. Louis accent was not a stretch for me. I walked in public with a limp, noticing and internalizing the way strangers regarded me, and how awkward and awful it felt to move through life so slowly and clumsily. I imagined every detail of a home in disrepair with shabby, torn curtains over the small, dusty windows. Recalling Stella saying, "Every prop has its own reality and truth," I endowed the little glass figures with souls and imagined myself having an important relationship with each of them. When we finished the scene, Stella pounded her fist on the table, stood up, and applauded us with a hearty "Bravo!"

I nearly died of shock. I had worked hard and applied what I'd learned, and it had resulted in a few moments of truth onstage. I'd left the self-conscious me to find a very differently self-conscious Laura. And I had not worried about how I looked. I was thrilled at Stella's praise, of course, but equally gratified at my own personal triumph.

Another personally significant scene I worked on in Stella's class was from Henrik Ibsen's masterpiece *A Doll's House*. Published in 1879, it was massively influential, and the moment at the end of the play when Nora leaves her husband, known as "the door slam heard around the world," stirred up in the hearts of women everywhere the courage to break out of the gilded cages in which they'd been living.

When I presented the scene for Stella in class, she said to me, "You must reach deeper, go further." And the more closely I examined Nora's character and circumstance, the clearer it became that I was living a similar experience. Mac, like Nora's beloved Torvald, was a good provider and an adoring husband. He was kind, supportive, and loved me, but we were not equals. Mac was a cardiac surgeon with a whole life of accomplishments behind him. I, meanwhile, didn't know who I was. I was going through the motions of being a wife, but inside was a well of untapped potential that I knew I would never explore if I stayed in the marriage. However, considering I had just had a baby, my instinct told me this wasn't the time to slam that door.

One of my favorite plays is Tennessee Williams's *Cat on a Hot Tin Roof*. I attempted the role of Maggie several times in class but to my great frustration could never really connect with it. Looking back, it makes perfect sense: Maggie, to put it bluntly, is a woman in heat, spending much of the play throwing herself at her unresponsive husband while using every tool in a woman's arsenal. Although I was twenty-six, married, and obviously not a virgin, my arsenal was basically empty. I had gone from pristine pageant contestant to a baby-faced Hollywood hopeful to wholesome doctor's wife, not exactly roles associated with heat. I couldn't access profound sexual energy because despite my experience I'd never been truly in touch with it. I tried to recall my feelings for Brian Hyland, but this did not get me far; there had been little that was sexual or lust-driven about my girlish crush. It was an innocent, romantic fantasy that quickly faded into disappointment. I didn't yet know what it was to deeply desire a man sexually. The closest I'd come was with Don Ho, but that had been short-lived and mutual. Maggie's fierce longing and aching I could understand intellectually, but I could not sufficiently connect to the feeling and bring the intention to life.

I had been calling myself an actress for years, but until Stella Adler came into my life I didn't know what acting really was. To act a character, one had to get behind that person's motives, requiring empathy and understanding, and this was precisely what I couldn't do for Maggie. And still being insecure, I allowed that one scene gone wrong to erase for myself the other successes I had had in that class—just as my good reviews for *The Grasshopper* had paled against my disappointment that I wasn't Jacqueline Bisset. I felt that I'd somehow failed as an actress because I hadn't pulled off that passionately charged scene.

Stella had a wicked sense of humor. Long after she died, I was in my dermatologist's office when the subject of conversation somehow moved to Stella. He told me she had once been seated beside him at a dinner party and had asked if he was married. "Yes," he had told her proudly, "forty years."

"Oh, darling, what a shame! No man should have to endure the same woman for forty years!"

Stella Adler's passion for acting was beyond inspiring. She said "Life beats down and crushes the soul, and art reminds you that you have one." One of the greatest pieces of advice I ever received came from her. She told me a character will reveal who he or she really is in a single sentence—listen for that sentence. This pertained not only to characters in plays, but to those out in real life as well. It changed how I would see and relate to others for the rest of my life.

CHAPTER 36

Dakota

....

W hen Vanessa turned a year old, Mac decided it was time for us to buy an apartment. Although seeds of doubt regarding the future of this marriage had already started to germinate, I didn't see this as the time to make that known. Mac wanted to live on the Upper West Side, so that's where I began my search. When our realtor showed me an apartment at the fashionable Beresford, I was smitten, and we made an offer that was accepted. A few days before we were to sign the contract, however, Mac read that an apartment in the nearby historic Dakota had been put on the market. He begged me to take a look before we committed to the Beresford. Not being from New York, the only association I had with the Dakota was *Rosemary's Baby,* and when I asked around I heard it was known for being haunted! But my husband could not have cared less and insisted I at least see the place before making a judgment.

The Dakota, on the corner of 72nd Street and Central Park West, is a large, elegant, Victorian-meets-Renaissance building with gothic overtones and ornate finials and Neptune heads along the outside rails. The east side of the building overlooks Central Park, where every type of New Yorker comes to enjoy Manhattan's version of the great outdoors— thespians rehearsing for Shakespeare in the Park, yuppies out jogging or walking their purebred dogs, kids playing Frisbee, nannies wheeling prams, drug dealers awaiting clients, and everything else in between.

Looking up at the daunting brass gates was like peering into a medieval fortress. I wondered what kinds of people would want to live there. *Rosemary's Baby* had been set there for a reason.

Entering the building with Vanessa in her stroller, I passed the doorman named José and asked him to point me to the office to meet the agent. Once we were in the office, a pregnant woman with wild black hair approached Vanessa and smiled. The man with her then knelt beside the stroller and started an animated conversation. It took me a moment to register that this sweet couple clucking at my daughter was Yoko Ono and John Lennon.

Four entrances to different sections of apartments surrounded the courtyard, in the middle of which sat a huge circular fountain festooned with sculpted art-nouveau lilies. Entering the building featuring the available unit, the agent mentioned that each floor had two apartments. As we crossed the inlaid marble of the foyer and climbed the imposing stairway with its wrought-iron banisters to the second floor, I marveled at the walls, also marble, their upper portions finished with bronze work, and the ceiling hand-carved in English oak. This was no ordinary building.

The apartment itself seemed dark and a tad gloomy. Of the two sets of mahogany pocket doors outfitted with solid brass hardware, the first led into a confined area and the other into a living room whose focal point was a massive baroque fireplace. From there another set of large mahogany doors led to the dining room, whose sixteen-foot-high ceiling made the place feel vast but still underlit, the windows being narrow and facing away from the park. Walking down a long and narrow hallway, we came to a space next to the kitchen so immense it could have been a small ballroom. From there were walked through a butler's pantry into an outsized kitchen, beyond which were two bedrooms and baths. The layout of the apartment was certainly unique, as I understood all the others in the Dakota were as well, each in its own way. I wasn't at all sure if this was for me, having imagined living somewhere more modern and bright. The broker mentioned that if we were to buy the apartment Leonard Bernstein would be our neighbor. I supposed she thought that would make a difference.

Mac rushed over from the hospital, still in his scrubs, to see the apartment for himself. After a quick survey he offered the broker the asking price right on the spot. "This is not how it ordinary works," she said, "but I will relay your offer to the owners."

After a few days of negotiation, the apartment was ours. Before we moved in, the couple we purchased the apartment from held a cocktail party to welcome us. I had my first glass of wine at that party, a French Pouilly-Fuissé, which to this day remains my favorite.

Life on the Upper West side had an easy charm to it. From Central Park West to Columbus and Amsterdam Avenues and all the way down to Broadway one could find grocery stores, little vegetable shops, delicatessens, children's shops, small bakeries, drug stores, tobacconists, a camera store, etc. I loved to browse the trendy upscale boutique Charivari on the corner of 72nd and Columbus, where Mac once got me a gift certificate for my birthday. I bought a green cashmere sweater with pants to match with it, and I wore that outfit until it fell apart! Of the ethnic neighborhood restaurants my favorite was the lively Victor's café, a Cuban place that had been there for years and where I would drink sangria and never worry about driving. This became my neighborhood, where I knew everyone and everyone knew me. I never wanted to live anywhere else; I was happy there and felt at home.

The Dakota, for all its alleged prestige, wasn't all sleek luxury. When I'd flip on the lights, scores of cockroaches scattered across the floors. The mice were more discreet, they just left little gifts in the form of droppings. A burst pipe was not uncommon. The walls were adorned with watermarks from consistent leakage, and bits of plaster fell with regularity from the ceiling. All that history and glamour—that "character"—came with a price.

I rarely called the super, because he was the creepiest man, next to Del Shannon, I had ever encountered. One day while I was moving things in, he came by the apartment and asked how things were going. I told him everything was great, to which he responded, "I'm sure you are great ... at sex!" I should have reported him, but it didn't occur to me. I was new to the building, and he had been there for years. I wouldn't have wanted to be *that* tenant, the one who moves in and immediately causes problems. Besides, I was embarrassed; I wondered if something I'd said or done had given him the wrong impression.

There was a mystical energy around the Dakota. She was a building rich with history and with all her faults I was inexplicably pulled to her—as were so many others. To live there, even for a short while, was to be given a rare and wonderful gift.

CHAPTER 37

My Neighbor the Maestro

······································

*L*eonard Bernstein, his wife, Felicia, and their three children, Jamie, Nina, and Alexander, were warm and friendly neighbors. Lenny, as he liked to be called, was a fascinating man—sexy, charismatic, and larger than life. He always carried the strong scent of cigarettes and was definitely what one would call "eccentric." He knew Stella Adler well, and when I told her I'd be moving into his building she said I must only call him Maestro. One day I found myself in the elevator with him and said, "Hello, Maestro!"

He burst out laughing and said, "How is that old broad Stella?"

Before Vanessa was born, Mac and I had gotten a dog named Natasha Whoo, or "Whoo" for short. (Mac named the dog, I named the baby; that was the deal.) The Bernsteins wanted to mate their family dog, Tooky, with Whoo, so we arranged for the dogs to have a date night over at the Bernsteins' apartment. The next day, Lenny brought Whoo back. The date had been a bust. Later that afternoon, we received a flower bouquet addressed to Whoo from Tooky, thanking her for the date and apologizing for his "performance issues." The note read: "My dear Tasha, I am mortified and feel a total failure! I hear talk of Spanish Fly—who knows—I'll try anything! Yours in misery and love, Tooky."

When Halloween rolled around, the Maestro wore a red cape and handed out popcorn and cider to children who came trick-or-treating. He was a lovely man; they were both wonderful to me, and they also adored Vanessa, who Felicia said reminded her of their youngest daughter, Nina, when she was small. Anytime Mac and I wanted a day off, she said, they'd be happy to borrow Vanessa from us. I took them up on that offer.

One afternoon I went to pick Vanessa up from a visit with the Bernsteins and found her sitting on the Maestro's lap while he played the piano. Vanessa didn't want to leave (who could blame her) and cried all the way back to our apartment. She may have been too young to know she was in the arms of greatness, but she knew good music when she heard it.

CHAPTER 38

The Unexpected

....

One morning in February, a few months after we moved in, I wasn't feeling well, so I headed to the doctor to see what the trouble was. A couple of days later he called to congratulate me; I was pregnant again. The news came as a shock. This would be my second unplanned pregnancy. I was starting to doubt the effectiveness of the diaphragm.

This pregnancy didn't go any smoother than the first, and in fact was even worse. I couldn't keep anything down and became dangerously dehydrated. Fortunately, I was married to a doctor who could put me on an IV so I wouldn't have to leave the comfort of my home, but at one point it became too much to take and I was hospitalized for a week. Released, I was feeling much better but noticed that my stomach seemed abnormally large for my being only three months along. My doctor agreed and scheduled a sonogram.

The technician spread some cold gel on my belly and began running the scanning wand over it. "There's the head," he said, "and—oh look! The second head!"

"What?" I jumped up in alarm. "My baby has two heads?"

"No," he said with a laugh. "Two heads, two babies. Let's see if there's a third!" There wasn't a third, thank goodness. I rushed down to Mac's office to tell him the news. He could not have been happier. My life was about to change from being a mother of one to a mother of three!

During the pregnancy I became so enormous that for the final six weeks I couldn't fit into any of my maternity clothes. Sheila Lukins, the co-founder of the Silver Palate food shop and a Dakota neighbor, lent me a huge tent dress that she had worn during her pregnancy. I wore it every day until I delivered, unable as I was to fit into anything else short of a shower curtain. I was constantly out of breath, with one baby lying high and squishing my diaphragm and the other's head so far down I didn't want to use the bathroom for fear of knocking it on the toilet seat and giving it brain damage.

In the summer of 1976, one of the hottest in the city's history, the Maestro stopped by to invite us to a Fourth of July concert he was conducting for the bicentennial. I was in no condition to brave the heat and crowds, so we had to decline. On his way out, he rubbed my belly and said, "I think you're having two boys, and you're going to name them both Lenny!"

The next week, meeting Mac at the hospital, I popped into the gift shop, where Ethel Merman volunteered. She walked up to me and said, "You're going to have two girls!" I asked her if I should name them both Ethel and she said, "Of course!" As it turned out, Lenny and Ethel were both right—or rather, they were both half-right. On September 11, I gave birth via caesarian section to gorgeous, full-term twins, a boy and a girl, Courtney Alexander and Caitlin Paige. (I figured, doing some counter-intuitive math, that since there was one of each sex, I was no longer obligated to name either of them Lenny or Ethel.)

With three children now and a husband who worked so much of the time, I needed an extra set of hands. Thank God we had the means to hire Ingrid, a Seventh-day Adventist from the island of Saint Kitts. She was the nanny of my dreams—a true gift from heaven without whom I surely would have lost my mind. Still, Ingrid would leave at four every Friday in order to be home by sundown, and from then until Monday morning, when she returned, I would stagger around in my pink bathrobe. I had no time for showering or much of anything else with a two-and-a-half year old and two babies. My life revolved around those babies, and at their first-birthday celebration, I could not stop crying. Why? Because they and I had actually survived a whole year!

CHAPTER 39

It's All about Who You Know

·······························

L iving in the Dakota, which was its own little community within
Manhattan, certainly had its advantages. When it came time to apply
for schools, the address alone was our "in." I guess the perception was
if we were good enough for the co-op board, we were good enough
for their admissions board. The letter of recommendation from Leonard
Bernstein didn't hurt either, and Vanessa was accepted.

Then there was the unforgettable Jimmy Martin, who in his nineties
always had a smile for me. Jimmy had once danced and sung for Flo
Ziegfeld, until he had an accident and hurt his eye. Jimmy was a character. He lived on the 8th floor, in one of what were referred to as the attic
rooms. One day as I was walking into the courtyard with one of the twins,
he asked what her name was. When I told him Caitlin, his response was,
"No, you mean Katy, like katydid." From then on we called Caitlin Katydid or little Did-did. This would last until she was a teenager.

In the fall, there was an annual potluck dinner in the courtyard to
which every resident bought a dish. John and Yoko arrived with enough
sushi to feed the whole building. One year, I sat beside Roberta Flack,
of whose music I was a fan. She regaled me with stories about her early
years as a gospel singer.

I got into a conversation about acting and the theater with a lovely
actress named Ruth Ford. She was thrilled to learn I was a student of
Stella Adler's and insisted I join her for luncheon at the Lotos Club honoring Tennessee Williams.

When I arrived at the luncheon, Ruth was seated beside Tennessee. I
recognized him immediately, his coal-black hair and mustache contrasting

with his pristine white suit. He had a smile that glowed from across the room. I located my table and took my seat, but moments later, Ruth approached me and asked if I'd like to switch seats with her for a little while. My legs shook as I crossed the room to sit down beside the legendary playwright. He smiled warmly at me, asked me my name in a slow drawl, and put me right at ease with his southern charm. I opened up to him about class with Stella and my work on *The Glass Menagerie*. He seemed moved by my appreciation for his work but told me that personally he saw me as more of a Maggie than a Laura. When I told him I had yet to really conquer Maggie, he looked into my eyes and said, "One day you'll make a great Maggie." I never got to test it, but I continue to hold his words close and dear to my heart as one of the greatest compliments of my life.

Being married to a world-class surgeon had many perks that extended beyond a financially comfortable life in Manhattan. Mac was rarely home, seemingly on call round the clock, but out in the world, he was something of a hero and treated accordingly. He was invited to speak at medical conferences all over the world. One of the first stamps in my passport was for Helsinki, Finland. We also went to Japan, where we attended a private dinner with a representative of the emperor, who presented us with a gift of a silver-and-enamel bowl. It was in this extraordinary country that I got my first taste of Eastern philosophy and culture. Traveling with children limited my options for sightseeing and sometimes I felt guilty dragging them away from their playmates, but occasionally things worked out. One time, the Lennons happened to be staying at the same hotel as us in Tokyo and they had brought their son. While John and Yoko were off working and Mac was educating the Japanese medical community, their nanny brought Sean over to play with Vanessa.

One afternoon in 1978 while I was having lunch with Nina, the Bernsteins' sixteen-year-old daughter, she mentioned that her mother had been ill. I didn't think much of it, but a few weeks later the Maestro, back with the family after a recent separation, showed up at our door in tears, asking for Mac. Felicia had lung cancer and was going to need an IV every night. For several weeks Mac would go next door to administer the IV to keep her heartbeat regular, and the Maestro would come to our place until it was done. He could not, he told me, watch his wife suffer. Sometimes we'd attempt small talk, but most of the time I would just sit with him in silence as he cried. It was apparent that he loved his wife very much. Once Mac came back, the Maestro would thank him and then return home. That was our nightly ritual until Felicia passed away, in the Hamptons, a few months thereafter. One afternoon, I passed Jackie Onassis leaving the Dakota. For a second, our eyes met and I could see that hers were full of tears. In that moment, I knew Felicia was gone. I rushed up the steps to find the Bernstein's door open and I went in to pay my respects to the rest of the family.

Before Felicia passed, I was fortunate enough to spend some time with her at her bedside. Looking like a fairy-tale godmother, in her frilly, white mop-cap, she gave me some valuable encouragement. She would tell me, "Work on your stage voice!" When I asked her how she kept it all together through the pain and trying to stay strong for her husband and children, she smiled and replied, "Love. It's all about love."

CHAPTER 40

The Center Cannot Hold

································

When the twins were around nine months old, Mac was seized with the need to leave Manhattan and move to the suburbs, specifically New Jersey. He was spending nearly all his waking hours in the hospital, and when he came home, sometimes with blood still on his shoes from the operating room, all he wanted to do was collapse into bed or catch up on sports. Physical contact between us had ceased, and I missed that intimacy. He had little energy or time for the children and less desire to be social or to make friends (especially with those in my acting circle), and he seemed uninterested in taking advantage of the city. I, on the other hand, had bonded with New York and my beloved Dakota. I was not ready to leave.

My resistance to abandoning New York for the suburbs was one of many tensions developing in our marriage. Mac, sixteen years older than I, was brilliant in his field, but we were only growing steadily farther apart. The more time I spent around him publicly, the more I noticed how difficult he could be around people and how abrupt he was and bereft of many common social skills. He would blurt out strange things at the most inopportune times and conduct inappropriate telephone conversations with my girlfriends. People would comment on how "eccentric" he was, which was the polite way of saying just plain *weird*. A doctor who once referred patients to him confided in me that he had stopped doing so because however gifted Mac was as a surgeon, his manner with patients had become too strange and erratic. When I tried to speak to him about it, Mac refused to discuss it, seeing nothing amiss. Having his behavior challenged or even questioned was completely foreign to him. He was lord of the manor, and though I was aware I had bought into this to some extent, there was less and less room for me to move, grow, and even breathe. Communication broke down between us.

I was still taking one class a week at Science of Mind and another with Stella. That was the most I could manage with three young children, even with a nanny's help during the week. Among other things, I sensed Mac was threatened by my attachment to Stella and suspicious of her influence on me, which drove him to press harder for us to leave the city. Mac was not wrong. Stella saw that being Mac's wife was stifling my potential. I was coming into my own and in the prime of my physical appeal. She encouraged me to break free. My world was profoundly different from Mac's, there was less and less for us to share. He wanted a normal life and a normal wife, but I, who had married young—perhaps too young, was not that girl.

For months I'd been suggesting a trial separation, but Mac wouldn't hear of it. The topic alone would send him into a rage; he'd threaten me with no support, that he'd move away and stop working, and then he'd reverse course and offer a million dollars for me to stay. It was getting crazy. And as it became clear that I had to get out of the marriage, it also became clear that in order to do so I would have to take matters into my own hands—and clearer yet that with three small children, it would not be easy for me do this. I would have to be prepared to be on my own with them for an indefinite period of time—it being highly unlikely that any man in his right mind would want to come home with me after a date to an apartment with baby toys on the floor and Cheerios stuck to the furniture. But truly, I felt it was for the best for all of us.

One day walking down 5th Avenue, I passed an attorney's office. I hated the idea of starting proceedings behind Mac's back, but he hadn't given me much choice. So in mid-February 1978, Mac was served divorce papers. After much arguing, Mac finally agreed to the divorce. But then, he refused to move out! As infuriating as his stubbornness was, it was for the best because he was there when the Bernsteins needed him. Every morning during that incredibly awkward time, I would pull out my Science of Mind books and treat for Mac's happiness.

A few months later as Mac was walking out of surgery, he ran into a woman named Sarah whom he had dated briefly after graduating from Princeton and whom he hadn't seen in nearly twenty years. Mac had wanted to marry her then, but Sarah's parents had talked her out of it, claiming, according to Mac, that as a broke medical student he was incapable of supporting a family. She married an attorney, breaking Mac's heart. He went on to marry his first wife, Phyllis (a lovely woman whom I came to know and like very much).

As Mac and Sarah talked, she revealed that she was in the process of getting divorced as well. And just like that, their old spark re-ignited. Mac, now a lot happier, agreed to move out of the Dakota so he could move in with Sarah in New Jersey. He had his first love and the suburbs with it. I stayed on with the kids in the Dakota.

As soon as our divorce was final, Mac and Sarah married. Our three children attended the wedding, and when Mac brought them back, he gave me some wedding cake to put under my pillow for good luck. I could not have been more relieved. I had full custody of our children, and Mac, who continued to pay for maintenance and the children's schools, camps, and health insurance, could take them every other weekend. It worked out beautifully because the children had the opportunity to get out of the city to a lovely house with a pool and lots of farm animals. Every once in a while when Mac had a late call he'd ask to sleep on my couch, and I readily agreed. Now that we had resolved things, it was all friendly and open and not the least bit weird.

CHAPTER 41

Bringing Up Babies

....

*L*ooking back, I can see how it all resolved itself, but there were times during the painful process of working through the divorce, with Mac occasionally irrational and threatening to cut me off, when I felt as though I was standing at the edge of a precipice. At the same time, however, I wasn't afraid. I knew deep inside that everything would be alright. My confidence wasn't based on anything tangible, just a gut sensation. I could take my kids and move into a loft in Greenwich Village, send them to public school, and get a real estate license to support them. I knew that if I had to I could make it on my own.

I may have been living in luxury at the Dakota, but the truth is I never quite fit into that extreme upper-class lifestyle. Unlike most of the people who lived there, I had no jewels, no designer clothes or summer houses, no decorators, no full-time housekeeper—and I was fine with that. When my one serious gem—the three-carat diamond engagement ring Mac had given me—got lost in the sandbox, I used the insurance money to purchase a piano, which the Maestro came over and tuned, declaring it "good enough." I was young and considered myself an artist. The people I liked best also shared those values. I knew who I was, and I also knew I was a work in progress. I was grateful to live in that building and to give my children a privileged life. Still, it was not easy being a single parent of three on a limited budget, despite Mac's covering the basics. What resources I had, I invested in my children's lives. I wanted to give them a magical life and expose them to every wonderful cultural advantage New York City had to offer. Like most parents, I wanted my kids to have all the things I never had.

Living across the street from Central Park, their playground, was a blessing. I would load up the twin stroller and have little Vanessa walk alongside it. Released from their stroller, the twins were especially partial to eating dirt, and Vanessa couldn't get enough of the old "cracker man," as the kids referred to him, who offered the children broken bits of stale saltine crackers from his coat pocket. Nervous about her eating those crackers, I told her they had poop on them. That solved the cracker problem.

Every kid we knew had a Big Wheel tricycle and my three were no exception—two pink ones for the girls and a blue one for Courtney. Sometimes I let them ride around the courtyard (our neighbors were most indulgent); other times they rode them up and down our long apartment hallway. It was constant chaos in that place, with toys scattered everywhere, but there was little I could do but to embrace it.

Summers I would put bathing suits on the kids and take them to the park, where they'd run through the sprinkler. I remember sitting there and watching them—Caitlin with her flaming red hair, towheaded Courtney, and Vanessa whose brown hair was sun-kissed with highlights—and marvel how lucky I was to have them. I also worried a bit about how they might have enjoyed a yard to run around in and even a plastic kiddie pool to splash in. When the city became oppressive, I'd take them to Maryland for a few weeks; we'd hop on the Metroliner to Union Station in DC, where my father would pick us up, and we'd visit my cousins, whose kids were about the same age as mine. As we enjoyed Sherry's beautiful big house with a baby pool in the backyard, I had a few twinges of guilt thinking of my own kids missing out. I started understanding—just a little—how children might benefit from leaving the city.

Mac felt guilty that the kids were not going on summer vacations, so every July he would generously send us to Bermuda for a couple of weeks and rent us a house on the water. It was paradise for the kids, and I loved it too, but but when I looked at the other families around me, it really hit me that my children were missing a father. Mac was there for them every other weekend, but he had a new life, and the children were only a small part of it. I felt guilty for not giving them more.

But the holidays in the city—that was something else, starting with the annual Macy's Thanksgiving Day Parade, whose route passed right below our window. The children always clamored to go down to the street, to be in the crowd, and so I would bundle them up and we'd watch from the corner, where they screamed with delight at the huge balloons—Snoopy, the Cat in the Hat, Minnie Mouse, Superman. The next day we'd head down to Macy's and stand in line for what seemed like hours to sit on Santa's lap and whisper a Christmas wish list. I would buy them gingerbread houses and arrays of sweets to be devoured on Christmas Day. We saved the gingerbread houses for our dessert on New Year's Eve.

Christmas morning, the kids would jump out of bed, run into the living room and open their toys; in the afternoon I'd hold an open house for all my actor friends who did not have relatives to visit. The kids loved the company and attention and of course the chance to show off their new toys, and my actor compadres got a dose of family life. It was a win-win.

Despite the occasional twinges of regret that I could not offer my kids wide open spaces, I loved living in the city with my children and treating them to Rumpelmayer's tea room and ice cream parlor at the St. Moritz Hotel on Central Park South, beautifully decorated like a Parisian café and displaying an array of toys and stuffed animals. Or Serendipity, on the East Side, where we'd share frozen hot chocolate and foot-long hot dogs.

I sent my children to a small neighborhood nursery school called the Morell School. It was located in the basement of a church on Central Park West, and I can still remember walking my kids up to the charming little red door that was the entrance. Many kids from the Dakota attended school there, including Paul Simon's adorable little boy, Harper, with whom we'd sometimes walk over together in the mornings.

One day I got a call from a fellow mom who introduced herself as Carly and explained that our two-and-a-half-year-old daughters had become friends at school. She asked if she could take Vanessa to the ballet with her daughter, Sally. "Are you nuts?" I asked, laughing out loud. "You want to take a couple of two-year-olds to the ballet at Lincoln Center?"

"Oh, I know it sounds a bit crazy," she replied, "but I'd like to try and see how they do. If it doesn't work, then we'll just leave and go to the park." I said sure and wished her luck, and we both laughed. Later that week, I told another mom from class, Maryanne about this crazy mother named Carly who was taking Vanessa and her daughter to the ballet, Maryanne screamed into the phone.

"What? That was *Carly Simon*. Didn't you know her daughter is in Elizabeth and Vanessa's class?"

"Who is Carly Simon?" I asked.

"Oh my God," she replied, "I'll pretend you didn't just say that."

She went on to name some of Carly's hit songs, but I'd been so out of the loop with babies and a toddler that I hadn't had time to listen to music. She mentioned that Carly was married to James Taylor (him I knew!) and added that other mothers had all been trying to arrange play dates with Sally Taylor with no success.

I did get to meet James Taylor at their apartment one afternoon, when I brought Vanessa over for a play date. Carly introduced me to him by saying that I had formally been a beauty queen. I was completely thrown and at a loss for words, so I stupidly said, "You must be impressed." I'd been kidding, of course, but I don't think he thought so, and when he replied, "Are *you* impressed?" it was one of those cringe-worthy moments I wished had never happened.

At that time I was seriously committed to feeding my children health food, even to the point of making some of their baby food. Eventually when they were old enough to eat pizza, I bought whole-wheat variations at the health food store rather than patronize the popular and ubiquitous pizza parlors all over the city (and my kids have never let me forget it). I did allow them sweets at birthday parties and on holidays, but during the week I was fairly meticulous and conscientious about what they ate, never even considering a stop at, say, McDonald's—which was difficult for me because when their father had them every other weekend, he gave them whatever they wanted, and McDonald's was high on the list.

One day, though, my kids begged and begged to go to McDonald's, and because I was too tired to argue, off we went down to Broadway and 72nd to the one nearest us. As we were sitting there with our burgers, French fries, and milkshakes, in walked Carly Simon with Sally. We locked eyes, and with a mortified look on her face, she came over and entreated, "Please, I beg you, never tell anyone you saw me in this place. I'm so embarrassed. I never come here, but Sally begged me and I relented."

"No problem," I told her, knowing exactly how she felt.

I was also embarrassed, of course, having violated the sacred oath of Upper West Side mothers to feed our kids only the purest of organic offerings. Of course I never told a soul about it—well, until now, that is. Carly if you're reading this . . . I'm so sorry but it's been almost forty years—I'm outing us both.

CHAPTER 42

Old Friendships to the Rescue

·······························

From time to time Garry Marshall would come to New York and fit in a visit with me. Garry's kindness to me during my three years in Hollywood made an impression that never went away—and we remained friends for the duration of his life. In fact, I had barely been in New York a month when Garry called and insisted I fly back to L.A. to act on an episode of his show, *The Odd Couple*. Not only did I welcome the work, but during that shoot I made friends with Jack Klugman and Tony Randall. In the coming years, Klugman too would check in when he was in town, meeting me for lunch at the Russian Tea Room or taking Mac and me to the racetrack. When Tony Randall and I were both living on the Upper West Side, I'd run into him constantly at the Pioneer market on Columbus Avenue. He was always very friendly. One time when I was in my ninth month with my twins, he saw me and yelled, "Kathalynn, is that you? You're huge! I think you're having twins!" Good guess, Tony.

One Mother's Day, when it was pouring rain and the kids and I were stuck inside, I decided we'd make cookies to keep them occupied. The phone rang and it was Garry Marshall, in town and wanting to come visit that afternoon. I said sure, and as soon as he came through the door he was attacked by three sets of little hands coated with cookie dough and icing. I will never forget the look of sheer delight on his face as they smeared their sticky little paws on his nice clean pants. He turned and said to me, "Okay, which one do you want me to make a star?" Then he asked if I could make him a tuna sandwich.

We had such a great time, he ended up staying for dinner. I baked chicken with spaghetti sauce, which he devoured. He didn't even bat an eye when I forgot to give him a knife and fork and napkin. There is not a restaurant in New York, (or anywhere, for that matter) who wouldn't have rolled out the red carpet for Garry Marshall—but there he was, choosing to sit in my my kitchen with three screaming toddlers in the background and eat baked chicken with his hands. He was as down to earth as they come.

On his way out, Garry noticed my living room mantle. He told me it reminded him of a house he had just visited where this woman had a similar-looking mantle displaying four beautiful vases. She saw him looking at them, came over and said, "I see you've met my family." He asked, "What?" She then proceeded to introduce him to her husband, brother, cat, and dog—whose remains were in the vases, and asked him to tell them all about the new television show he was developing. Never wanting to offend, Garry stood there and spent the next twenty or so minutes talking to four dead people in vases. There is just no other way to put it—Garry Marshall was the best.

Kay and Warner LeRoy were also neighbors at the Dakota. Warner owned the Tavern on the Green and Maxwell's Plum, two of the most popular restaurants in the city at the time.

The Tavern on the Green, on 66th Street, just into Central Park and not far from the Dakota, looked like an enchanted fairyland with crystal chandeliers of just about every color and the most beautiful Tiffany stained glass. From the glass-enclosed Crystal Room one could look out at trees with tiny white lights outlining them.

One day an Israeli actress friend of mine (whose name I can't recall) asked me if I would go with her to a wedding reception at the Tavern, since her boyfriend was sick and she didn't want to go alone. When we got there, she instructed me to walk in as if I was invited.

"Excuse me?" I asked.

She looked at me with a straight face and replied, "I wasn't invited, but I love to crash fancy weddings, so just follow me."

Terrified, I followed her into the Crystal Room with all the other invited guests drinking Champagne and dancing. We both guzzled some of the bubbly potion and danced with guests we did not know. One man I danced with asked, "Do you know the bride or groom?"

Shit, I thought, *I should have at least found out their names!* I quickly responded, "Both."

Afraid he would question me further, I excused myself to the ladies' room and stayed clear of him after that. Half loaded, we laughed our asses off all the way back to the Dakota. But I never crashed another wedding again.

Years before, while living in L.A., I had met Warner's director father, Mervyn LeRoy, through my friend Gordon Bau, the head of makeup at Warner Bros., who thought Mr. LeRoy might be able to use me in his next picture. Walking into Mr. LeRoy's grand office, I was struck by the paintings of Thoroughbred horses on the walls and used it as a conversation starter, telling him how my father loved horse races and would take me along to them when I was a child.

He listened intently to me, smiled, and then asked, "Have you studied acting?

"Not yet, but I plan to start a class very soon, Mr. LeRoy."

"An acting class?" he said, slamming his fist down on his huge desk. "No, do not join a damn acting class; either you got it or you don't. Acting classes spoil actors! I want you pure, and I will direct you."

I was shocked. I had never heard anyone go off on acting class like that before. Next, he went on to tell me about *I Never Promised You a Rose Garden*, a book he was trying to acquire the rights to. He said he thought I might be right for the role of the sixteen-year-old lead and suggested I read it, which I did. The character Mr. LeRoy saw me playing was that of a schizophrenic girl who lived in a fantasy world and wound up spending three years in an institution. I wasn't sure exactly how to take that.

The book was eventually made into a movie in 1977 with Kathleen Quinlan in the role. Mr. LeRoy neither directed nor produced it. I never ended up working with Mervyn LeRoy, but it was an honor to meet him at all—and it was a charming coincidence, finding myself on the opposite side of the country, neighbors with his son.

Warner's wife, Kay, was as wonderful a lady as I ever knew. One day, she saw me on the elevator when I was wearing a bandage after just having fallen and cut my chin. Looking concerned, she asked me what had happened. Later that afternoon, I arrived home to a gorgeous bouquet of flowers with a note that read "Chin up!"

CHAPTER 43

Methods to Access Madness

·······························

With the emotional burden of the marriage lifted, I felt able to turn my attention toward acting again. Stella Adler was very supportive through my divorce, and we'd occasionally meet on Fridays at the Stanhope Hotel on 5th Avenue to have drinks and talk about life. Despite our thirty-five year age difference, Stella and I always found plenty to talk about. She was kind to me and interested in my life, especially now that I was single. I think she enjoyed living vicariously through me—being a young single woman. She always encouraged me to date, but warned me to stay away from actors—especially the ones in class who she knew to be 'player' types and not worthy of my energy. When I held parties at the Dakota for my actor friends, she would sometimes come by and hold court. This made my parties very popular. I admired her greatly and continued with her script interpretation class, but I felt I lagged behind the other actors with my resistance to accessing deep emotions. When an actor friend suggested a class with Warren Robertson, a teacher known for his ability to open actors up emotionally, I was intrigued.

It was known that there was some competition among New York's elite acting studios. However, Warren Robertson's approach to acting was complementary to Stella's—and I knew she wouldn't see my training with him as a betrayal. Had I decided to study with Lee Strasberg, on the other hand—that would have been a different story. Stella and Lee were rivals. Their respective twists on the Stanislavsky Method of Acting were fundamentally incompatible and most actors I knew stayed solidly in one of those two camps. Stella trained actors to create truthful behavior within the constructs of the imaginary circumstance of the play—while

Lee urged his students to use their own private experience to hook into the emotional life of a character. According to Stella, Lee's approach overemphasized the emotions while neglecting the story. Another famous acting teacher of the day was Sanford Meisner. Unlike Lee, Stella adored Sanford Meisner and the two of them were lifelong friends.

One day, I was invited to a party honoring Lee Strasberg at the Lotus Club. Devout 'Adler-ite' that I was, I seriously deliberated over whether I should even go. Eventually, though, I came to the conclusion that there was no harm in meeting the man, (he was after all, a legend) as long as I stayed far away from his class. When I was brought over to be introduced, Lee's daughter, Susan told me she'd heard of me. Upon hearing that, Lee shook my hand and told me he was glad to meet me. Most likely what had happened was that she mistook me, *Kathalynn* Turner for the sensuous and beautiful up-and-coming star *Kathleen* Turner. I did not go out of my way to correct her. At some point, Lee invited me to sit in one one of his sensory classes. I accepted the invitation because, well, I wanted to see him in action! Stella, I imagined (obviously I couldn't know for sure because I wasn't about to ask) would not have approved. However, my guilt over going behind her back was trumped by my curiosity about Strasberg.

The first thing I noticed about Lee Strasberg when I entered the studio was that he was all business. He barely acknowledged me when I came in, which surprised me a little, considering how friendly he'd been at the party. He simply waited in silence for everyone to be settled, then he went to work. His class strictly revolved around a technique called 'sense memory,' which is another derivative of the Stanislavsky Method of Acting. The object of sense memory is to be able to experience on command the effects of various external conditions on the five senses. Because the memories of how things look, taste, hear, smell, and feel are all stored within our subconscious, they can technically be accessed at any time. To do this work well requires a tremendous amount of concentration and dedication. To watch it as a spectator requires the patience of a saint because it is about as entertaining as watching paint rust. Sitting in that studio, I yearned to see some actual acting, or at least reading— anything! I know sensory work is something many actors swear by and I hate to disrespect it, but I would have sooner blown my brains out than spend hours just sitting there drinking imaginary hot tea out of an imaginary teacup like those actors did. If I needed any more reason not to study with Lee Strasberg, that class provided it. When it was all over, I thanked him for allowing me to sit in and left, never to return again. Stella—thank God—was none the wiser.

I did, however, decide to join Warren Robertson's class, where I found ways to sharpen my technique, tap into my emotions, and supplement what I'd been getting from Stella, who by then was spending months at a time teaching in Los Angeles. My first assignment for Warren was from John Pielmeier's *Agnes of God;* I got to an emotional point in the scene and just froze. Warren stopped the scene and told me to get onto my hands and knees and beg. "I don't beg," I told him.

"Do it anyway," he replied.

I went down on my knees and I started to beg. It was one of the most difficult and humiliating things I had ever done. But once I submitted to the physical action of begging on the ground, the emotion followed. Once it was clear that the demons of judgment and self-consciousness were overpowered by the fierce current of raw emotion that was flowing through me, Warren said "Start the scene."

What happened next was was nothing short of a breakthrough. Warren had all kinds of methods for unlocking an actor's emotions without violating him or her psychologically. Under his expert tutelage, I felt safe delving into my own well of feelings in order to pull out the emotions necessary to do my characters justice. I reached levels in that class that I didn't even know existed within myself—tackling roles I never thought I'd be capable of. Like Stella, he was a genius in his own way. The way Warren worked with people emotionally was truly exceptional. However, Stella's script interpretation class was invaluable for not only acting but for life itself. There was nobody who could break down a script like Stella and nobody understood characters like she did. In that way, she was still in a league of her own. It was all coming together for me and between the two of them, I felt well on my way to becoming the actress I wanted to be.

CHAPTER 44

Warren and the Gurus

....

One night after class Warren asked me to go to a party with him. Surprised and flattered (Warren was considered a cool guy who was plugged into an equally cool scene), I accepted. We started spending time together, morphing into unofficial dating. He was divorced and would occasionally bring one of his daughters Vanessa's age over to play, and on weekends when Mac had the kids, I'd spend the night with Warren. When I woke up I would find him in the living room, contorting his body into all kinds of bizarre positions on the ground. "It's called yoga," he said. "It's an Indian practice, but I never studied it. When I wake up in the morning my body just starts to move into these poses on its own." He was an interesting man who was dedicated to spiritual quests that would enlarge his awareness and deepen his experience, and I, as ever, was eager to expand my own world as well.

Warren practiced Dynamic Meditation to a tape that had been developed by guru Bhagwan Shree Rajneesh (later called Osho), and he even brought me to Greenwich Village to meet a group of Rajneesh's disciples who taught the practice. The meditation was supposed to help rid you of unwanted habits, deep-rooted beliefs, and conditioned self-concepts. It began with breathing—in through the nose and out through the mouth—followed by a few minutes of screaming, jumping, kicking, and shaking along with music to rid yourself of your "stuff." When you finally felt that the "stuff" was gone, you would freeze in silent reflection in whatever position you were in and stay frozen until the music resumed, which signaled free-style dancing. This was considered a spiritual discipline, which I did every morning for an hour, and when I spent nights with Warren, we would do it together. As bizarre as the process sounds (and it was bizarre), it allowed me to start my day feeling freer and more centered. I just thank God that it was conducted in the privacy of either the center or an apartment because we looked like a bunch of lunatics and otherwise surely would have been committed.

Warren often talked about visiting Rajneesh's ashram in India, but for me, a single mother with a life in New York, this was an impossibility. A weekend was one thing, but I wasn't leaving my three kids behind to follow a guru—not to mention the fact that Rajneesh's ashram was notorious for orgies and other excesses I had no interest in. Still, I found his teachings promoting meditation, self-awareness, creativity, and humor to be profound. "The real seeker of truth," he said, "never seeks truth. On the contrary, he tries to clean himself of all that is untrue, inauthentic, insincere, and when his heart is ready, the guest comes." He had a unique way of teaching, and to this day I read his books.

One Friday afternoon Warren invited me to join him for the weekend at an ashram in the Catskill Mountains, where Swami Muktananda, an Indian guru who founded Siddha yoga, was in residence. It being a weekend for me without the kids, I met him at the bus station the following morning at 6:00.

When we arrived at the ashram, set on a gorgeous lakeside property, we passed under a large white stone archway that read SEE GOD IN EACH OTHER and headed for the main office, where three friendly women greeted us. Warren explained that he'd been having a strange experience with his body, which would automatically contort into yoga positions, and requested a private meeting with Muktananda to discuss why this might be happening.

The woman who seemed to be in charge said, "This is an unusual request; I'll have to consult with the Master," then turned to me and asked, "Would you like a meeting too?"

I declined.

"Are you sure?" she asked again. "You don't want to meet the Master?"

"No, thank you," I insisted, "I'm just here with him."

"Come back this afternoon and I will have an answer for you. In the meantime, you can do a yoga class and have lunch."

I wanted to try the class, but Warren had no interest. We went to lunch, which of course was vegetarian, took a walk along the grounds and down to the lake, stopped in the bookstore, and then returned to the office.

The woman we'd spoken to earlier told Warren, "I'm sorry, Mr. Robertson, but the Master will not be meeting with you. However, you are both welcome to attend the darshan this evening." Then she turned to me and said, "The Master has asked that you sit in the front row so he may have private time with you."

"What?" I asked, confused. "Are you sure?"

"Of course."

I was mortified. I couldn't even look at Warren, who was doubtless boiling mad inside. When we arrived later that night to the darshan for a viewing of the Master, Warren was led to a seat in the back, while two women ushered me to the front row. I turned around and mouthed "I'm sorry" to Warren, who just stared back. On a small platform before me a man in a bright orange robe with a red dot between his eyes sat smiling, surrounded by artfully arranged fruit and roses. I assumed this was Swami Muktananda. Suddenly, I was pulled up from the floor (yes, we sat on the floor) by the same two people who'd escorted me up front. They led me onto the platform and had me kneel in front of the Master.

As I knelt, he looked at me as if fascinated, and then placed his thumb between my eyes and pressed hard for at least a full minute. He pushed so hard I thought I was going to fall backward. Finally, he released his thumb from my forehead, picked up a feather, and began hitting me repeatedly. Then he put down the feather, looked into my eyes, and nodded once. The two women who'd been standing to the side came over, assisted me onto my feet, and escorted me back to my spot.

"What just happened?" I whispered to one of them.

"Don't you know? He opened your third eye!"

Warren was so jealous of my experience with Muktananda that he barely said a word to me the entire bus ride home. He had spent years studying Hinduism and the power and significance of the third eye, while I hadn't even known I had a third eye before that day, let alone what I was supposed to do with it. After a long silence, Warren turned to me and said, "You're not even *spiritual*. I should have been the one whose third eye was opened." *Right, Warren*, I wanted to say. *And what would you like me to do? Close it up again?*

After the fact, I did some research and learned that the third eye is a kind of meta organ that sees spiritual energy as opposed to physical light. And after my third eye was opened, I indeed noticed my intuitive sense sharpened and my connection with the movement of my surroundings stronger. One day as I was walking through Columbus Circle, the sensation of walking suddenly disappeared—no feeling the ground under my feet, no wind, no temperature against my skin. Instead, I *became* the wind. There was no separation; everything blended together—trees, cabs, streets, noise. All one. Crazy, I know, but a true out-of-body experience. For that moment I wasn't taking the world in via my body; I was outside of it. Of course, the moment I became conscious of this I was jerked right back into more familiar reality, and to this day I have no way of knowing for certain if that had anything to do with my third-eye experience, but in any case I was grateful.

Warren, a believer in alternative, holistic forms of healing, convinced me to try a technique called Rolfing, a technique which addresses the emotional trauma of life that can take root in our muscles, causing deformities in our bodies we don't even know about. The idea is to aggressively work out the tension so the body can regain its natural shape. Warren sent me to Patrick, who worked out of his apartment on 72nd Street and West End Avenue. Like anyone new to Rolfing, I had to commit to ten sessions, each focused on a different area of the body. Each session felt as if Patrick was pulling my insides out through my skin and shoving them through a meat grinder. I walked out with bruising that might have resulted from being hit by a bus. I thought back to Winnie from Louise Long's studio in Hollywood, who next to Patrick seemed like a mere amateur. Theoretically, Rolfing evokes deep emotional catharsis once old energy is released from the body, and though this was not my experience, the physical results were remarkable: my body indeed felt stronger and more supple and flexible. I found I could move in ways I never knew possible.

Eventually, at Warren's suggestion, I agreed to get him and Stella together. By then Stella knew I'd been studying with Warren and that we'd been seeing each other, and so I arranged for the three of us to have dinner together at a restaurant on the Upper West Side. I wasn't certain the mix would work, but the two geniuses of the theater got along famously. Warren charmed Stella, and Stella loved being charmed, especially by such a nice-looking man.

CHAPTER 45

EST

....

After Warren's class, a group of us would typically adjourn to a coffee shop down the street. A few students had just completed something called EST (Erhard Seminars Training). They were going on enthusiastically about how it was transforming their lives. Naturally, I was curious. One of the girls offered to take me to an introductory meeting. At that meeting we were told that the purpose of the training was to "transform one's ability to experience living so that the situations one had been trying to change or had been putting up with clear up within the process of life itself." I couldn't resist signing up for the training. I was open to anything new that might expand my consciousness and make me more effective as an individual, a parent, and an actress.

The training was held over for two weekends, in between which was a Wednesday evening session. The weekend training, held in a huge ballroom in midtown Manhattan, went from nine in the morning to well after midnight.

As soon as I arrived I was given an agreement to sign pledging never to be late, among other things. Then I was asked to turn over my watch. Had there been cell phones then, I'd have had to hand that in as well.

After signing the agreements I was led inside, where hundreds of people sat nervously in their chairs. There were no clocks in the room, and we were told there would be no meal intervals and few bathroom breaks. So far, it was feeling more like prison than a self-help seminar.

Our trainer, Randy, was one part enlightened being, two parts drill sergeant. He began by shouting at and demeaning us, calling us "assholes" and asking about our "acts" or "labels." According to EST, everyone goes through life acting out a certain "role"—mother, friend, victim, lover, and so on. That "role" gives us an identity which makes us feel important, as though we belong. As we broke down and pledged to let go of our dependence on our so-called "roles," Randy would dole out little grudging doses of approval.

Each role requires a different mask. Because we spend so much time operating from behind these masks, most of us have lost touch with the person underneath. Of course, we can't drop all our acts or identities completely; we must remain accountable to the people and responsibilities we have taken on. But must these acts or identities run us every minute of every day? I began to see all the so-called identities I had taken on— baton twirler, beauty pageant winner, actress, wife, mother, student—and had held onto for dear life because without them who would I be?

At one point I became exceedingly anxious, checking my wrist for the time on the watch that wasn't there. I couldn't stand not knowing what time it was or having access to a phone. My brain created terrible scenarios about what was happening outside that room. I started to panic. I *needed* to know what time it was. I *needed* to call home and check in with my kids. I *needed* to go to the bathroom. *Now.* I didn't know why it was so important to me, it just *was.*

All my life I'd heard people talking about being in the "now," but until that day I didn't know what that meant. I realized that I spent ninety-nine percent of the time avoiding the now and living in the past and future, obsessing and analyzing what had already happened or planning to control what was to come. And right at this moment of course I didn't *need* to know what time it was, my children were perfectly fine, and I'd used the bathroom before I left, so I stood no risk of going septic. These compulsions—to get up, make unnecessary phone calls, go to the bathroom when I didn't even need to—were a means of avoiding exactly what I was there to do. I understood that the purpose of taking those options away was to force the participants to drop the "acts" for a little while and actually surrender to the time and space of the moment.

One of the issues we were charged to tackle right away was clearing things up with our parents. I realized during this seminar that I had never truly allowed myself to acknowledge how my mother's drinking had affected me. I never talked about it and rarely even thought about it. And though I never consciously or overtly held it against her, my emotions surrounding the issue included anger, shame, and embarrassment, all kept inside as a dark, ugly secret. The seminar provided a safe, nonjudgmental atmosphere in which to explore truths about my life that I'd so carefully avoided or ignored.

CHAPTER 46

Coming to Terms with Mom

·······························

D ealing with issues around my mother was not easy for me. It was in the past, and I felt we had a good relationship in the now, so *why dredge that crap up?* After listening to other people's stories about their addictive parents, siblings, husbands, wives, or children and the trauma and hardships they endured, I began to relax and allow myself to fully experience the emotions regarding my mother's alcoholism and face up to the truth I'd been burying since childhood. Once I could do that and work through the feelings of humiliation, disappointment, rage, and guilt, something miraculous happened: I no longer tried to hide it or hide from it. I began to find emotional peace, as opposed to mere intellectual understanding.

I called my mother after that session and told her that I knew she loved me, and that I loved her back, and it came from a place of honest appreciation and acceptance. All my life I had wanted a perfect mother and been secretly furious that I'd gotten a flawed one instead. EST gave me the ability to see her as the exceptional and powerful woman she was, who had overcome tremendous disadvantages and addiction (she had, I had to remind myself, stopped drinking when I was eleven and had not touched a drop since). I never looked down on her again for the rest of my life.

Facilitators were ready with microphones in case people wanted to "share." Although the term is now used freely, this was the first time I'd ever heard it in that context, to impart your thoughts to the group and make it a collective experience. EST had many jargon words and phrases, almost a language of its own. *I got it* was what you said when someone told you something. You could always identify fellow ESTian when you heard them say *I got it* or *I want to share something with you.*

In one of my seminars a man shared that he liked to molest little girls. Everyone clapped and congratulated him on his strength—we had all agreed, after all, to check our judgment at the door. But when this guy started to talk, I picked my judgment right back up; I couldn't help it. I sat there, picturing my two daughters. I felt like taking a knife and slitting his perverted throat. My transformation, such as it was, went only so far.

Some years later I dated a former EST trainer and told him about the child molester. I said that I had a real problem with everyone hugging him and telling him how amazing he was. He didn't say a word for a while. Then he told me that he had led lots of the sex seminars, and that sharing was about giving space for a person to expose their demons and whatever came with them, and that if you could get them out into the light, the darkness had a chance to dissipate or dissolve. Well, okay, I said, sure, that's the idea and the ideal. But I still wondered if that sex offender had actually changed after the seminar.

When EST offered a six-day intensive in upstate New York, my mother came up to help Ingrid with the kids for a week so I could go. This seminar was so intense, it made the weekend seminars look like loosey-goosey rehearsals. Every day began with a nature walk at 5:00 a.m., regardless of how late the session had gone the night before. After the walk we were given a thoroughly horrible breakfast of no cholesterol, no sugar, and no caffeine—the only things I wanted in the morning.

On the first day, we were taken to a mountain to be strapped into a harness to zip-line across to the other side. In theory, it sounded like a breeze. I laughed and joked with the other trainees while we waited for our turn, but when I started getting close to the front of the line, everything changed. As I looked across the canyon, the pounding of my heart got so loud I couldn't hear a thing around me, and my body started to shake in its first and only panic attack. I tried to back out, but on that mountain with those people, this was not an option. I climbed into the harness, closed my eyes, and pulled my knees in close. I felt a shove and off I went. At no point did I relax, enjoy myself, or take in one inch of scenery. In fact, I didn't take one breath until I reached the other side where I was met with helping hands, smiles, and applause. "You did it!" they all shouted. "You're amazing!" But I didn't feel anything like amazing. I'd handled the whole situation with nothing but resistance and thus had had a terrible time. What I did on the ropes was supposed to symbolize how I responded to life, which meant I held my breath and closed my eyes and got through challenges. Instead of stopping to smell the roses, I stomped them into the ground.

One evening we were brought into a room and informed that the theme for the night would be sex. The instructors got the ball rolling by putting on a not-so-soft porn film depicting different variations, from three-ways to people screwing animals. I found the whole thing appalling, but the part that disturbed me most was watching an old couple going at it. I'd never thought of seniors as sexual, just imagined them baking cookies and reading by the fireplace, and I would have much preferred a movie about that. The film was supposed to change my point of view. Did it? Not back then.

Following the movie came a group discussion prompted by questions: Had we ever had anal sex? Did we prefer it standing up or lying down? What were our thoughts on group sex; had we experienced it? Were we attracted to the same sex? Had anyone ever had sex for money? We were reminded that this was a judgment-free space and encouraged to share. A gorgeous older actor whom I recognized from television stood up and disclosed that he kept a plate of vegetables next to his bed to shove up his butt before he could orgasm. My first thought was, *how in the world could he get up and tell strangers this stuff? Had he lost his mind?*

Earlier that week I'd noticed a very pretty, petite blond with a charming Irish accent and a perfect figure. I could see that the men all had their eye on her and I was admittedly, a little jealous. During the sex sharing, she stood up and revealed how she was sexually attracted to little boys and had molested several of them she babysat for. She became hysterical and had to be calmed down. I was deeply shaken by her confession. She was so pretty and sweet, what mother would suspect she would violate her son? It terrified me, thinking of my own young children whom I entrusted to babysitters, and it reminded me yet again not to trust appearances. Needless to say, there was nothing there to envy.

Throughout the event, I questioned just about everything I had done in my life, and especially my sanity. At times the seminar felt more like an insane asylum than a place to evolve. I heard the term "inner child" a lot. We had to love, embrace, and care for our inner child. That was a bit too much for me. I thought, *inner child*? Seriously? I already had three children, for fuck's sake; I didn't need another one to take care of!

On the last evening, a hairdresser and makeup artist arrived to help us complete our "transformation." I took the plunge with a radical haircut. This was the new me, with short hair. Everyone was hyped up, telling one another how great they were and how much they loved them, caught up in the camaraderie of having survived this week together. There we were, all transformed, even in our appearance.

After dinner we went into a room to share our experiences of the week. The trainers went row by row, one by one, sometimes taking as long as an hour a person. It was so late that I'd gotten my fifth wind by the time they called on my row, which happened to be the last. By now, at three in the morning, they rushed though most people, and when they finally got to me, the first trainer said a couple of things and was happy to proceed to the next person. I'd gotten my two minutes, and that was fine with me. Then, out of the blue, the other trainer asked me a few questions. I still had a baby face and looked very young, so when I told him about my three children, he smiled in surprise and then commented on the huge responsibility I had with them and how difficult it must be to be a single mother. If I did nothing else in my life, he said, I had already created three beautiful beings, and I should be immensely proud of myself for that. This kind recognition brought tears to my eyes. It was the first time I'd felt appreciated and acknowledged.

The next morning we were up at 6:00, and despite having gone to bed around 4:30. Though operating on almost no sleep, I still felt fresh and rejuvenated. The six-day seminar was one of my most powerful experiences thus far. I came away from it with a completely different perspective on my past and a newfound strength with which to approach the future. However, I still recognized that transformation would require ongoing effort. Did it give me the everyday tools and techniques that Science of Mind or some other practices would eventually arm me with? Maybe not, but it provided important discoveries and insights I could take with me on my super-charged self-help journey.

My mother's drinking, meanwhile, continued to be the elephant in the room when I was with her, never talked about. I was now ready to address that elephant, and once I started the process, it was as if the universe had shown up to help me, allowing a beautiful thing to happen.

After my six-day seminar, I asked my mother to plan to come back to New York and try EST herself, and miracle of miracles, she agreed. She stayed with me for two weeks, during which we finally discussed her drinking. She told me how sorry she was and that I was the motivation for her quitting; she'd wanted to be a good mother and be there for me.

I will never forget being there with her the night she completed her EST training. It was about three in the morning, as those of us there to support someone waited outside the ballroom where the training was held, long after we'd thought it would wind up. When the time finally came, we all walked into the ballroom and applauded the graduates. It was an amazing feeling, being there for my mother. Afterward we tried to hail a taxi, but too many other people were also calling for them—at that hour few were on the street, even in New York City. So both of us, exhausted, walked through the city hand in hand, back to the Dakota, in silence.

I'm still not sure about EST. But I am sure about one thing: I'd gladly spend a hundred weekends of EST torture for just one more walk in the city with my mother.

And Warren? After about a year, our relationship came to a natural end. Neither of us had any real investment in the other or intentions toward a future, so when the romance fizzled out, there were no hard feelings. I even continued to study with him for several months afterward.

CHAPTER 47

The Sedona Method

....

One Saturday I was rehearsing a scene for Warren's class with my actor friend Michael, who had just booked a Broadway show and was beginning to make serious money. When I asked to what he attributed his recent success, Michael mentioned Science of Mind (which of course I knew all about) and something called The Sedona Method, which he said dealt with feelings, while Science of Mind dealt with thoughts. He considered them a great combination. Intrigued, I decided to sign up and take the course the following weekend.

I walked into the room and was introduced to Lester Levenson, the method's founder, and Virginia Lloyd, the master teacher. Virginia was seated at the head of a table, with ten or so other beginners like me around it. The vibe was casual and intimate, very different from EST. We began by introducing ourselves, with no pressure to divulge anything more than our names unless we chose. After her introduction about the method and its origins, Virginia delved into discussing feelings, which she explained are sensations we hold onto that exist completely independently of the truth. Anger, for example, is a feeling that emerges from resisting an event or circumstance; it has nothing to do with the event itself but is proportional to the level at which the person resists it. To break this down and make it personal, we were all asked to consider some of the things in our lives that we wanted to change.

As soon as I let my mind go there, I realized my list was about a mile long. I wanted to change that my acting career hadn't taken off, I wanted to change that I wasn't five-eight and ninety pounds, I wanted to change that I wasn't married to a prince, I wanted to change that I'd had to let Ingrid go because my ex-husband didn't want to pay her what she was worth and now I was alone and scrambling to manage three small children. The list went on and on. Virginia then reiterated that the anger we were all feeling was not a result of any of those things, but rather the degree to which we wanted to change them. The next step was an exercise in letting the feelings go by letting the desire to change our circumstance go.

Every time I let a feeling go, my heart would lighten and my head would clear. The circumstances did not necessarily change, but once the veil of emotion was lifted, I could assess situations for what they were and find new ways of taking action to handle them effectively. Releasing recharged and replenished my energy so that I felt I could take on literally anything that came my way.

EST and the Science of Mind, wonderful gifts as they were, had not helped me address the feelings that had been attached to my thoughts, and only by letting my feelings detach from my thoughts would those thoughts naturally start shifting in a positive way. Over the course of my life I had resisted myriad aspects of myself, which led to feelings I then translated into my own personal brand of truth, inseparable from my identity. Without a proper technique to release these feelings, I was constantly maneuvering around them. It was as if my mind was a house, and a full-grown elephant was sitting in front of the door. Instead of calling animal control, I threw a blanket over its head and used the windows for entering and exiting.

Lester was present at the seminars, but it was Virginia who did most of the teaching. One day in class, while watching Virginia guide another student through a release, I became visibly disturbed. Something she'd said had triggered some latent feeling in me. Noticing this, Virginia gently asked me if I wanted to work on something. Unable to speak, I nodded yes. Could I name the feeling and welcome it? Yes; it was grief. I welcomed the grief then, and as it came up I felt I was going to suffocate, as though I'd broken the seal on a package containing poison gas. I felt a heavy cloud rising and wondered if I was losing my mind. Virginia assured me I was not going crazy and asked me to describe the cloud. It was brown. She invited me to welcome the cloud, stop resisting it, allow it to be there, and give it its moment. She explained that it was coming to the surface so that it could leave. Pressure started building in my chest, and I started to cry. Virginia instructed me to imagine a window or opening so the cloud could escape. I focused hard on the window, and before I knew it the cloud was gone, and my body felt so light that I erupted into laughter. Virginia started laughing as well, and soon the whole room joined in, like hyenas around a table, laughing at nothing.

Virginia then led me through the process of releasing my resistance, and once that resistance was gone, there was nothing left but a centered and easy feeling. Nothing on earth, the teaching goes, can resist an absolutely nonresistant person.

Looking around the room, I admitted to myself that I'd been judging everyone from the moment I'd sat down. When I released my feelings about these individuals, I was able to bond with them and grow, sharing their experiences as their energies transformed, and they allowed feelings they'd carried for years to rise and dissolve. I was astounded at how such a simple exercise could have that effect. Releasing was the perfect complement to the work I was doing with Science of Mind.

With Science of Mind, one learns the process of "spiritual mind treatment," to direct the conscious mind toward welcoming and accepting life's infinite abundance.

The Sedona Method, meanwhile, teaches a practical technique for identifying and dissolving the feelings that stand in the way of our clarity and joy. While EST emphasizes being in the moment, The Sedona Method offers a process that *puts* you in the moment. Once I could let go of the feelings that were in my way, I could choose clearly where to direct my mind without interference.

I remembered a girl in Luigi's dance class who'd had a stroke at the age of nineteen. She told me that when she was growing up her parents had allowed only positive thinking in their home; neither they nor their children could express or acknowledge negative thoughts. A good idea in theory, but there was only one problem: to never have a negative thought is simply not human. No wonder she'd had a stroke; she'd suppressed all her feelings and beaten herself up for having them.

We cannot control the thoughts that come up, but we can let go and not dwell on them. The beauty of The Sedona Method, which I rely on to this day, is that when I release my negative feelings, my thoughts naturally become positive, and I become centered and have more clarity. When I don't push down a feeling and actually welcome it, it dissolves itself. It's a daily practice that calls on the technique of releasing pretty continually, but it gives me the tools to help me handle whatever comes my way.

On the second weekend of The Sedona Method training, Virginia introduced the concept of every feeling being driven by a "want." To want literally means to "not have," which of course implies resistance to a current condition, which in turn ignites feelings of anger and inadequacy. When we hold on to wanting, we are literally, with our consciousness, pushing what we want away. This concept stood in stark contrast to what I'd been taught, that if you didn't achieve something it meant you hadn't wanted it badly enough.

My biggest revelation was that above all, I wanted my own approval, yet my never having given it to myself had resulted in a woeful lack of self-confidence. And it made perfect sense: I'd grown up associating beauty with approval. Every compliment I'd gotten had to do with appearance, so appearances were critical. My mother had a good-looking family, and all four of her sisters were beautiful, a source of great pride in those days. I never heard them comment about education, career, or culture; it was always *Don't we have a beautiful family?* My father stressed education and cultivation of my talents, but he was just one voice among those of my mother's huge clan. And having only one, mostly absent sibling, Donald, I wanted desperately to fit in with my many beautiful cousins.

According to The Sedona Method, wanting approval of others is part of the human condition—but it is one of the trickiest aspects of the human condition because when we act on wanting approval, we make giant mistakes that bring conflict and discord to our lives. The point of releasing is to literally let go of wanting approval, control, and security before making decisions. Once again, the point is that wanting equals lacking, or not having.

As I examined the feelings of wanting when they came up, I noticed them start to recede. Finally, I had a secret weapon to handle life, and more important, myself.

Like many leaders, Lester attracted his share of sycophants who approached the method with expectations of achieving total bliss. They hung onto Lester like gullible townspeople clustered around the wagon of the man selling snake oil.

The deifying of Lester was bothersome because I felt it undercut the real intention and value of the method. Lester didn't create this for self-aggrandizement; he was simply trying to spread his discovery for the betterment of anyone who wanted his help, encouraging people to go beyond the body and mind to get in touch with our true nature, which would yield peace and joy. The personal growth he espoused was not designed to be dependent on external forces. His intention was to free people of negative emotions turned beliefs that hindered them from living fully, so that eventually they would lead themselves. I loved learning from Lester, even if a few things did go over my head.

Lester and Virginia offered a weeklong intensive seminar in Sedona, Arizona, the week Mac was taking the kids on vacation. The timing was perfect. I had never been to that part of the country and had no idea what to expect. All I knew was that Lester loved it there and raved about its beauty and energy.

Flying in, I was overwhelmed by the majestic red rocks against the crystal-clear blue sky. Sedona was established on the site of "vortexes," or energy spots that some say have special powers. Native Americans believed Sedona was sacred and performed rituals in and around the area. It was an ideal setting for a spiritual retreat. I could feel its power as soon as we touched down.

Our retreat was held uptown, in a motel across the street from the famous Bell Rock, the most renowned vortex in Sedona, shaped like a bell from which energy rose upward. Tourists flock to Bell Rock for the energy it is known to emanate, and it has been reported that some visitors have seen moving images foretelling their future. Though I never saw such images or glimpses into the future myself, I remained, as ever, open.

Our class was held each morning in the atrium of our motel, around a long table for twelve people (just like in New York) with Virginia at the head and Lester in attendance. The focus of the intensive was releasing our "programs," or the inner beliefs keeping us in resistance and holding us back from freedom.

During one of the sessions, a door flew open on its own and Lester said, "Oh look, Jesus just walked in!"

"Right, Lester! Right!" I said, shaking my head skeptically.

"Kathalynn, that's your problem; you don't *believe*."

"That is correct, Lester," I replied, "I do not believe that Jesus just walked in!"

Lester shot me a disapproving look, which I ignored. I may have been committed to growth and expanded awareness, but I had to draw the line somewhere!

The next day, however, I asked Lester if we could talk, and Lester, ever ready and there for me, suggested a walk. He told me I had earned this method from my past life, and he was confident that I would, indeed, if I continued to release, gain freedom in this lifetime. It was gratifying to hear and inspired me to continue practicing.

When the intensive wrapped up on Friday night, my friend Michael invited me to join him in renting a car and taking in some of the sights. One destination was the famous Slide Rock Park, a beautiful rocky stream set amid awe-inspiring rock formations known for the natural waterslide that flowed into a watering hole. One look at the slide told me that this was not the sort of thrill I went for, but Michael was urging me to go for it, and he was the cool guy in my acting class and the one who'd introduced me to Sedona—not to mention the fact that he was gorgeous. I wanted his approval badly, so, after a couple of minutes of playful goading on his part, I acquiesced.

Coming off a week of round-the-clock releasing, I should have known better than to run down Slide Rock just to impress some guy, but that's exactly what I did. I ran to the start of the slide, realizing too late that it was becoming increasingly slippery, and as soon as my foot hit the first stone I flew up in the air. But then something remarkable happened. Instead of tensing my body to resist the fall, I let go, released, and relaxed into it. When I hit the ground, thinking to myself *Not my face!* I landed with a big splash, walking away with nothing more than a small bruise under my eye. I had somehow managed to internalize all that teaching and put it to valuable use! That was not the first time I had circumvented a potentially harmful experience.

Six months earlier in New York, I had been waiting for a cross-town bus late one night on my way home from an EST seminar when a good-looking young man in an old, semi–beat-up car pulled over and asked if I needed a ride. Anxious to get home and violating rule number one about accepting rides from strangers, I said yes and hopped in. While fastening my seatbelt I noticed in the backseat a rifle, a long pipe, a hammer, and ropes. In that moment, it registered that maybe this guy was dangerous. I started fiddling with the door handle, but he was driving too fast for me to jump out. In Central Park heading east to west, he took a sudden sharp right onto a dark side-road, the bumpy ground forced him to slow down. In that moment, I screamed out loud, "No, not me!" With that, I lifted the handle, pushed open the door, and jumped out onto the gravel. I heard him saying, "What are you doing?" but I was already on my feet running west like a bat out of hell toward the main road we'd just left. I looked first behind me to see if he was following me and then ahead for any cars I could hail down. There wasn't a car in sight, and I felt like a sitting duck. Closing my eyes for a moment, I took a deep breath and centered myself. And though at the time I wouldn't have known the word for it, I *released*. There was no room for fear or doubt or self-flagellation. I repeated *No, not me*. And when I opened my eyes, I saw headlights heading my way and started waving my arms. A taxi pulled over and a man in the backseat said, "Get in." The passenger asked where I was headed and then instructed the driver to take me home. Once safely in the cab I began to process the close call and started to panic. The man just kept repeating, "Breathe, breathe," and before I knew it I was home.

We hear about people who in extreme, life-threatening situations have been able to summon some unknown reserve of courage or strength, abetted by the fight-or-flight hit of adrenaline that momentarily endows us with superhuman ability. And I too had been in what I perceived was a life-or-death situation, in which I had no choice but to drop fear, doubt, and impulse to criticize myself. All those feelings being moved aside left room for only pure, unencumbered courage and a kind of animal intelligence. If I could train myself to function that way when my survival *wasn't* on the line, I thought, nothing would be impossible. Releasing could even apply to dealing with wild and crazy children, and when I could keep my wits about me enough to employ it, it did help me keep calm and restore order.

While driving with Michael after the seminar, in Sedona, I noticed (as I practiced releasing) a tremendous sharpening of my senses and awareness of my surroundings. En route to Slide Rock, I'd looked out the window and consciously thought, *There should be daisies here,* and within moments we passed a field of daisies. I don't think I created or manifested the flowers, but I was somehow aware of them before seeing them. Later as we passed a forest, I thought, *How magical it would be if it rained right now.* Less than half a minute later, it started to pour for a short while. On our last morning, Michael came to my room to invite me on a helicopter tour of the Grand Canyon. When I told him I'd love to go, he looked at me, laughed, and said, "Great! Now whatever you do, don't think 'crash'!"

CHAPTER 48

Releasing Mom

....

*E*ven though The Sedona Method was now my primary spiritual practice, in August 1980 I decided to attend an Actualizations seminar with Stewart Emery, one of the original EST trainers, who had created a new, more informal and relaxed version of the practice. Having convinced my mother to take The Sedona Method just a few weeks before, I encouraged her to join me for this as well, but between EST and The Sedona Method, she'd had about as much self-improvement as she felt she needed.

During the Actualizations seminar, Emery led us through a series of guided meditations. At one point, I went into what I can only describe as a trance. I heard my voice repeating, *Mommy, don't die. Please don't die.* On our break when I phoned my apartment to check on the kids, the sitter told me my father had called. With a sick feeling in my stomach, I immediately phoned him back, and he told me my mother had had a stroke and was in the hospital.

The next morning I packed up the three children and headed to Maryland and my mother. On the drive to the hospital, not a word was spoken between my father and me. It had been years since I had visited Bethesda Maryland Naval Hospital, and the sights and smells there bought back a flood of terrible memories of my long stints there as a child.

We met with the doctors to discuss the results of the MRI. The prognosis was grim: 80 percent of her arteries were blocked. Back then there was no cholesterol medication, so if she was to pull through, a complete diet and lifestyle change would be necessary. I asked, "Should we bring her to a Pritikin clinic, where her diet would be monitored?" The doctors agreed that would be her best chance. It would cost at least $25,000, but my father didn't flinch because he cared about one thing only, and that was my mother—any sacrifice was worth keeping her alive. But soon her kidneys failed, and we were down to two options: letting her go peacefully or trying dialysis, which might give her another three months. I wanted to let her go in peace, knowing she wouldn't want her life prolonged under those conditions, but my father wouldn't hear of it, so dialysis it would be. Watching her being hooked up to that machine, I saw her flinch and knew she could feel the pain. It broke my heart.

Around noon my father said he'd go home for lunch. I wanted to stay, but my aunt urged me to accompany him; she'd remain there until we got back. Once again my father did not say a word in the car. When we reached the house, he went into the kitchen and fixed us some sandwiches as if nothing out of the ordinary were happening. At a loss, I went into the bedroom and called Ernie, a friend and The Sedona Method teacher in New York. Ernie gently asked me to let go and allow my mother to have what she wanted. I released with him on the phone for a while and felt my mother's presence. When I hung up I said out loud, "Mommy, I love you. I want what you want." Within seconds the phone rang. It was my Aunt Annie calling to tell me my mother was close. I stayed on the phone in silence. A few seconds later she said, "She's gone."

I felt numb and my mind went blank. I sat there for maybe ten minutes, drained, and then got up to tell my father. I stood there in the kitchen for a few moments watching him eating his sandwich and drinking his Kool-Aid. When he noticed me standing there and our eyes met, I blurted out, "Daddy, she's gone." He looked up at me and said, "What?" His eyes were devoid of emotion, so I thought he hadn't heard. I repeated, "Mommy just died." His face did not change, he continued to eat as though he had heard nothing more momentous than a weather report. That was my father—a man who kept himself to himself. I can only imagine what was going through his mind then. I do know without a doubt that he loved her greatly and was utterly devoted to her.

Feeling there was nothing more to say to him, I left the house and walked around the neighborhood for hours, dry eyed and still feeling numb. Everything had changed, I didn't have a mother anymore. There was a void in my life that could never be filled.

I turned off inside, just the way I had as a child when I couldn't handle my feelings. I wanted to run from the pain that hovered but had not yet settled. Unfortunately, I did not have anywhere safe to unleash the tornado of emotions brewing within. Three young children were expecting me to care for them. There was no time for grief and no place to fall apart. So I plugged on ahead and helped with all the arrangements for her small funeral and burial.

My mother had been very clear that she never wanted me to see her face after she died. She believed that the ones we love ought to remember us happy and alive, so it was no wonder that she passed away while I was home having lunch. To honor her wishes, I did not return to the hospital that day but stayed home and made the necessary calls. She was buried at Arlington National Cemetery. At Arlington, husbands and wives shared one plot. My mother used to joke that she wanted to outlive Joe so he wouldn't be on top of her for the rest of eternity.

A few days after the funeral, my children and I boarded the Metroliner back to Manhattan, and I stepped right back into my role as a single mother of three. The experience of that last meditation, when I felt my mother's death, haunted me. I wouldn't meditate again for years.

CHAPTER 49

The Unimagined

....

*I*didn't know Yoko Ono well, but she would always say hello when
we'd run into each other at the Dakota. The Lennons gave birthday
parties for their son, Sean, at Tavern on the Green, a kind of combination
celebration since it was John's birthday too. Vanessa and I were invited
for Sean's fourth- and fifth-birthday parties (John's thirty-ninth and for-
tieth). Every woman who walked in was given a white gardenia to wear,
a lovely gesture on Yoko's part and an indelible association I now have
with that flower.

Once, on John and Sean's birthday, Yoko hired a sky-writing plane to
fly over the Dakota and wish John happy birthday. When I heard about
this I ran up to the roof just in time to see it fade. John, who apparently
was asleep in his apartment, missed it entirely.

At the last party at the Tavern on the Green, I was seated beside John
for lunch, and we got into a heated debate about music school, of all
things. When I told him I was planning to send my children for music
lessons, he turned to me and said, "Why would you ever do that? They
don't need music school!"

"How can you of all people be opposed to a child learning music?" I
asked him in surprise.

"I'm not opposed to music! I'm opposed to music *school*! I think it
ruins kids."

"Last time I checked, my kids don't have a music icon as a father, and
I don't even play an instrument! How else are they going to get music in
their lives? Do you want to teach them?" I said jokingly.

"Any time!" he said. "Just don't send them to music school!"

"Deal," I agreed.

When the party ended, I collected my daughter and approached John and Yoko to thank them. John gave me a hug and told me he'd keep seeing me there at parties for the next eighteen years. Without thinking, I blurted out, "Oh, John, no you won't."

"Why not?" he asked, looking confused.

At that moment, an eerie feeling washed over me, as though I was implying something awful. I hoped he hadn't felt it.

I quickly amended my statement. "Do you really think Sean will want to spend his birthday here with us for the next eighteen years?" I asked.

"Oh!" John laughed. "I get it now. No, I suppose he won't!"

I left the party feeling strange, as though I'd said something off-color, but I couldn't quite put my finger on why.

The following December 8, 1980, around three months after my mother's death and two months after I'd sat next to him at lunch, John Lennon was shot and killed in the archway outside of the Dakota.

When I was leaving the building sometime that afternoon, I ran into John and Yoko, and we said hello as they got into their limousine. I noticed a group of people standing outside the building, which was not at all unusual. Among them was Mark David Chapman, whose name I didn't know at the time.

That evening I went out to meet some friends for dinner, and when I returned home around ten o'clock I noticed that Mark Chapman was still there talking to José, our doorman. Again, I didn't think anything of it because it was common for fans to gather around the building's entrance in hopes of catching a glimpse of their idol. I said hello to José and proceeded through the archway into the courtyard and into my apartment.

After paying the babysitter, I changed into my pajamas, climbed into bed, and turned off the lights. I had just closed my eyes when the sound of three gunshots jolted me out of bed. My first thought was that someone was shooting at the building.

The shots were coming from the direction of the courtyard, which my twins' bedroom overlooked. I crawled into their room and pulled the two of them out of their cribs and onto the floor for safety. I moved over to the window, looked down, and saw two policemen hauling what looked like a body into their car. Apparently, John was in such bad shape there was no time to wait for an ambulance. Just then my phone rang.

I answered, and a voice said, "Somebody just shot John Lennon." I had no idea who it was and was too shocked to ask. I put my sleeping babies back into their cribs, then threw on some clothes and headed down to the office to find out if it was true. John was already on his way to Roosevelt Hospital, where all my children had been born. I felt sick to my stomach when I saw blood on the ground right by the archway.

Many residents were standing in the office waiting for news of John. It didn't take long before someone called to let us know John had died. Everyone was in shock. The men in the office who saw the whole thing were so badly shaken that a neighbor kindly brought down some brandy to calm them. Everyone just kept asking each other if they were all right. It was surreal.

One evening shortly after that night, someone knocked on my door and asked to come in. It was a fellow named Elliot Mintz, a dear friend of John's who'd flown in from L.A. to be with Yoko but had been so overwhelmed by the parade of mourners passing through her apartment that he sought temporary refuge from the sadness. We sat for a while as he told personal stories about John, mostly about how much he adored Elvis Presley. Elvis was dead and now John. It was like a very bad dream.

Once John was killed, living in the Dakota became a different experience altogether. The building had always been famous for its architecture and for being home to celebrities, but now it was an international household name. Crowds gathered in the freezing cold all through the night. People held candles and with arms around one another sang "Imagine." Reporters were merciless about shoving their cameras and microphones in the faces of residents trying to enter and exit the building. For our own security, we were issued photo IDs and allowed in and out only through the basement. An aura of gloom hung around the place like never before. The building had not just lost John, it had lost its innocence.

Over the years, I've heard unkind things said about Yoko Ono from people who never even met her. I can only say that in every interaction I had with her, she was kind, loving, unfailingly polite, and extremely generous.

Once while I was having lunch in a little café on Columbus Avenue, I noticed her come in with her friend Elliot. The two of them were taken to their table, and I continued to eat my lunch. Suddenly I heard a familiar voice say, "Hi there." I looked up and there was Yoko. "I noticed you sitting here," she said, "and I wanted to come over and say hello. I didn't want you to think that I was ignoring you."

"Of course I would never think that, Yoko. Thank you for coming over. Please say hi to Elliot for me."

That was just the way she was. Always polite and considerate.

CHAPTER 50

Enter Brad, Stage Right

································

When January came, I was glad 1980 was over. Between the death of my mother and the murder of John, it had been pretty much the worst year of my life. After the new year, I still wasn't in any mood to go out much until Michael, my Sedona friend, urged me to come to his party to celebrate his first million. The place was buzzing with actor-types. As I was leaving, I heard a voice behind me say in a thick Australian accent, "Hello, you," and turned to see a devilishly handsome blond in a tweed hat, seated comfortably on a sofa and eyeing me intently. I had noticed him earlier, along with the crowd of women who'd flocked to him all night. He stood up, walked over, and said, "I'm Brad England." He asked me to stay and talk to him, but I had to rush home to relieve my babysitter, so I gave him my phone number. Though not my type, Brad was one of the most beautiful men I had ever seen, and I was frankly surprised when he called the next morning to invite me to dinner.

Brad and I dined at a little café down the street from the Dakota. At one point during the meal, I picked up some food with my hands and apologized. "Sorry," I said, "I'm used to eating with my kids."

"I don't care if you eat with your hands or your feet!" he said with a laugh. "You don't have to apologize for anything when you're with me."

Brad and I continued to talk. People passed by and looked at us—and by us, I mean him. He had been a regular on a soap opera for years and was used to attention, so it didn't faze him a bit. After dinner we walked to my apartment. Intrigued by his sexy accent and sense of humor and not wanting the evening to end, I invited him up for a drink. Once inside, I pointed him toward the alcohol and told him he was welcome to pour himself whatever he wanted while I slipped into something more comfortable. He laughed heartily. Brad seemed completely amused by whatever came out of my mouth. He even loved that I had three children!

As our relationship took off, Brad's devotion anchored me, his kindness to my children heartened me, and his creativity and joie de vivre couldn't help but rub off on me. Before I'd met him, food had been a necessary evil to be avoided lest, I God forbid, gained a pound. Brad approached every meal like a holy communion—from cooking to pairing the wines to arranging flowers for the table (roses with daisies? Yes!)—and I learned to share his deep appreciation. As for my body, to him it was the proverbial temple, and he worshipped at it. He made me feel perfect, whole, and complete as a woman, and I felt safe enough with him to let my guard down and relax. Also, while I'd always been drawn to art and design, I had no real knowledge of fashion or style, while Brad, a master in this regard, taught me how to combine colors and pull things together. And beautiful as he was—for reasons I could never understand —he had eyes only for me.

Unfortunately, despite all his good points, Brad England had a side to him that was disconcerting. He paid hundreds of dollars a week to a psychiatrist who had him lie down on a small cot in his underwear and then poked him in the stomach until he screamed with pain, and Brad trusted this doctor with a zeal that made me question his stability. I believed in confronting one's issues and letting them go, that's what The Sedona Method was all about, but this was taking it to the edge. Brad also seemed to have intermittent frenzied episodes where he lost control of his emotions. Something might trigger a memory of a trauma and he'd start to shake and cry out wildly, appear to be having a seizure, and then erupt into a kind of primal scream. I didn't dare touch him or try to reason with him when he was in one of those states but would sit there and wait for it to pass, which it generally did after ten or fifteen minutes. He'd come out of it exhausted, then return to his normal, delightful self, laughing and smiling as if the whole episode had never occurred. Thankfully, this never took place in front of my children.

After we'd been together for nearly two years, Brad got frustrated with New York, feeling he wasn't getting enough work, and decided to move to L.A. Of course that wasn't an option for me, since I was tied to the East Coast with the children, so Brad became bicoastal. One mid-October afternoon, during one of Brad's stints out west, I came home to four dozen roses and a first-class ticket to Hawaii. He had booked a job on *Magnum P.I.* and wanted me to join him for the week he'd be filming. I arranged for Ingrid and her daughter to stay with the children, and off I went to island paradise.

Being on the set of *Magnum P.I.* was a blast. I even got to have dinner with the cast, including the show's handsome star, Tom Selleck. Hawaii was even more enchanting than I'd remembered. The only thing not quite right was being with Brad. In addition to his random emotional collapses, a different and frightening facet to his personality had emerged when he had twice gotten violent with me, once pushing me hard against a wall and injuring my back, another time slapping me across the face and bruising my eye. I was shaken, mortified, and alarmed. No man had ever hurt me physically before, and by the second incident, I realized I could not afford to hang around for more. Despite his abject apologies and vows to never let it happen again, I could not be sure it would not escalate.

In an agony of indecision as to how to proceed, in mid-November I paid Brad's doctor a visit, seeking advice on how to handle the breakup. I felt for the man who had given me so much, and I wanted to separate as humanely as possible. The doctor seemed shocked at first but soon understood. He'd concluded from Brad that our relationship was strong, but once I explained how things were on my end, the scenario modified. He asked me if I would wait until after Christmas to let Brad return to New York and enjoy the holidays. Then he suggested we come to the office together so that he could be there to support Brad when I broke the news. I agreed to this plan, and the doctor thanked me and wished me well. Brad came back and spent Christmas with the children and me. After New Year's, as arranged, we went to see the doctor, and I ended the relationship. Brad was, as I expected, devastated. I felt terrible, but there was no way around it. He flew back to L.A., and that was the last I ever saw of him.

My children were growing fast, and Mac was only in their lives every other weekend. I was basically raising them alone. I longed for a partner, however finding the right one was not proving to be easy. Before Brad, I had dated some men who worked in the finance industry, but they bored me and the romances were always short-lived. I was more attracted to creative people, but they rarely offered any kind of security, and I worried about foisting that instability on my children. I decided to consult Eric Pace for treatment on the subject. Eric looked at me and said plainly, "Why can't you find a man who is both? Creative *and* stable?" I didn't know what to say. I hadn't thought of that.

CHAPTER 51

Enter Bob, Stage Left

·····························

*E*very December, I would start off my holiday season with Eric's Science of Mind workshop on prosperity. The Wednesday night it began, I arrived early and found a seat toward the front. Looking around the room I caught the eye of a slim fellow of about average height with dirty blond hair who was standing in the doorway, staring at me. He smiled, I politely smiled back, and then I turned back. Next thing I knew he was seated beside me.

"Hello," he said, "Wow! Yours are the first eyes I've ever seen that are even more beautiful than mine! I'm Bob Edwards, what's your name?"

Nice pick-up line, I thought. I had just the day before experimented and gone blond—was this the kind of thing I could expect as a blond, I wondered? He continued to stare at me throughout the workshop, which I found distracting and a touch off-putting. When it was time to leave, he asked if he could take me home in a cab. I told him I'd been planning to walk. Could he join me, he asked. As it turned out he lived on 83rd and Central Park West, so the Dakota was on his way home. Unable to concoct an excuse on the spot, I agreed.

As we walked, Bob told me about his actor parents, who had discovered Science of Mind when he was a teenager. He'd been involved in the teaching ever since and could not get over the fact that we'd never met. "It's destiny!" he kept saying. I had to admit that despite my mixed feelings about him, it piqued my curiosity to have this in common.

When we finally reached my door, he asked if I would go with him Friday to a Dizzy Gillespie benefit concert for Eric's church. I'd already been planning to attend it, after a cocktail party at my son's school.

"Great!" he said, "I'll join you at the cocktail party and we can go on to the concert together."

Bob seemed so excited I did not have the heart to refuse. I gave him my number and hoped he wouldn't follow up. But when Friday afternoon came and I was packing the kids up to spend the weekend with their father, Bob called.

He picked me up at the Dakota and we headed over to the cocktail party, during which he told me more about his parents and how great they were. He said he had set out to be an actor and a singer—he even still took dance lessons!—but a tarot card reader told him that he had to make money in this lifetime (I am not making this up), so he gave up his dream and became a stockbroker. Strange as it sounds, however, there was something about him that I liked—plus, with his background in the arts we had more in common than just Science of Mind.

When we got to the concert, a group of Bob's friends were waiting to meet me, and after the show we all went back to Bob's apartment. They were a mixed bag, his friends—some genuine, some hangers-on who seemed to take advantage of his generous nature. When Bob was in the kitchen serving up expensive takeout from a nearby gourmet shop, I noted that not one of these good friends offered to help or contribute. I was happy to pitch in, but they seemed accustomed to being taken care of by him. He was a great host that night, though, and I was touched when he took a break from playing his guitar and singing and brought out a sweater for me to put over my blouse against the winter chill. He was looking more and more attractive and definitely starting to grow on me. The music continued into the early hours of the morning, and when everyone else had gone, Bob walked me home along a deserted Central Park West. Arm in arm, we discussed the concert and Science of Mind, and when we reached my building, his good-night kiss was just right.

At 8:00 a.m. I was awakened by the phone. Bob wanted me to meet him for breakfast down the street. "Are you crazy?" I said. "I just went to bed four hours ago, and so did you!" But he insisted, and I agreed to meet him, but not until ten. Over breakfast he asked me if I had plans for the evening, and I said I was going to a party with friends. I could tell he wanted to be invited, but my instinct told me not to bring him. He had a corniness about him that gave me pause when it came to the idea of introducing him to my friends. Plus he seemed overinvested in me in too short a time, and I didn't want him to assume that by introducing my friends to him, I was ready to be as serious as he was. He promised to wait by the phone in case the party wrapped early or I got bored. No, I told him, he didn't need to do that, but again he insisted.

After breakfast, he was walking me back up to my apartment when we passed a camera store, and he asked if I'd mind coming in for a moment, he had some photos to pick up. He tore open the envelope and proudly showed me shot after shot of his parents and asked which ones I thought he should blow up to 8 x 10s.

"Oh, is this for them?" I asked. "Are they having an anniversary or something?"

"No," he replied, "they're just for me. I love having pictures of my parents around my apartment. I have a few more errands. Would you like to join me?"

Join him on a few more errands? I politely declined and headed back to the Dakota.

Later that afternoon Winnie from downstairs called to tell me a package had arrived for me. It was a bouquet of flowers and an exquisite blue topaz necklace with a note inside: "Just a token of my appreciation for having breakfast with me." This was a full-court press. I had to admit that it was awfully flattering.

That night at the party, I couldn't erase the visual of him waiting for me to call. I broke down and asked the host to use his phone and called Bob to invite him over. A guy that generous and interested in me maybe deserved a bit more of a chance. Within ten minutes he was there, all smiles.

Bob introduced himself and got into a conversation with the host's sister. When the host, probably a little drunk at this point, suggested to Bob that he ask his sister out, Bob pointed to me and shouted, "Hey, man. I'm here with this woman. I'm not asking anyone out ever again. I'm in love!" If dying of embarrassment was a real thing, I would have dropped dead then and there.

Still, I continued to date him because despite his gaucheness he had a certain charm, and we two had a certain chemistry. It may seem bizarre in retrospect, but there was something there that could not be denied. Moreover, at that time I had been treating both on my own and with Eric for a man to come into my life who was stable, age-appropriate, loved children, and was passionate about culture and the arts. Bob was all those things. The manifestation had worked—or so it seemed.

Bob was not thrilled about having to lie low during the holidays while I dealt with Brad, but he understood the situation and was flexible. After I had disengaged and was free again, we had a belated Christmas celebration. Bob bought my son his first bike and taught him how to ride it on a freezing Saturday afternoon. Courtney, oblivious to the cold, was in heaven. The two of them were clearly bonding.

As we continued getting to know each other, our relationship began making more and more sense. We started taking some Science of Mind classes together, talking for hours afterward, and we went to church together every Sunday, after which we'd go to the theater, a passion we both shared. I introduced him to art, and he began to love it, and we got a kick out of being drawn to the same paintings. We traveled well together. His parents, about whom he'd initially seemed so overenthusiastic, turned out to indeed be interesting people, and I'd talk to his actor father for hours about the theater. We both loved going to psychics and would compare notes if we didn't go together; it was a source of great entertainment, exploration, and more commonality. Not to mention, Bob was a fabulous lover who brought great sparks to our physical life. Lastly, and perhaps most importantly, Bob adored my children, and they adored him back. Having been married twice before, he had an older daughter, Nan, who lived in upstate New York with her mother and whom he missed having a closer relationship with. Kids were not foreign to Bob; on the contrary, he was devoted, enthusiastic, and unintimidated. We all had great fun together, going to shows and amusement parks and dinner. We were becoming a family pretty fast.

Not too far into our relationship, Bob planned a romantic weekend at a Manhattan hotel. He had the suite preset with rose petals scattered over the floor and bed, pretty candles everywhere, an assortment of essential oils on the table next to the bed, and a magnificent bottle of Dom Perignon on ice. There was a recorder on the nightstand with a tape he'd created of him singing an original song he'd written for the occasion, "Hey, Hey, You're My Woman Now." I passed on the oil massage and went straight for the Champagne, drinking so much of it in the first fifteen minutes that I passed out. An hour or so later I woke up and changed, and we went downstairs for a dinner and cabaret show. At the table, Bob pulled out a hefty diamond-and-sapphire ring that had been a family heirloom. He asked that I wear it until he could afford a proper engagement ring.

I was taken aback. We had known each other only a month or so by then. But my children had fallen in love with him, and he with them. And although the children were provided for financially, thanks to Mac and his conscientiousness, I saw in Bob the father figure that was missing from our family. He was devoted and seemed stable. He fit the criteria.

Could I have used more time before making such an important decision? No doubt, but unfortunately time was of the essence. The lease on Bob's sublet was ending, and he needed to decide quickly where he was going to live. The choices were either to move all his things and sign a year's lease someplace new or to move in with me and give it a real try. I weighed what I thought were my options and found that I couldn't justify letting this man go on the off-chance that someone better would come along, especially given all he'd already come to mean to my children.

From that day forward, I would do my best to ignore Bob's irritating qualities and look for the good. This was not always easy.

A few evenings later, I went to meet Bob for dinner at a neighborhood café. When I arrived I was surprised not to see him, since he was always early for our dates. The hostess said, "You must be Kathalynn! Right this way, please," and escorted me to a table on which a single rose lay across my plate. I asked for a glass of wine, and as I was taking my first sip, Bob appeared from behind a partition, holding a microphone and wearing a white dress shirt unbuttoned to his stomach with a long necklace and tight black leather pants. I hadn't seen an outfit like that since the night I'd taken Harold to Studio 54! Bob then cleared his throat and thanked the audience (actually, customers just trying to enjoy their dinner) for coming. Then he instructed the men in the room to give their "darling ladies" a kiss. No one budged but instead awkwardly looked around or down at their plates. At this point he started going table to table, insisting that the men put their arms around their dates. When he got to me he kissed me on the cheek, announced that I was his sweetheart, and pulled me out of my chair to stand up and wave to the "crowd." Just when I thought it couldn't get any worse, Bob strutted to the front of the restaurant, inserted the microphone into a stand, brought out his guitar, and started singing "Teenager in Love." He instructed the room (most of whom had by then called for their checks and were inhaling their meals at lightning speed) to clap and sing the *ooh-oohs* and the *wah-oohs* as backup. There was nothing I could do but order more wine to drown my humiliation. By the end of his "set" we pretty much had the restaurant to ourselves. He finally came over and joined me at our table, looking as proud as if he had just won a Grammy award.

One evening as I was walking out of the Dakota, Leonard Bernstein pulled up in front of me in his limousine. "Get in!" he called, opening the door. "I'll drop you wherever you're going." As soon as I hopped in the car, he started drilling me about Bob. "Who's this new guy? I don't think I like him." The Maestro had met Bob only once briefly, when we passed him in the hallway on our way to an event. Bob had wanted to stop and chat, but I made a big fuss about us being late and practically shoved him out the door and on our way. The Maestro loved Mac and was automatically suspicious of anyone who came after, but the real reason I didn't want Bob anywhere near him was because though Bob had never published or recorded a piece of music in his life, he considered his songwriting to be of Bernstein's caliber. I knew that if Bob trapped the Maestro in a conversation, he would have insisted on playing his silly songs for him, and the Maestro, out of respect for me, would have listened. I was not strong enough to bear that level of embarrassment, so I did everything in my power to keep them apart.

When the Maestro asked me what I was doing with Bob, I didn't know what to say. I downplayed the relationship and made all the generic excuses I could think of on the spot. Sensing how uncomfortable the conversation was making me, he finally dropped it. But before he let me out he said, "Look, I'm sure the guy is very nice, I just think you can do so much better. Please don't sell yourself short." I nodded awkwardly, thanked him for the ride, and got out of the car.

After that conversation, I realized that if I was to go forward with Bob, I could never, ever introduce him to Stella Adler. Even though I was no longer taking her classes we continued our acquaintance. She would have not only seen right through Bob but also through my feeble excuses, and she'd have forced me to confront what I wanted to avoid, which was a good hard look at the man I was going to spend my life with and who seemed so perfect on paper. I felt self-conscious and truthfully couldn't face her, so I let things drift and didn't see her again for many years. I just didn't know how to handle it.

Nothing was happening in my acting career, though the truth is I wasn't putting very much into it. My focus was on my children. I would do some small, under-five-line parts in soap operas, while many of my friends at Stella's were getting cast as regulars on the same shows and others were working in movies and network TV. I'd flown to L.A. a few times to audition for something, and I would book the occasional commercial, but it wasn't enough for me not to feel I'd essentially failed. Jack Klugman, my buddy from *The Odd Couple* job I'd had a few years before, would encourage me to continue my acting career when he'd come to New York, but I hadn't developed the requisite thick skin any actor needs to survive that kind of life, and I needed a break from the rejection and the pressure. I was overly sensitive, easily discouraged, and for me to survive emotionally and be there for my children, I felt I needed to plunge ahead and completely change my focus.

CHAPTER 52

More Family Matters

. . . .

On a hot day in the middle of June, Bob and I and the children were on our way home from Jones Beach when I suddenly began to vomit. I figured it was from something I'd eaten or too much time in the sun.

When I woke up the next day, I felt worse and went to the doctor. Once again, sure enough, I was pregnant. I was shocked; clearly, relying on coordinating a diaphragm with the rhythm method had been naïve. The timing was awkward, and I was completely unprepared. But the fact is I was also thrilled and excited, and I had a feeling Bob would be thrilled as well. By then his daughter, Nan, was eighteen and still living upstate, and their relationship was not as strong as he would have liked. One of the reasons I loved Bob was that he adored children and had made it clear he wanted more. With this baby, he was going to get another shot at real fatherhood. Also, as inconvenient as this baby might be, I was, at thirty-five, considered old at that time to be carrying a child, and this might be my last chance for one more. In a strange way, many pieces were falling into place.

When I told Bob he was to be a father again, his first concern was that we were not married. I couldn't have cared less, but if it meant that much to him, I told him we could push up the wedding date. What Bob had left out when he proposed and moved in, though, was that although he and his ex-wife, Bonnie, were separated and living apart, he was still technically married while she, he said, held out for a bigger settlement. He was terribly uneasy about having a child out of wedlock, but the circumstance was, at the time, immovable. Eventually the excitement of the new baby overcame his fear of social stigma. Then again, by the mid-'80s, people didn't care the way they once had about that sort of thing.

Genevieve Joy was born on Friday, March 23, 1984, at 10:00 a.m. via C-section. Bob watched her birth while leaning against a wall for support in case he passed out. Gradually he made his way close enough to snap some pictures. After the delivery, he stuck around long enough to see me out of the Operating Room and back into my room, then headed out for an appointment with a realtor in Connecticut.

The following morning, while I was recovering, Mac brought Vanessa over to meet her new sister. Later that day Bob came by, and when I mentioned that Mac had been there with Vanessa, Bob suddenly darkened and became incensed, screaming, "Why would you let Mac into this room? *Why?*"

"Could I have stopped him?" I asked, baffled at this unexpected explosion. Up till then, Bob's relationship with Mac had been cordial.

"You should have told him to get the hell out! You planned it that way, didn't you; you wanted him here!"

His anger persisted; I sat there, stunned, unable to make sense of his rage. Then he stormed out, not even glancing at the baby. That evening he returned with a bag of muffins and some tuna salad from my favorite café. I thought he was coming to apologize; instead, he took the items out of the bag, tossed them at me, and said, "These aren't for you, they're so you can nourish my child." Then he left in a huff. I cried until the nurse called my doctor. The nurses and my doctor just assumed the crying was a mild case of postpartum. I didn't dare tell them what really happened because I was way too embarrassed. A little later, once the crying subsided, my friend Dorcas called to congratulate me on the baby. Needing to get it off my chest, I told her everything. The event was so traumatic to me, I told a few friends about it. I also did a few releasing sessions on it with a Sedona Method teacher, Ernie. I needed all the support I could get at the time.

The next evening Bob came over with Champagne and apologized, and though it felt less than sincere, I went through the motions of accepting the apology because there didn't seem to be a better option. Bob told me about the house he had chosen to buy with the money I'd get from selling my apartment—because contracts had already been signed for the sale, and it was too late to reverse the process. It didn't look like I was going to have a say. By then, though, I felt trapped, in far too deep to walk away. So I adjusted my blinders and pushed forward, hoping eventually he'd change. And at the age of thirty-six, with the mileage I'd already accumulated, I should have known better.

Three months after Genevieve was born we moved to Greenwich, Connecticut: the land of men in Docksiders and coral-pink Bermuda shorts and women in bright little Lilly Pulitzer minidresses, sipping white wine at—where else—their country clubs. If this sounds trite, it's because it is.

It was one of the hardest decisions I'd ever make. I was a mother of four and wanted to do what was best for my children. The city just wasn't going to work anymore. As large as the apartment was, it was still crowded with two adults and four children, and in 1984, New York was roiling with crime.

I accepted the new reality that I was marrying Bob and wasn't going to be an actress anymore. Bob had little money at the time, but he was a stockbroker on the rise in the industry, and there was hope and potential. I bought the house in Greenwich without a mortgage with the money from the sale of the apartment, setting aside what was left over for furniture, renovations, and a car, and thereby setting Bob and me and the family up for our new chapter.

I gave up my beloved Dakota, my alimony, my acting, and my city. I convinced myself that Bob and I had enough in common to make it work, and I didn't have time to worry or question the decision. I cried all the way to Greenwich.

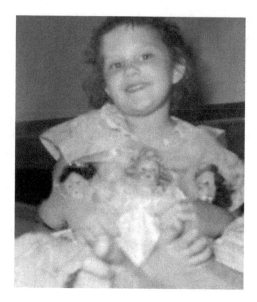

At five years old I was really into dolls.

Splits. (Just don't ask me to do them now!)

Learning how to sit properly at the Patricia Stevens Finishing School. My smile indicates how natural that felt.

With my dad at the Miss Dixie Pageant in Florida. That makeup case went with me everywhere.

The suspense was almost unbearable as
each beautiful girl competed for the
crown of MISS AMERICAN TEENAGER...

*A photo from the Miss American Teenager competition—I am in the
front in the dress with the black top and white bottom with flowers.*

*My dad and me in my motel room
in Palisades, New Jersey,
on the way to the Miss American
Teenager pageant. That was the
night I met Brian Hyland.*

*Sitting with Brian in the locker
room of my high school the night
he sang for the school. I was the
envy of all the girls!*

My skit for the talent competition of the Miss Maryland Pageant.

My mother congratulating me after I was crowned Miss Southern Maryland.

The evening gown competition at the 1968 Miss Maryland Pageant. I didn't win, but the girl who did copied my gown and wore it at the Miss America Pageant. (And yes, I was steamed!)

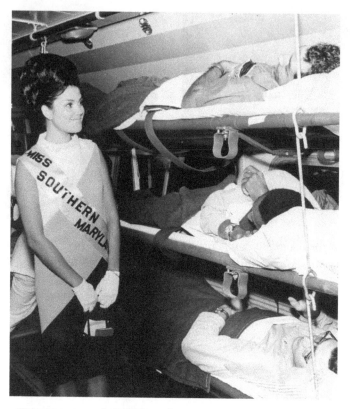

Greeting wounded soldiers from Vietnam at Andrews Air Force Base, part of my duties as Miss Southern Maryland.

The motel where I met Gary Loizzo, of the American Breed, and got my tutorial on sex.

In my bedroom in Los Angeles while dog-sitting little Malibu for my friend Stanley Beck. It came furnished and I didn't do much to make it any homier. (Note the baton in the corner.)

My first Hollywood headshot.

My majorette group at the national competition.
(I'm in the middle).

Going full-on Hollywood here!

Left photo is me on the set of The Grasshopper. *The photo on the right is me with Jim Brown while we were filming. A representative of Hugh Hefner approached me while on set and asked if I wanted to pose for a Playboy centerfold for $10,000. He assured me it would be "very tasteful," but all I could think of was my parents' reaction, so I declined.*

On the Richard Nixon campaign tour. The president-to-be's brother Donald is standing in the back.

Two unhappy people on a date for The Dating Game. (Lesson: Don't choose someone solely on the basis of a charming English accent!)

My "lucky" outfit for The Dating Game, complete with the white go-go boots!

Fooling around with Troy Donahue.
(Who were we calling, anyway?)

Trying to be the next Lolita.

Me doing a scene in The Odd Couple *with Tony Randall.*

With Jack Klugman and Mac's kids at the race track in New York. Jack, like my daddy, loved horse racing.

With Mac at Vanessa's baby-naming ceremony at the First Church of Religious Science, New York City.

Hands and arms full with
newborn twins Caitlin Paige and
Courtney Alexander.

Me with my little redhead Caitlin.

Playing around with my old
costumes at my parents house
in Maryland.

My first subway ride in
New York City.

The twins in the courtyard of the Dakota. Look at the lilies!

The kids playing on the roof of the Dakota.

Brad in the kitchen with Courtney. They adored each other.

The kids with the amazing Luigi at a party at the Dakota.

Dakota annual potluck dinner, with Sean Lennon.

Princess Mommy birthday celebration.

My New York headshot (taken while I was sick with the flu).

I just turned blond! (Brad hated it.)

MERRY
CHRISTMAS

LOVE & KISSES
CAITLIN, COURTNEY & VANESSA

Courtney always was a ladies' man. Kisses from his sisters at the Dakota.

In Nice, France, while I was
pregnant with Genevieve. It was
here that I found out the baby was
a girl and gave her a French name.

My nanny, Ingrid with her
daughter, Anthea, holding
newborn Genevieve. I couldn't
have survived without her!

With newborn Genevieve in the Dakota courtyard. Paul Simon once
asked me how I managed to live in that super-gloomy building;
he had lived there a short time with his ex-wife, Peggy, and had
no regrets about leaving it behind. (I had dyed my hair back to brown
right before Genevieve arrived so she would see me exactly as I was.)

Me with my cousin Sharon.

With Genevieve, looking Good
Housekeeping *perfect.*

My college graduation. I was so happy that my father was alive to finally see me graduate—one of the highlights of my life.

With Vanessa on vacation at Club Med before her mental break. I love this picture.

With my son, Courtney, celebrating the Fourth of July at Caitlin's house in Greenwich.

Caitlin and me at Courtney's swearing-in for the New York Bar Association. My son, the lawyer!

My kitchen compadres at the Le Cordon Bleu—a rollicking, fun group of chefs.

From left to right: Vanessa, me, Genevieve, Kelly (Mac's granddaughter), Caitlin (in the middle), Sussie (Mac's daughter), Allie (Mac's granddaughter holding Kaylie Paige).

My cousin Marie, me and her husband Dennis at Caitlin's rehearsal dinner.

With my niece Michi.

With my children and my beautiful niece Michi at my sixtieth-birthday party.

Caitlin and me on her wedding day.

Me performing at Caitlin and Drew's wedding.

With Kaylie Paige, my first grandchild.

*Hanging loose with Jas at a
Manhattan soiree.*

*My favorite shot of Jas
and me, taken in 2010.*

Meditating with Buddhist monks in India.

My "destiny or choice" swami.

Participating as guest of honor at a beautiful, stirring ceremony on the Ganges River in Varanasi, India.

Visiting an orphanage in India. These children were as inspirational as they were beautiful.

My favorite swami of all.

Riding in Petra, Jordan, a truly extraordinary, awe-inspiring place.

Church of the Holy Sepulchre, in Jerusalem, where I yearned for the holy moment that eluded me.

Wearing the shawl I was given in Israel, not far from the place where I finally did have my holy moment.

With Garry Marshall in his office in Burbank, California. How I miss this wonderful man!

Genevieve and me at the opening of her play she wrote and starred in. So proud of her.

With Bill Cunningham at the eightieth-birthday dinner for his assistant, Angela Dupine.

In Sedona with Hale Dwoskin at one of his retreats.

Genevieve and me with Garry Marshall at dinner before one of her performances as Libby in the Neil Simon play I Ought to Be in Pictures *at the Falcon Theater in Burbank.*

My grandchildren, Caitlin's children.
Back row: Shai, Kaylie, Aliana
Front row: Camille and Ireland

Turning seventy with my adorable kids in Greenwich.

This really sums up life on a Beverly Hills morning: beauty queen runner-up indeed!

PART IV

Greenwich: A World Apart

· ·

All changes, even the most longed for,
have their melancholy; for what we leave behind us
is a part of ourselves; we must die to one life
before we can enter another.

—ANATOLE FRANCE

CHAPTER 53

God and Money

. . . .

M ost people have heard of finding God in prison or in a foxhole. I
had to find God in Greenwich, Connecticut . . . or die.

Greenwich is essentially the Holy Grail for some, but for me it was
a gilded cage in which I could hardly breathe, let alone fly. Greenwich
was where Wall Street's top dogs moved their families, where investment
portfolios thrived and incomes staggered ever upward. For most people,
the point of living in Greenwich was to surround yourself with the best—
having your kids attend the best schools, belonging to the best clubs,
vacationing in the best spots.

Hollywood, Manhattan, and Greenwich were three very different
worlds; all worlds away from the place I came from. That being said,
back home, wishing on stars from my childhood bedroom window, I
had envisioned for myself a lofty future and here it was, playing out in
real time. I experienced the glitz and glamour of Hollywood, the rich
and diverse culture and spiritual/personal-growth community of New
York. And then, in Greenwich, my life suddenly centered around shopping, entertaining, and country clubs. Wanting to feel part of the community, I got sucked right in.

It's not as if I'd been living in penury in the city. Like most parents,
I'd wanted my children to have the best, and so I'd sent them to private schools, enrolled them in extracurricular activities, and threw them
extravagant birthday parties in keeping with those of their friends. But
prior to moving to Greenwich, it had never occurred to me to spend
much on myself. I had a few nice outfits in my closet, but my personal

style was more bohemian and eclectic, and I'd never even considered designer clothes or envied the women who wore them.

In Greenwich, that would all change. Not many women, at least in the private-school crowd, wore anything that didn't boast a high-end label, and the quilted leather Chanel bag with the thick chain and interlocked Cs was a staple of most purse collections. Of course, Greenwich also had its share of old-money eccentrics who wore clothing from thrift shops just to prove they didn't need to prove anything, as well as those who were just, well, thrifty. But as a newcomer who wanted to establish herself in this culture, I found the pressure fierce.

I bought into much of it, and in so doing I felt my wit dull and my brain shrink. Needless to say, I was no longer reading great plays and learning lines, and I even stopped reading poetry. The more time I spent in that energy, the more I began to forget my heart's true purpose. I kept thinking of the Marcel Proust line about snobbery as "the greatest sterilizer of inspiration, the greatest deadener of originality, the greatest destroyer of talent." How did I get so complicit?

CHAPTER 54

A New Life and Apple Pie

·······························

Unlike the case in Manhattan, you absolutely need a car in Greenwich. The station wagon Bob selected for me was a far cry from the red Fiat convertible I'd driven around Hollywood. I was now a suburban mother of four kids and a white German shepherd named Tucker (who'd come with Bob). My mommy-mobile—the best Bob would spring for— was an unsightly, clunky Buick in navy blue, Bob's favorite color. I hate navy blue. Bob drove a silver BMW.

The house we bought with the proceeds from the Dakota sale was also Bob's choice. Small and brown, it looked like a beach house, minus the beach. The first thing Bob did was paint the outside of the house cobalt blue and christen it My Blue Heaven. I hated the house, but it was on a picturesque little street walking distance from the schools and Greenwich Avenue's shops and restaurants.

The New York City private-school application process, starting as early as pre-pre-kindergarten, was a rat race that made Wall Street seem like a churchyard bake sale. When Vanessa had been not quite two years old, I had attempted to sign her up for the Susie Prudent program. I'd called the office, and when Susie herself answered the phone she was sweet and friendly until I told her how old my daughter was. "What?" she shrieked in my ear. "Why wasn't she registered a year ago? How do you expect your child to get in to college at this rate?" I felt like the worst mother who'd ever lived.

Suspecting that Greenwich would be just as bad as New York City, I decided that the first order of business—even before the actual move— would be to get the kids into the right schools. Bob, having joined the family after the Susie Prudent fiasco, had no concept of this diabolical process. For months before we moved, then, I schlepped back and forth to Greenwich, visiting all the local private schools to find the best fit for the kids, as well as nursery programs for Genevieve. Eventually I settled on the all-girls Greenwich Academy for Vanessa and Caitlin, the all-boys Brunswick School for Courtney, and Putnam Indian Field School for Genevieve. Genevieve would have to wait until she turned two, but the application was in. The concept of paying tuition for a baby's education blew Bob's mind, but wanting to fit in and please me, he relented.

Our first day in the house, our next-door neighbor, Mrs. Mason, a sweet elderly woman living with her forty-something son, Charlie, welcomed us by stopping over with an apple pie—yes, an actual apple pie that she had baked herself. I'd thought that happened only on TV shows from the '50s.

That evening I told Bob all about our neighbor Mrs. Manson and her son Charlie. He shook his head. "Mrs. *Mason*!" he said, laughing, "Please don't tell people we live next to Charles Manson and his mother!" Oops! Easy mistake!

Right before we'd moved into the house, Bob and I had driven Vanessa, Courtney, and Caitlin to Stage Door Manor, a performing arts camp in the Catskills (which Vanessa loved and the performing-averse twins didn't). We timed it so they'd be out of our hair during the move and wouldn't have to endure the necessary renovations—the house had to be painted, the floors refinished, the side-porch replaced, and the dirty kitchen with its old cabinets and hopelessly out-of-date appliances needed to be updated. Bob had rented a house nearby for us to live in during the renovations, but I'd still have to be at the new house by 8:00 a.m. to let the workers in and stay there most of the day supervising. Not to mention, I had a three-month-old who was getting up at least three times a night.

Bob was working long hours in Manhattan and sometimes had meetings that ran late. On the nights when he didn't, he'd meet friends in the city for a meal, go for long jogs in the park, or take a ballet or jazz class at Broadway Dance Center. Getting back home to have dinner with me was not a priority. So there I was in the heat of the summer, with a baby at my breast and my sole companions electricians, plumbers, and painters, in a house with a temperamental air conditioner and an oven so old the electrician cautioned me that should I smell something strange to grab the kids, call 911, and get the hell out because it could be a gas leak.

CHAPTER 55

There Are No Lice in New York City

. . . .

In mid-August, we drove upstate to pick up the children at camp and bring them to their new home. All their things were waiting for them in their new rooms, which I'd had wallpapered in their favorite colors. We were the perfect little family with our perfectly wallpapered house and our perfect little porch on the side. Bob used to call us the Brady Bunch, and it was all I could do not to visibly cringe. The only thing I had on common with Carol Brady was that I'd gone into the marriage with kids. Bob's dreams seemed to be coming true, while mine were, one by one, getting stuffed deep down inside me.

One day on a hot August morning (still no air conditioning), I noticed Caitlin scratching her head. I looked closer and saw a tiny black dot scamper down her face. We both freaked out and screamed bloody murder.

Avenelia, my housekeeper, came running into the kitchen to report thousands of lice crawling all over the kids' sheets and pillows. I called a friend who'd been through this with her kids, and she recommended a special shampoo that would destroy the lice. Rather than create a bathroom full of dead bugs to deal with, I brought the kids into the yard and washed their hair with the special shampoo. As I was hosing down my children, old Mrs. Mason dropped by (with a cherry pie this time) and congratulated me on my brilliant idea. "How clever! Washing their hair in the yard! I should have done that with my kids!"

I thanked her for the compliment and didn't bother mentioning the lice. I wish I could say that was the end of them. It wasn't. They had infiltrated the kids' rooms, and by the following morning they had returned with a vengeance to all three of my babies' pretty little heads. I was at my wits' end. My doorbell rang, and it was the electrician. He said good morning, and I burst into tears about the lice. The poor man listened to the whole story and then suggested maybe I could use a cup of coffee. We went into the kitchen together, he poured me a cup, and then suggested I get out for the day, do some shopping, take myself to lunch. He would take over the house and get an exterminator to eradicate the bugs. Then he called his wife for the number of the doctor she'd used when their own kids had had lice.

"Does everyone in this town get lice?" I asked him.

"Pretty much," he said with a laugh. "Consider it a rite of passage. It's just what happens when kids get back from summer camp. You're not alone."

"There are no lice in Manhattan!" I cried.

"I am sure there are not any lice in Manhattan, Mrs. Edwards," he replied with a straight face.

I brought the kids to see that doctor, who gave me a prescription for some powerful lice-killing solution and a list of young girls who offered "nitpicking" services (nitpicking literally meaning plucking out individual microscopic lice eggs from hair and scalp before they have a chance to hatch). Between the exterminator, the prescription lice-killer, and a team of nitpickers, we managed to get the lice situation under control by the time the kids started school the following week.

So this was the suburbs.

CHAPTER 56

The Country Club of Hospitals

· ·

The first morning of Labor Day weekend I woke up to a nearly empty house. Bob, as usual, had gone off at the crack of dawn for his morning jog, while Mac had taken the older kids to New Jersey. It was just Genevieve and me. I poked my head into the nursery, and seeing me she smiled and reached out her arms to be picked up. As soon as I lifted her out of the crib she started projectile vomiting over my shoulder, clear across the room, and then pulling her legs in tight, started to scream. Bob heard her as he came in from his jog and rushed up the stairs to see what was wrong. We tried all the usual means of calming her down, but nothing worked. I called Dr. Larkin, the head of one of the pediatric groups in town, who told us to bring her right over. Dr. Larkin gave Genevieve an examination and explained that she had contracted a virus and would be fine in a couple of days. We took her home, but she did not improve. When I attempted to feed her, she moaned and grunted in pain. The next morning she looked pale, and with nothing in her system left to vomit kept gagging and spitting up bile. I brought her back to the doctor, who repeated his original diagnosis and sent us home.

The next day there was still no change. I took her once again to the doctor. He examined her a third time and with a hint of irritation, probably because we'd disturbed him on the holiday, insisted that it was just a nasty virus and the only thing for us to do was wait it out. But by the next day, when Genevieve still wasn't showing any signs of improvement, I knew something was seriously wrong. I brought her in a fourth time, and the doctor still refused to believe this was more than a virus. The following morning Genevieve had lost so much strength and color, my instincts told me I was going to lose her if I didn't do something, and fast. Desperate, I called Dr. Larkin yet again, and this time he listened.

He told me to go straight to Greenwich Hospital, where they would X-ray her abdomen. Seeing my baby that pale and weak, my fear became so great that all logic deserted me. On the way to the hospital, I passed some storefronts and spotted a cozy-looking pink-and-black sweater in a window, and was seized with the notion that I had to have it. I pulled the car over, picked up my sick child, and walked into the store and bought the stupid garment right off the mannequin. As the saleswoman packed up the sweater, I told her how there was no time to try things on because we were on our way to the hospital for an emergency. She must have thought I was out of my mind. She would have been right. I was.

Dr. Larkin met me at the hospital and reviewed the films. "It looks like intussusception," he said, sounding somewhat in shock. I looked at him blankly and he explained that intussusception is a rare condition in which part of the bowel collapses into another part, blocking anything from passing through the intestines.

Bob rushed home and joined us at the hospital just in time to hear the diagnosis. Dr. Larkin apologized profusely for his misdiagnosis and urged us to bring Genevieve to either Yale New Haven or Columbia Presbyterian, since Greenwich Hospital was not equipped to handle this kind of thing. We agreed on Columbia Presbyterian, and Dr. Larkin excused himself to call the pediatric department and make the necessary arrangements. On the drive home from the hospital, I was so undone that despite the fact that I had not smoked for years I told Bob to stop for some cigarettes. He looked at me as if I had grown three heads and ignored my request. Thankfully, Avenelia was a heavy smoker and always had some on hand. I told her the news and she happily shared her pack with me. We paced around the house smoking one after another until the doctor called to tell us we could head in to New York.

We were greeted at Columbia Presbyterian by a competent and compassionate team of doctors and nurses. While Bob was filling out forms, the pediatric surgeon came over and introduced himself. "I'm Dr. Stolar. I will be taking care of Genevieve." I burst into sobs and threw my arms around him. I knew that my child was in safe hands.

They took Genevieve in for an examination. There they discovered that the obstruction had unfortunately become too large to blow out via barium enema, making surgery the only option.

A nurse came and took my daughter out of my arms and into the operating room. The surgery didn't take long, and all went well. During the few days she remained in the hospital for observation, I slept in the chair next to her crib, while Bob went home to help with the other children and relieve Avenelia. Finally, we brought our baby home to Greenwich. New York, as usual, hadn't failed me.

Apparently, Greenwich Hospital had never seen a case of intussusception before. Whenever I recounted the ordeal, no one seemed surprised. I soon learned that Greenwich Hospital was nicknamed the "country club of hospitals" because many of the doctors took every Thursday off to play golf. Then, a few weeks after she was home, Genevieve began showing symptoms of intussusception again. Not wanting to jump to conclusions, I brought her to Greenwich Hospital once more. Dr. Larkin was out of town, but the doctor on call assured me it was nothing but an upset stomach and that I was paranoid. This time I decided to go with my instincts and brought her straight back to Dr. Stolar, who confirmed that it was, in fact, a resurgence of intussusception. Thankfully, this time we caught it early enough for the barium enema.

During those weeks I barely ate or slept at all. My weight dropped to ninety-nine pounds. I was convinced there was something wrong with me. I insisted on being tested for every type of cancer. When they came up negative, I thought maybe it was this new disease I'd heard was taking a lot of people out called AIDS. My doctor assured me I did not have cancer or AIDS, and most likely this was all just a result of stress. In addition to the trauma of almost losing a child, I was becoming acutely aware of the lack of support in my life. I didn't want to burden my elderly father in Maryland, but Bob's family were local, and though they were in the loop and knew exactly what was going on, they never showed up at the hospital nor offered any help.

CHAPTER 57

The Ugly Green Monster

....

When I was acting and my social life revolved around the theater, I'd never felt envious of anyone—not for their money or their talent, or their jobs. But once I left that world and stopped being that person, I picked up the dangerous habit of comparing what I had with those around me. Bob and I were out of our league in the wealth department, and for the first time ever it bothered me. There I was a mere run-of-the-mill housewife, surrounded by impeccably dressed women who lived in mansions with maids, butlers, and personal chefs. While they'd all spent their summer in the Hamptons or the South of France, I'd spent mine in a sweltering matchbox, now painted blue, with three lice-ridden kids.

When your children attend prestigious private schools in Fairfield County, the beginning of the academic year is nothing but parties, luncheons, and fundraisers. We were thrown into a circle of wealth beyond what Bob or I had ever known existed, let alone imagined for ourselves. And as if the tuition to these places wasn't outrageous enough, we were expected to donate large sums as well, and that was not going to happen. Compared to the ninety-nine percent of the world, we were doing very well, but I felt poorer than I ever had before—even since I was a child. It was not an enjoyable feeling.

CHAPTER 58

Toxic Gas and Child Molesters

· ·

School had been in session for a week, and I was finally feeling I was getting the hang of things. One night after I'd tucked the kids into bed and gone down to the kitchen to wait up for Bob, a putrid odor infiltrated my nostrils. At first I thought I must be imagining it, but then the kids came running down the stairs in their pajamas, one after the other, gagging and screaming about the smell. Remembering what the electrician had said about the stove, I shoved the baby into ten-year-old Vanessa's arms, herded them outside, and told them not to panic but to wait for me on the lawn. I ran down to the basement to grab Tucker and called 911. Within minutes, four massive fire trucks were lining the street.

We watched as the firemen stormed the house. One by one our neighbors emerged from their houses and gathered around. After about fifteen minutes, the firemen walked back to their trucks and the chief came over, chuckling a little and shaking his head. "I understand you're new to the neighborhood."

"Yes, we are; we moved in this past July."

"Where did you move from, dear?"

"Manhattan."

"I knew it!" he said, laughing. "Ma'am, have you ever seen a skunk—or let me rephrase that, have you smelled skunk before?"

"No sir," I replied.

"Your oven is fine," he said. "My guess is someone left the basement door open, maybe one of the kids, and a skunk slipped in and got startled by the dog."

Mortified, I apologized profusely. He smiled broadly and told me never to be afraid to call if I ever thought something was wrong; that's what they were there for.

I gathered up the children and went back into the house, opening every window in an effort to air out the stench, then poured myself a glass of wine and waited for Bob to return from dinner with his city friends. It was after midnight when he finally sauntered in. "Ugh, what is that smell!" he demanded.

"It's a gas leak," I told him. "Our oven's leaking toxic gas."

"What?"

"It's a skunk, you idiot—don't you know what skunk spray smells like?" I said, and then told him the whole story.

"Oh, Kathalynn, next time call me first; I would have told you it was just a skunk!"

About two weeks later I received a call from the mother of one of Caitlin's classmates. I figured she was calling to invite me to another party. Instead she said, "I'm sorry to tell you that it appears a child molester was seen prowling the Greenwich Academy campus. One of the girls claims a man with black hair and a mustache, wearing jeans and a red shirt, tried to molest her. We have no further information at this time, just wanted to warn you to be on the lookout."

Not only did two my daughters go to that school, but our house was less than three blocks from the campus. For all I knew, that guy was in my backyard at that very moment. I hung up and called Bob in a panic. "You dragged me out here to this boring-ass town because you said it was 'better for the children,' and guess what, there's a child molester on the loose! A fucking child molester at the Greenwich Academy! I mean, are you fucking kidding me? I could kill you! Goddamn it, Bob, I didn't move here for this shit!"

Bob let me rant for about three minutes, then in a tone devoid of emotion told me to calm down, lock the doors, and be mindful. *Be mindful?* Easy for him to say from his cozy little cubicle in the safest place on earth, Manhattan. Meanwhile, I was stuck in the rabid wilderness of Greenwich, battling lice, skunks, and now child molesters!

Around five o'clock, as I was sitting down with the kids for an early dinner, the doorbell rang. I called, "Who's there?" and a voice told me he was a rep from the landscaping company I'd phoned earlier in the week, coming by to give me an estimate on some yard work. I breathed a sigh of relief and opened the door. Standing before me was a young man with black hair and a mustache and wearing jeans and a red shirt. Just as he reached for a handshake, I screamed and slammed the door in his face. I ran down the hall in the kitchen. "It's him!" I shouted, "It's the child molester!" Courtney pointed at the girls and laughed, "He's coming to get you!" We all barked at him to shut up. Nobody thought it was funny. Caitlin burst into tears and bolted upstairs to hide under her bed. Vanessa ran to get the baby, who'd been jolted awake from her nap by the commotion and was now howling. I called the police, and they rushed over.

The young man had not hung around after I'd slammed the door in his face. He moved on to one of his other appointments on my block. The police found him and questioned him outside a neighbor's house. As it turns out, he was not a child molester. In fact, there was no child molester. The whole thing had been a big misunderstanding. The little girl who'd originally reported it had met a man she hadn't recognized on the path near the school playground. He was an older man who lived in the neighborhood, out for some exercise. He'd smiled at the child, who had probably seen too many "stranger danger" videos and had jumped to the wrong conclusion. Needless to say, I was going to have to continue looking for landscaper.

CHAPTER 59

Ungaro Unchained

·······························

Courtney had befriended a boy in his class named Jamie. Jamie's mother, Susanne, was one of the few Brunswick School mothers I liked. One day Susanne pulled up to my house in a sleek black limousine to drop Jamie off for a play date. She popped in to say a quick hello and asked me what my plans were for the rest of the day. I told her I was on my way out for a luncheon in Manhattan. It turned out she was on her way into the city herself and offered me a ride. Sitting across from her on the plush backseat of the limo, I couldn't help staring at her skirt. I finally broke down and asked her where she got it.

"Oh, it's Ungaro!" she said.

Ungaro? I didn't know whether Ungaro was the name of the store or some exotic animal on the endangered species list from which the skirt was made. I was not about to embarrass myself by asking, so I just nodded, "Oh! Ungaro. Of course."

"There's a place not far from here called Reman's where they sell designers' collections at a discount. I'm thinking of going next Monday, want to come?"

Oh, yes, yes, did I ever.

The following Monday, Susanne picked me up and off we went. As we stepped through the doors, an impeccably dressed woman rushed over to greet us. "Madam Sus-ahhhhn!" she exclaimed in a god-awful attempt at a French accent. "Soooooooo mag-nee-feek to see you!" And then the two of them exchanged air-kisses. Her nametag read Simone, which made me wonder, but I didn't say anything. Susanne was clearly one of her regulars.

Susanne couldn't wait to show me everything. We headed over to the Ungaros (which, it turned out, were not animals but the labels of a high-end fashion designer). Susanne started grabbing things off the rack, holding them up to me, then tossing them to Simone, who was never more than three steps behind with the ever-growing pile. As soon as we were alone in the dressing room, I asked Susanne what part of France Simone was from. "Flushing," she said with a laugh.

I laughed so hard I nearly peed all over the Escada pantsuit I was trying on, which, by the way, looked phenomenal on me. Everything did. It was impossible not to look good in these clothes. Susanne kept throwing options at me. She never checked the price tags, so I didn't either. By the time Simone had finished ringing up my new wardrobe, the tab came close to $10,000. My first impulse was to try to put some of it back, but I was not about to humiliate myself in front of my first Greenwich girlfriend, not to mention the uppity Simone. The only option I saw right then was to hand over my card and pray that it went through. It did.

For the next few weeks I dreaded going to the mailbox, anticipating the American Express bill that would be lying in wait. And then sure enough, one evening Bob came into the bedroom and calmly asked, "Kathy, who's Reman?"

I felt a surge of panic. "It's, um, it's not a person, it's a store."

"Yeah," he said, smiling, "I figured that."

And that was that. Bohemian, not-impressed-by-labels me was suddenly hooked on designer clothing. Thankfully, Bob who was doing better and better as a stockbroker, was fine with it. He wanted me to be happy, and if that was what it took, he was reconciled to it.

CHAPTER 60

Country Clubbers

. . . .

B ob slipped easily into the Greenwich lifestyle and made friends fast. One day our new neighbors, Chip and Janine, came to our door and invited us to join them at their country club for dinner. Bob was thrilled, and as soon as he laid eyes on the place he wanted to join. Chip and Janine sponsored us, and a few months later we were members of the Millbrook Country Club.

The club offered every activity imaginable for kids, and I went to a few wives-of-members luncheons (women themselves would not be allowed membership until much later). The women, perfectly nice, would give me one-armed half-hugs when they saw me and blow air kisses when I'd leave, but I wasn't one for boozing in the afternoon, and how many discussions about window treatments or the benefits of granite versus Corian countertops could one be expected to sit through stone-cold sober?

The following spring I was invited to try out for the ladies' tennis team. I had no interest in tennis, but Bob thought I might like it if I learned, so I took a few lessons. First thing I did was head to the pro shop and purchase a little white skirt and top to match those that the women on the courts were wearing. Rather than chance having me make an ass of myself in front of the Millbrook community, Bob arranged for me to take private lessons from a local pro at the public tennis courts behind our house. My instructor was a hulking Swede. I made the mistake of asking him what he'd done for a living back home. He told me his family business was embalming corpses! This freaked me out so much so that, irrational as it may have been, I declined further lessons, thus ending my tennis career.

The Millbrook Club had a golf team, and because I'd never so much as held a golf club, Bob signed me up for lessons for that as well. I bought the most charming golf outfit, complete with knee socks and a hat. Half an hour into my first lesson, however, my hand started to cramp up and blisters started to form. The pro laughed and told me that used to happen to him before he developed a good callous, then he proudly showed me the disgusting mound of hardened skin on his palms. Golf, I decided then and there, was not for me. My new golf clothes, worn once, were cast into the back of the closet with my tennis whites, never to see the light of day again.

Bob became frustrated at my resistance to embracing the country club lifestyle. "You just want to be miserable, Kathy," he'd say, pointing his finger.

"Yes, I do!" I'd holler back, "I want to be miserable! Okay? Now leave me alone." And so he did.

Bob played on the men's tennis team, learned golf, and jogged every weekend morning. He even found time to do some community theater. One time he talked me into doing a play with him, Jules Feiffer's *Hold Me!* Bob had the lead, and I was one of the female leads. On opening night Bob had not learned his lines, so he held the script and read them. It was a disaster for him. His parents had come all the way from New Jersey to see it. His father, who was a professional actor, turned to me and said, "You are an amazing actress. I'm so proud of you. You project and take over the stage when you're on it. You belong on Broadway!" The review that came out in the *Greenwich Times* praised my performance but was not very kind to Bob.

These activities might have taken Bob out of the city and into Greenwich, but he was not in the house much except to change his clothes. In the rare event that he spent an evening at home, he'd be barricaded in his office writing songs or working on the self-help book he was writing, which happened to be about integrity (move over, Jack Canfield!). I was living with a possessed man who felt compelled to squeeze ten lifetimes into one and expected me to be his cheerleader, muse, and number-one fan. He loved our new life so much and couldn't understand why I was so miserable. "How can you be so ungrateful?" He'd ask. I couldn't help it; we were only a short hop from my beloved New York, but it felt like a different universe, and I felt like an alien.

That said, I dutifully showed up at his god-awful musical performances and was at the finish line when he completed his marathons, half-marathons, and 5Ks. I threw parties for his friends and family, most of whom I found to be ungrateful leeches who'd stink up my house with cigarettes and never once lend a hand or offer a hostess gift. These parties were hardly last-minute suburban get-togethers with beer and cheese and crackers but rather catered events with hors d'oeuvres and elaborate centerpieces, which were, Bob felt, expected. For Halloween one year I had pumpkins filled with vegetables and autumn floral arrangements. I bought the finest wines and labored over finding just the right background music for each event. I thought nothing of the expense; Bob, who was by then thriving financially, was happy to foot the bill.

Then there was the annual Millbrook Club talent show. Bob, without asking me, signed us both up. As new members, it was important to him that we really make a splash. I had made the mistake of telling him I'd taken hula dancing lessons when I was a kid and then again on my visits to Hawaii. I had held on to my old fringe skirt and sequin halter, thinking maybe I would wear it some Halloween or one of the girls could use it for dress-up.

Bob decided that for our act I was going to dust off the costume and do a hula dance while he sang "The Hawaiian Wedding Song." My first response to this was a resounding **NO**, but Bob sulked and pouted so much that I eventually relented. "All right," I said, "I'll try the stupid thing on, if I can even find it." And with that he went running downstairs and pushed all our living room furniture against the wall to create our rehearsal space. I found the outfit. The good news was it still fit perfectly. The bad news was . . . it still fit perfectly. When I came down the stairs, Bob's eyes lit up. There was no getting out of it.

The show was everything I expected it to be and worse. I did the hula for the longest three minutes of my life as Bob stood center stage in a jacket and Hermès tie and sang "The Hawaiian Wedding Song" while miming playing the ukulele. I had gone from performing Strindberg for Stella Adler to dancing the hula in an amateur variety show at this godforsaken country club. I let Bob know that night that this would be my last talent show. I told him he could keep doing them if he wanted to, but he was going to have to go solo from now on. Which he did. Year after year.

CHAPTER 61

Tying the Knot at Last

....

*B*ob and I had been living in Greenwich for a year and a half when Bob's wife finally agreed to give him a divorce, and to Bob's relief we could now legitimize our union. Eric Pace came up to perform the ceremony at our little "blue heaven" on February 13, 1986. The event was small: us, the kids, Bob's parents, and a few city friends. Most of our Greenwich acquaintances were under the impression we'd been married all along. Afterward, we all went to the Catskills for the weekend. It wasn't much of a honeymoon, but we didn't really need one, and the kids had a good time.

CHAPTER 62

Unity

....

On Sunday mornings, Bob, the children, and I went into the city to hear Eric Butterworth, a Unity minister, speak at Lincoln Center. Unity, like Science of Mind, is a part of the New Thought Movement. While the two schools of thought are alike in principle, the teachings of Unity are rooted in scripture. The two also differ in their approaches to prayer. Science of Mind, as mentioned earlier, emphasizes Spiritual Mind Treatment, an active movement of mental energy toward a specific purpose. Unity's primary methodology is positive affirmation, affirming what one *wants* as what *is* and then embodying the affirmation and therefore manifesting its result.

On what would have been her deathbed, Unity co-founder, Myrtle Fillmore discovered the power of affirmative prayer. When, after accepting into her heart the belief, "I am a perfect child of God; therefore, I do not inherit sickness," she reversed the effects of her tuberculosis. After this happened, people everywhere wanted to learn this technique for themselves. The Fillmores opened up a prayer ministry they called Silent Unity to offer people the faith and strength they needed to affirm whatever they were seeking to make happen. Silent Unity still exists today, providing support day and night to anyone who writes or calls in with a request for prayer.

While I witnessed countless astounding results of this practice, I personally had a hard time with affirmations. Most of the time when I attempted it, I'd just find myself repeating words I didn't really mean that were in contrast to my actual circumstance. Spiritual Mind Treatment gelled with me more naturally, and in my own experience, the results from it were more powerful.

Eric Butterworth was among the greatest Unity ministers of all time. His talks encouraged a practical approach to life's challenges through spirituality. Bob and I became friendly with Eric and his wife, Olga, who also lived in Greenwich. Eric performed Genevieve's christening, or "naming," as it's referred to in the Unity tradition, at our house.

Occasionally the four of us would get together for dinner. During one of these dinners, Eric asked if I would be interested in earning an advanced-study degree in Unity so I could teach for him. This would entail taking two week-long courses at the organization's headquarters, Unity Village, located just outside Kansas City. Naturally, I jumped at the chance. Since the Unity philosophy focused around a metaphysical interpretation of scripture and my knowledge of the Bible then was rudimentary at best, I was excited to learn more about it. Plus, Eric being the giant he was in the New Thought community, an opportunity to teach at his center was an honor.

During this period, the Butterworths asked Bob and me to teach Sunday school for him at Lincoln Center, so every Sunday we would head into the city and teach, with Genevieve's playpen set up in the corner. We knew nothing about teaching Unity to children, but it wasn't that difficult; mostly we just read them children's books from the church gift shop. Bob loved the idea in theory, but it meant missing Eric's sermons. In addition, we would have to leave for the city that much earlier, which meant Bob couldn't do his Sunday morning jog, so our teaching Sunday school lasted only about six months.

Bob was a huge supporter of my going out to Unity Village. He thought spending time there would make me a better person, which meant a more forgiving one. He'd leave pamphlets around the house about forgiveness because according to him, my inability to forgive was our only real problem as a couple. I have to say that on some level Bob was right. I harbored an irrational amount of resentment toward his friends and family, whom I felt he had given carte blanche to pretty much walk all over me. But the truth is, these people really didn't deserve my anger. All they were guilty of was accepting the gifts and invitations Bob all but forced on them. They didn't reciprocate, but Bob didn't expect or even want them to. Bob took enormous pride in being the guy who always picked up the tab and gave the most expensive gifts. Out of desperation to keep the family together, I directed my anger toward these other people, when my real issue was with Bob himself. I felt lonely, unappreciated, and unloved. I yearned to be part of a team in which we made decisions together. When I tried expressing myself with Bob, he would shut down. I never felt heard. He simply wouldn't connect. Were the red flags there? Of course. Did I willingly sign on for this marriage? Yes. Should I have made a different choice? Possibly, but here I was, and I was not going to walk out now. The kids filled much of my life, but I couldn't rely on them for all that was lacking. I suppose it's this kind of emptiness and disconnect that drives people to have affairs, but I wasn't interested in doing that. Instead, I threw myself into shopping and more spiritual study.

One of the first classes I took at Unity Village focused around forgiveness. I shared with the group what I was going through with Bob. The woman who spoke next was seeking help forgiving her neighbor, who had hired her son to clean his pool and attached weights to the boy's ankles so he wouldn't float up while scrubbing the bottom. Her son had drowned, and she sought guidance on forgiving this man, who in wanting to save money had hired a kid for a job a professional should have done. At the end of the workshop that woman threw her arms around me and told me how sorry she was that I had to go through that with my husband and that she would pray for me. My issues paled so profoundly next to hers that there wasn't anything to say.

I graduated from the Unity School of Christianity in 1987. Bob flew in for the ceremony, and we had a lovely weekend together. Eric immediately invited me to do the noon lectures at his center. It was a wonderful experience, but though I was great on the outside, I felt like a hypocrite standing at the podium teaching people spiritual principles to use in their lives while I wasn't putting them into practice in mine. I could not manage to "let go" of my distaste for the things Bob would do.

CHAPTER 63

Reinventing "Rudolf"

....

One Sunday morning during the holiday season, Bob, the children, and I were at church to hear Eric. On our way out, I ran into Ruth Warrick, who'd played Phoebe on the soap opera *All My Children*. Ruth and I had become friendly at Unity Village, where she also took courses. She asked me if I had received her invitation to her Christmas party that afternoon. When I told her I hadn't, she pulled an invitation out of her purse and handed it to me. I told her I would have loved to go, but we had matinee tickets and dinner plans after the show. She insisted that the family come by after dinner, as the party would be going into the night.

When we all arrived at Ruth's exquisitely decorated apartment, the party was in full swing. A man in a pristine tux played background music on her grand piano, and the place was crawling with celebrities. Out of the corner of my eye, I spotted the queen of daytime herself, Susan Lucci, who looked every bit as fabulous off-screen as she did on.

Ruth, knowing what a huge fan I was of Elizabeth Taylor, introduced me to her daughter Maria. Then Ruth telephoned Elizabeth and after a few minutes told her that there was someone she'd like to introduce her to over the phone. I was shaking when she handed me the receiver and couldn't get much more out than a quick "Hello, Ms. Taylor, you don't know me, but, um . . . I think you're wonderful!" Then I shoved the phone back at Ruth, feeling like a complete idiot and yet not caring, as I savored the rush of having spoken to *Elizabeth fucking Taylor*.

I grabbed a glass of Champagne from one of the impeccably dressed servers, and while I sipped in private celebration over just having exchanged words with one of my idols, I noticed Bob sulking against a wall. Oh shit, I thought, he's not enjoying this. I had forgotten how uncomfortable Bob always became when he was around famous people. A frustrated artist himself, his envy and resentment made it impossible for him to relax. No sooner had I turned around to chat with another party guest than I heard a familiar voice asking for everyone's attention. My heart started racing and my stomach contracted. I prayed it wasn't what I thought. It was. Bob, standing beside the pianist, started belting out "Rudolf, the Red-Nosed Reindeer," adding lyrics like "Rudolf, baby, Rudolf, you red-nosed Reindeer, I said Rudolf, baby, Rudolf!" The pianist had no choice but to follow along. During the musical interludes, Bob yelled out, "I'm Bob, everybody, now give it up for the gingerbread man on the piano!" A few people clapped politely, but most of them just stared. It was like that night in the restaurant, but a thousand times worse because I actually *knew* some of these people and they knew me. He gestured for Vanessa to join him because of all my kids, she was the only one who sang. Vanessa, who did not want to sing, ran into the bathroom to hide with me, and then came Courtney, banging on the door demanding to be let in as well. Finally Bob's performance was over and he asked his captive audience to join in singing Christmas songs, which some reluctantly did.

After it was finally over, he thanked the audience and found his way back to me with a huge smile on his face.

"Get your coat," I said. "We're out of here."

"Why?" he asked. "I haven't eaten."

"Should have thought of that before you decided to humiliate us all. I want to go, *now*."

"Oh please, Kathy, everyone was bored to death until I livened the place up! They loved it."

"No one was bored, Bob. Only you."

I found Ruth, thanked her for inviting us, and left. Not a word was spoken on the drive back to Greenwich. Bob genuinely believed he had saved the party. I never heard from Ruth again.

CHAPTER 64

Into the Fire

....

One of our favorite places to vacation with the children was Saint Martin. On one of our trips, Bob and I met a couple named Ruth and Chuck. Chuck, a handsome chiropractor, was a connoisseur of self-help seminars and had decided to go out on his own and start leading some himself. When he brought his seminar to New York, he invited Bob and me to attend. It was a weekend event, out by LaGuardia Airport, that would culminate in a fire walk, wherein participants proceed barefoot across a bed of burning coals. The fire walk was something Chuck had picked up from Stuart Wilde, who used them to illustrate mind over matter. To me, it sounded like a bunch of New Age nonsense, not to mention dangerous. I had absolutely no desire to partake, but unfortunately this was the big event of the weekend and we were special guests of the hosts, so I felt I couldn't very well back out. When my turn came, I took a deep breath, held it, and, focusing my attention on the end, moved as fast as I could across the coals. When I finished, Bob was right there to give me a hug and kiss; he could not have been prouder. Not only did I not burn my feet, but I learned a valuable lesson about the power of concentration. Ruth and Chuck sent us pictures of the event, which Bob framed and hung in his office. The next time we saw Chuck and Ruth in Saint Martin, they'd changed their names to River and Rainbow.

CHAPTER 65

Another President's Grandson

....

The following spring, I found out that I was pregnant with my fifth child. I wanted a boy for Bob and imagined giving him a pair of blue baby booties, all wrapped up. One Saturday morning, sick as a dog, I was in the kitchen making breakfast when Bob said we had a dinner date with another couple that evening. I told him I didn't want to go. I felt sick, my stomach was sticking out, I had nothing to wear, and it was unfair of him to spring that on me when all I wanted was a night in with the kids, who'd be leaving for camp the next morning.

"We have to go, Kathy, it's business. You'll look fine, just throw on something, maybe that loose white dress of yours. Anyway, these people are so down-to-earth, they're not going to care what you're wearing. We're meeting them at their house for drinks before dinner and it's an hour away, so we'll have to leave here by six."

Around 4:30 I took a quick shower, dried my hair, and slapped on some makeup. I hardly recognized the gaunt and pale woman starring back at me in the mirror. I put on my little white dress, the only one that fit, and went downstairs to the kitchen to boil up some spaghetti and heat sauce in a pan for the kids' dinner, which was the best I could do. I rushed to get them fed, and as the babysitter walked in the door, Bob and I walked out.

After driving for about an hour, Bob turned off the main road and headed toward a set of magnificent gates. "Bob," I said, as the gates opened for us, "who are we having dinner with? This place is huge!"

"Oh! I didn't mention this earlier because I wanted it to be a surprise. President Roosevelt's grandson is thinking of doing some business with our firm. This is his place."

"Which President Roosevelt?"

"Franklin D.," he said, "I think."

"You don't know?"

"I do! It's Franklin D."

"Great."

Bob parked the car, and as I reached down to grab my purse I noticed little red dots all over my white dress. Spaghetti sauce. "Bob, I can't go in. We have to go home right now."

"What? Why?"

"My dress is dirty; I hadn't noticed before, and I need to change."

"I don't see anything," he said, casting a cursory look my way.

"Bob, you're either blind or a liar, and I know you're not blind! Now, I am not meeting Franklin and Eleanor's grandson with sauce stains all over my dress. Take me home now!" Ignoring me, he turned the motor off and got out; I just sat there. He came around to my side, opened the door, and with a big plastic smile, told me I looked fabulous.

"To hell with you," I muttered, as I followed him begrudgingly to the front door.

We were indeed greeted by Franklin Roosevelt's grandson and his wife. Decked out in a Chanel from head to toe and with jewelry to die for, she was the most put-together woman I'd ever seen. The embarrassment I was already feeling over my Ragu-spattered dress was magnified a thousand times.

We moved into the living room for a pre-dinner cocktail. If ever I needed a glass of wine, it was then. Of all times to be pregnant. Mr. Roosevelt, whose first name has since escaped me, was a charming host. While Bob flirted with his wife, he and I talked about FDR and my father, who'd been captain of his yacht during World War II. All the while I prayed that I wouldn't get an attack of morning sickness and puke all over their gorgeous Persian rug.

Mrs. Roosevelt was as gracious as she was stylish. As we were about to head out to their country club for dinner, she disappeared for a moment and came back with an exquisite shawl. "Kathalynn," she said, "it gets so very cold at the club with the air conditioner on. I thought you might want to have this for your arms."

"Oh, how thoughtful!" I replied gratefully. "I can't believe I forgot mine at home."

"I figured you had," she said with a smile. If tact had been a category in the Olympics, that woman would have taken the gold.

However ungainly my appearance, though, it could not have hurt prospects too badly, as the two men eventually did end up doing business together.

CHAPTER 66

No More Babies

·····························

ecause I was thirty-eight years old, my doctor insisted on an
amniocentesis to make sure the baby was okay. I consented mainly
because I wanted to know the sex ahead of time; it hadn't occurred to
me that there might actually be a problem. Back in the '80s, similar tests
in earlier stages of pregnancy had either not been developed or were,
like chorionic villus sampling (CVS), an alternative to amniocentesis,
still too new for my doctor to be confident that it would not put me at
risk for miscarriage.

Bob and I wanted to take a vacation together before the baby came,
and we had a short window in early July, while the kids were off at camp.
Avenelia agreed to watch Genevieve, and we headed to Sedona. I had
been dying to get back there and knew Bob would fall in love with it as
I had.

Knowing we'd have some time to kill in Phoenix before our connecting flight to Sedona, I'd reached out to Virginia and Lester, who were
living there most of the time. They suggested we all meet for breakfast
at the airport between flights. Over coffee, Lester asked, "What are you
having, a boy or a girl?" I told him we didn't have our results yet, and he
said, "The mother always knows." At that moment, my stomach started
to churn. Lester and Virginia walked us to meet our plane, Lester carrying my bag the entire way. Just as I was about to board, I vomited all
over the tarmac right in front of everyone. Lester gave me a hug, wished
me good luck, and told me to reach out if I there was anything I needed.

The flight into Sedona was bumpy, and I continued to be violently
nauseated the whole way. Part of what drew me to Sedona was that
every time I was there, the alignment between intuition and conscious

thought became stronger; it was as though whatever was going on with me internally, good or bad, was magnified. I was no stranger to nausea during pregnancy, but this was different, and in a sickening flash I wished I was not pregnant. The thought was fleeting, but it came from a place deep within. Something was wrong. Determined to enjoy this vacation, however, which I knew would be my last chance to be alone with my husband for quite some time, I worked to put all negativity out of my head.

Before we'd left Connecticut, I had scheduled massage appointments for our first day in Sedona. A friend who lived there had recommended a woman named Cumilla. When I told Bob, he almost ran off the road. "You must mean *Cam*-illa, Kathy," he said.

"No, Bob, it's *Cum*-illa, accent on *Cum*."

"Well, I'm not calling her that!"

"Fine, don't!"

We arrived at her house, which was decked out in Buddhist art and reeked of incense, and New Age music playing in the background that sounded like one hundred wind chimes clanking together while somebody tortured a cat was playing in the background. The tall woman with scraggly gray hair who greeted us wore sandals made of a hemp-like material and a floor-length, strapless sundress that drew focus to the little black tufts poking out from under each armpit. Extending her long, bony hand toward Bob, she said, "Welcome, I'm Cumilla,"—as in *Cum*-illa. It took every ounce of strength in me not to erupt into laughter. Bob did not so much as crack a smile.

"Who would like to go first?"

Bob still needed time to get over the name, so I went first. I mentioned I was pregnant and she assured me she was not going to touch my stomach. I lay on the table waiting for her to begin, and after about ten minutes I asked when she was going to start.

"What do you mean, dear? I started ten minutes ago."

"Oh!" I said, confused. "Could you go a little deeper?"

"I'm only allowed to go as deep as they tell me."

"What? Who's 'they'?"

"I am massaging your ethereal body, and am going as deep as the guides allow me."

The guides? I couldn't wait until Bob's turn.

"Jesus Christ!!" she screamed.

"What?"

"Jesus is here!"

"What?" I asked again, wondering if I'd heard her correctly.

"I am channeling Jesus! Oh, no! I'm wrong, it's not him, it's his master!"

"Jesus's master? You mean God?"

"No!" And then she murmured some name that I'm pretty sure she made up on the spot.

"Oh, him," I muttered. Jesus Christ, all I wanted was a massage.

"This is very rare, you are so blessed!"

When the session was over, I sat in the waiting room just picturing Bob on the other side of the door, having his ethereal massage. I wondered if he too would be blessed with a visit from Jesus's master, and I started to laugh. The more I thought about it, the harder I laughed, until I couldn't stop.

A nice-looking man came through the door and saw me curled up in the chair howling like a hyena. We locked eyes for a moment, and then he started laughing too. The two of us never exchanged a word; we just kept glancing at each other and laughing until Bob emerged from the room. He did not join in the laughter but just gave me a look and shook his head.

On the way back to our hotel, we drove passed Bell Rock. Thousands of people were crawling up the mountain in a gigantic human ant pile. Bob pulled over to ask a passerby what was going on and why it was so crowded.

"You don't know? Bell Rock is going to open up its top in a few hours, and UFOs are going to come out."

Opting not to wait for the UFOs, we instead stopped along the way at a place offering aura readings, which turned out to be a full-service psychic lair with a smorgasbord of options from tarot cards to astrology; past-life, clairvoyant, palm, and tea-leaf readings; as well as healings of the shamanic and crystal variety. Bob and I chose basic psychic readings. When I asked my reader if she would predict the baby's gender, she told me I'd have a healthy baby girl. Bob was told that he would be a famous singer in this lifetime. He left in a great mood.

We were staying at Enchantment Resort in Boynton Canyon, which was considered the most mysterious of the vortexes. Legend had it that the goddess of the land still lived there. The views driving up to Enchantment lived well up to the name, and as I was admiring the magnificent spread of juniper trees and the vibrant red rocks that seemed to touch the endless cerulean sky, Bob stopped the car.

"Why are you stopping?" I asked. Bob gestured to a narrow, towering rock that was undoubtedly phallic in appearance.

"Just look at that thing," he marveled. "They should call it Dick Rock, or Cock Rock! I'm going to meditate on it, see if it improves my stamina!"

"Are you serious?"

"Of course not; my dick is magnificent. But I will tell David about this place." David, a friend of Bob's who I never liked, was apparently having trouble keeping it up for the twenty-three year old he was dating. "We should send him here to release on wanting to control his dick!"

That was one of the rare times Bob truly made me laugh. He couldn't get over "Cock Rock," and it became a favorite inside joke for us in times to come. Sedona, with all its beauty and mystical and metaphysical offerings, was a kind of spiritual Disneyland that was just what we both needed. We were having fun together, laughing, kidding around, and really connecting.

I called home the following afternoon to check on Genevieve, as usual. Avenelia told me the baby was fine and that Dr. Jacobson had phoned and was looking for me. At first I assumed he was calling to tell us the sex of the baby, but when I thought it over, it seemed odd that Ivan himself would phone. Sure that it had something to do with the amniocentesis, I started to panic that something was wrong and urged Bob to make the call for me.

"Hi, Ivan, this is Bob Edwards." After a minute or so, his countenance became grim. "Are you sure?" he asked.

"Is he sure what?" I cried. "What's wrong with the baby?" Bob started to say goodbye, and I snatched the phone away from him. "Ivan, what's the sex of my baby?"

"Boy," he replied, sounding sad. "I am so sorry, Kathalynn." I hung up and looked at Bob.

"Kathy, we have a challenge," Bob said softly and with great love. "Our baby has Down syndrome." I began to sob. Bob wrapped his arms around me and could not have been more compassionate. After I calmed down, I called Ivan back. I was in a welter of grief and shock, but I knew that for me and for my family there was one choice to make here, however wrenching. I asked him what I needed to do.

"When are you coming home?" he asked.

"Monday, but we can head back today if you need me to."

"No, it's Friday already and nothing can happen until next week. Stay through the weekend and try to have a nice time. I will take care of all the details. Come to my office on Tuesday for an examination. On Wednesday, I'll check you into the hospital to terminate the pregnancy."

Ivan had known what I'd wanted to do without even asking. He worked at Roosevelt Hospital just like Mac, and had not only been my doctor since I was twenty-three and delivered all four of my children, he was also a friend.

I felt angry, ashamed, heartbroken, and completely betrayed by my body. I felt I had failed Bob for not being able to give him the son he so badly wanted. That night I had a nightmare in which I saw eggs dying all around me. I woke up in a sweat, went into the bathroom, and stared into the mirror. The face reflecting back at me was that of an old woman. A voice echoed inside my head, hissing, "Your eggs are all rotted; you can't even have a healthy child! You're just an old, unlovable thing." I collapsed onto the bathroom floor and cried until I fell into a deep, dreamless sleep.

I understand that many women would have opted to keep the baby, and my hat is off to them. For my part, I already had four children, one of whom was only two years old. I weighed 104 pounds and was already stressed to the limit. Bob, who bounced in and out of the house and was rarely home on a weeknight for dinner, let alone available for child care or homework help, could not be relied on to show up when I most needed him. Weekends, he'd typically go to his parents' apartment in New Jersey to hang out with them after his Sunday morning jogs. I couldn't see how it would have been fair to the kids with my attention already stretched thin, to bring in a special-needs child who would require constant care. Had I been married to a more present husband, might the decision have been different? I will never know. What I do know is that I made what I thought was the best choice at the time for my family and myself.

The next morning in Sedona, Bob, well rested and bright eyed, suggested we take a ride over to the Chapel of the Holy Cross, a beautiful little structure nestled in the Sedona red rocks. We entered the space and sat down to take in the energy and pray. After a few minutes, Bob reached over and took my hand. "I just did a treatment on the baby's health."

"What?" I asked. Did he mean the baby we were terminating in three days? He couldn't be serious.

"I've decided we should go ahead and have the child. I've done a treatment, and with our powers combined, we will heal his condition inside of you."

"Excuse me, Bob?"

"Yes, Kathalynn! This is the ultimate test of our faith in the power of the Science of Mind! It's our chance to prove it works."

"Oh, you mean the way Jesus healed people?"

"Exactly!" he said.

"Bob, you're crazy. I have seen wonderful things come to pass via treatment, but I'm not Christ, and neither are you."

"It's worth a try! Worst-case scenario, the experiment doesn't work and we have a beautiful Down syndrome child. We can handle it."

"You mean I can handle it."

"What does that mean?" he asked, looking bewildered.

"I mean are you going to give up all your activities? Your sports, dancing lessons, community theater, dinners with your city friends?"

"If I have to," he said, but I knew better than to believe him. "Just tell me you'll consider it."

"No. I won't."

The next morning Bob took me to the Unity Church in Sedona. I cried through the entire sermon. After the service, Bob suggested we speak to the minister. What I didn't know was that he had called her the day before, told her everything about our situation, and scheduled us a counseling session.

When I entered the office, the nice woman smiled and, just as Bob had, tried to assure me the baby's condition could be reversed through prayer. She was certain that with the right attitude and faith, the whole thing would clear and I would deliver a perfectly healthy baby boy.

"And what if it doesn't work?" I asked.

"But it will, dear. If you have faith," she counseled.

I stood up and walked out of her office. Bob came chasing after me. I told him I would not have any more of this. I was terminating the pregnancy, and he could either support me or not, but either way, my mind was made up and the subject was closed. He got the message and relented at last.

That evening we went out to dinner and I ordered my first drink in months, a glass of Champagne. This was by no means a night of celebrating, but the alcohol helped me relax, and the bubbles settled my stomach. The next morning, we flew back home.

Bob and I drove in silence to Roosevelt Hospital, where Ivan was waiting for us. Bob had intended to head to his office after dropping me off, but when I started to throw up and shake uncontrollably he changed his mind and decided to stay.

After the termination, I was so physically and emotionally exhausted I could barely move my arms. Bob checked me into a hotel to relax and recuperate. The next evening he took me to see *Heartburn,* during which Meryl Streep gives birth to a beautiful little baby. I looked over at Bob right there next to me; he was emotionless, watching the screen he showed no indication that he took in the sad irony of it. I don't think it was intentional; however, it was an example of just how mindless Bob could be. A few days later, I felt ready to go home.

The following Friday, we drove up to the Catskills for family weekend at the camp, and the twins didn't notice anything wrong, but Vanessa, who was extremely intuitive even at the age of twelve, asked me right away what had happened to the baby. "We lost him," I told her. She threw her arms around me and told me how sorry she was.

I was depressed after the termination, and my weight started dropping so rapidly that at one point it went to ninety-nine pounds. Although I was functioning, I was not myself. Every time I saw a mother with a baby I found myself fighting back tears. I told myself that I'd made this choice consciously and had no right to grieve. But logic was no match for my emotions. The day I'd found out I was pregnant, I had run out and bought a few baby outfits. Every time I passed the drawer where they lay, I would spiral into despair. Bob was concerned and suggested I do a week-long intensive in Sedona to release and regroup. Mac was planning to take the older kids on a vacation, and Avenelia could stay to help Bob with Genevieve, so the timing worked out, despite it being just three weeks after the procedure.

When the seminar wrapped up, the participants all went back to Virginia's house in Oak Creek for lunch. Lester, who was always there,

came up to me and said, "Kathalynn, I heard what happened. I'm proud
of you for being so strong and doing what you felt was the right thing.
Life is full of challenges as it is without a double whammy like Down
syndrome. I also don't believe life really begins until the umbilical cord
is actually cut."

Lester was the only person who directly addressed what had happened with me. Most people never mentioned it, probably not knowing
what to say, but I felt supported by him. He truly understood the complexity of such a choice.

Did this event influence my marriage? I don't think it did, although
had we had the healthy baby boy Bob wanted, he might have adored the
child and been around more.

Some people believe that spiritual work will protect them against
hard times and challenges. Others believe that challenges are a test for
your spiritual growth. I don't think that the universe tests. With every
challenge there is an opportunity for growth. Spiritual work does not
guarantee that your life will be smooth and without challenges, and it
doesn't stop the process. Sometimes bad things happen. Being on a spiritual path gives you tools to cope with what comes your way.

CHAPTER 67

Full Circle with Don Ho

·····························

A few weeks after I returned from Sedona, feeling better but still shaky, we took our annual family vacation, this time in Hawaii, splitting the time between Waikiki and Maui. Bob insisted that we go to the Don Ho show with the older children—Bob, without my knowledge, sent a note to Don telling him that his old girlfriend Kathalynn Turner and her family would be in the audience (the note also mentioned our recent loss). Don, with his customary grace, invited us all to meet him backstage before the show.

Don arranged for us to have pictures taken with him and invited the kids onstage to sing with him during the show. Bob was ecstatic at the attention and acted as if he was the former lover and not me. At one point Don took me aside and told me how sorry he was for what had happened. He also reminded me of his philosophy, which he had spoken of all those years earlier.

"Do you remember my old theory about how for every good there is a corresponding bad?"

I nodded yes.

"Well," he said, "look at the good in your life and look at what just happened."

He continued dwelling on how darkness was inescapable and how we must prepare and accept it in equal measure with the light and the good. This did not help me feel better about my situation, it made me feel worse. It also made me feel sorry for Don.

"I have had so many highs in my life, but I have had some tragic things happen too," he continued. "For instance, someone very close to me was just hit by a car and is a vegetable." And then he continued to give me more examples to support his point of view.

I listened to his litany of examples, and though I felt sympathy for his misfortune, I did not buy his theory. Life is not always easy, but that did not mean to me that suffering must or should be part of it. What would be the point in striving for anything good if it meant that a tragedy of equal magnitude was guaranteed to follow?

Despite our gloomy little talk, it was a wonderful evening. His show brought back beautiful memories. The children felt honored to be asked onstage, and of course Bob was thrilled at the special treatment. When we got home, Bob bought the sheet music to the beautiful song "I'll Remember You," which Don had made famous. Bob would sing it constantly around the house for months.

CHAPTER 68

Still Spiritual with Sedona

....

When fall rolled around, I started joining Bob in the city Thursday nights to take classes with him at Science of Mind. We both became practitioners and then went on to pass a fifth-year test at Asilomar in Monterey, California, which qualified us to be ministers. Bob proposed that we start our own church. I told him he was nuts. The classes and training were fascinating and definitely beneficial, but I had to draw the line somewhere.

In addition to Science of Mind, I continued to practice The Sedona Method and attended retreats. When Lester passed away in 1994, the rights to the method were handed over to his protégé Hale Dwoskin. Having met Hale back in my original class in New York and knowing him over the years, I felt Lester couldn't have chosen a better successor.

On one of our trips to Sedona, Bob tried The Sedona Method himself, but as soon as the concept of confronting feelings came up, he immediately became resistant. The whole thing, he decided, was bullshit, and so was Hale. Hale was neither offended nor surprised; having met Bob years before, he understood. The tenets of The Sedona Method undermined and threatened the foundations of how Bob functioned, and surrendering to this teaching would have meant a massive change he was simply incapable of making.

Hale was a tremendous help to me in releasing my desire to change Bob from being that way. Although Bob never got onboard with the method himself, he never hindered me from continuing to go out to Sedona for retreats, for which I was grateful. Vanessa and the twins were becoming more independent and old enough to need less constant supervision, and between Bob and Avenelia there was always coverage for

Genevieve. Also, with me out of his hair, Bob could relax and pursue his ten million activities guilt free, which I'm sure he enjoyed.

CHAPTER 69

Shopping for Revenge

....

Wen Bob started making some real money, we upgraded our residence to a gorgeous Georgian Colonial. The house, being a stone's throw past the Greenwich border, technically placed us in Stamford. Our kids went to private school anyway, so it didn't matter to me. Plus, the absence of a fancy Greenwich zip code made it all the more affordable, and that made Bob all the more happy.

My life was looking great from the outside, but as Bob never ceased to remind me, he was the source and the controller of our finances. He refused to consider any of my ideas on investments. When, for example, I proposed buying an apartment in Manhattan, he dismissed the idea with "taxes are too high."

I didn't feel I had any influence or control in the relationship, so running up bills on the credit card was my way of grasping at a semblance of power. It was crazy, it was pointless, it was wasteful, and in no way was it going to bring my desired result, which was to be respected and seen by Bob as an equal. But at the very least, I rationalized, I'd get to spend some of it on myself before he blew through it altogether.

Blowing through money was something Bob did with tremendous force and abandon. He spent tens of thousands of dollars on his music, his tennis and golf lessons, and memberships to expensive private clubs that he didn't even neccessarily go to but for some reason had to belong. He also gave thousands away, often impulsively. Bob seemed unable to hang on to money or save it, and coming as I had from a financially prudent father who avoided debt at all costs, this disturbed me, It also led to a need to be in the mix myself because there was no mutuality in any decisions as to where that money went. Bob simply did what he wanted

271

to do when he wanted to do it. He would give what he wanted to give when he wanted to give it. It seemed to me that he had little regard for our bank account or concern about our future. I realized how absurdly counterproductive my own actions seemed. I could not control him, but I still had some agency over myself.

CHAPTER 70

Digging Deeper

. . . .

As the children were growing and becoming more independent, I asked myself how I could turn my own experience and training into something more broadly useful. What was it I truly wanted to do? What was my purpose?

Now that I had my Science of Mind practitioner's license, I was invited to perform the noontime services at the center, which I found greatly fulfilling, reaching out and connecting with people I could actually help. I was discovering how much I loved to teach, getting a taste of it when lecturing and leading meditations before and after the service; it came easily and seemed to be effective. I had, over the years, taken pleasure and satisfaction in contributing resources and time to various organizations—helping needy families at Christmas, sending aid to India—but here I was able, via teaching spiritual principle, to give something even more meaningful: tools with which to help people cope and feel powerful. Sharing this work I so fervently believed in tapped into those powerful feelings I'd been filled with as I'd observed the dying child in the hospital when I was a little girl.

As these small revelations started to take form, I recognized that helping people would bring the reward and fulfillment I had been so earnestly seeking. I also realized I would have to collect some mainstream credentials to make that happen—starting with the college degree my father had wanted for me all along.

Bob was completely onboard. Our marriage may have floundered in many ways, but he deserves credit and gratitude for supporting pretty much anything I wanted to do and giving me the space to pursue my goals. There would be money for my school, no problem, and though this would only deepen the inroads of our separate, parallel lives, it seemed to work as long as I suppressed the desire for real connection and partnership.

CHAPTER 71

Studying for Salvation

....

In 1992, I enrolled in Manhattanville College in Purchase, New York, roughly forty minutes from where we lived. My intention was to major in religious studies with a minor in philosophy. Vanessa was eighteen and away at college in Rhode Island. Courtney, having shown promise as a tennis player, was developing his talent at Bollettieri Tennis Academy in Florida. Only Caitlin and Genevieve were left at home. Caitlin, who was in high school at Greenwich Academy, was a social butterfly and fiercely independent. Little Genevieve was in second grade, and on days when I had late-afternoon or evening classes, I would pick her up from school and bring her along with me. A future student of philosophy herself, she loved being included and sitting in on the lectures with me, even as a young child.

In 1997, five years after I started, I graduated Manhattanville magna cum laude alongside Vanessa, who had transferred from Roger Williams and was graduating with honors in history. My father, who almost never left Maryland, came to attend. Finally, he would see his daughter receive the diploma he had so badly wanted for her over the years, a symbol of the education and independence he'd valued so highly.

CHAPTER 72

Mental Illness Hits Home

....

*F*rom the time Vanessa was a little girl, I suspected that she was different from other kids. All children express themselves uniquely, but something about Vanessa's behavior seemed outside the realm of what would generally be considered normal. For example, when she was in second grade I was sitting on a park bench watching her jump rope with some other little girls and I saw her, out of nowhere, jump out of the line and start laughing hysterically, pointing at nothing and then skipping in circles. The other kids stared for a minute and then resumed their game, barely surprised, as if this wasn't the first time. It occurred to me then that she may have some emotional issues.

One theory about Vanessa's occasional oddities was they might have been a byproduct of her being gifted. Vanessa had an exquisite singing voice, was a phenomenal dancer, and showed promise of being a very good actress. She loved to perform and stood out in every recital like a star. Everyone agreed she was on her way to becoming one hell of a triple threat. But as time went on her behavior got weirder and more difficult to explain. She'd become a nervous wreck over seemingly inconsequential things and sometimes exhibit signs of severe paranoia. My instinct told me something was off, but both Mac and Bob refused to take it seriously. Mac didn't see what the big deal was, figuring most teenagers act out in some form or another, especially those who are products of divorce. Bob considered Vanessa spoiled and chalked up her "moods" to not having had enough discipline in the house. I took her to a psychiatrist who suggested medication, but I was hesitant to go that route because she was so young. I really thought she just needed someone to talk to, never imagining that she was actually sick.

It wasn't until Vanessa had to pull out of college, having frightened her roommates about the voices whispering in her ear that celebrities were stalking her and trying to kill her, that Bob and Mac agreed there was a real problem. On our way to pick her up from school, I called Mac in a panic. He suggested bringing her to a psychiatric clinic in New Jersey. There she was put on a low dose of medication, which actually seemed to help. The following fall she began Manhattanville College and moved onto campus, not too far from where we lived, and came home most weekends.

Vanessa struggled a bit socially there, but she majored in history with a minor in art history and enjoyed it. I loved getting to see her every day. We shared meals in the cafeteria and even had a few classes together. In the spring of 1997, we celebrated our joint graduation with a massive party. Vanessa then got a job at a local art gallery, which she also loved. Every day when she'd come home from work happy, I'd breathe a sigh of relief that the medications were working and Vanessa was going to be okay.

I applied to the Columbia University School of Social Work for a master's, and to my great surprise I got in. My classes were to start in the fall. Then in August, when Bob, Genevieve, and I were vacationing in Spain, I got a distraught call from Caitlin. She said Vanessa was acting crazy, accusing her of stealing flowers Brad Pitt had left for her. I flew home right away. Caitlin had not exaggerated Vanessa's state of mind. The moment I walked in, Vanessa insisted I turn on the TV. Uma Thurman, she explained to me, was devastated because Ethan Hawke was leaving her to marry Vanessa Harris, and the news would be broadcast shortly.

I called Vanessa's psychiatrist, who told me he'd meet us at Stamford Hospital. Since the days when I twirled batons for patients in the psych ward as a young girl, I remember such places as being just like *One Flew Over the Cuckoo's Nest*. In a million years, I never could have imagined someday returning to drop off my own child in one of them. I took a deep breath and reminded myself that mental health had come a long way since the '50s (thank God) and brought Vanessa straight there.

Because Vanessa was over eighteen, I needed her to agree to be admitted. I told her I loved her and that it was very important to me that she give this a chance. She said, "Okay, Mommy, if it really means that much to you." The doctors diagnosed her with schizophrenia.

It was a fortuitous coincidence that Vanessa's psychotic break took place just as I was about to start at the Columbia School of Social Work. The Master of Social Work degree would qualify me to become a therapist, which meant that for three years following my daughter's diagnosis I would be surrounded by experts in the field of mental health. We tried various medications, some of which worked better than others. Vanessa took the pills, but only reluctantly, as they made her gain weight. And, as often happens, once she started to feel better she'd decide she didn't need them anymore and go off them, resulting in, among other things, insane phone calls to us at all hours of the day or night. Once Vanessa called everyone she knew and told them I was having an affair with the actor Brendan Fraser from *The Mummy* movies. It was greatly unnerving for us all.

By some miracle, Vanessa realized that the damage she was causing to the people around her outweighed her resentment about living on medication. She swore to the family that she would never take herself off it again, and I can happily say that she hasn't had an episode in close to twenty years. With the support of family and some amazing doctors, the illness has been pretty much under control. And though it hasn't been easy, she has managed to pull off a more or less normal and happy life. The medications have in fact put unwanted weight on her, and that's been difficult for her, but she's handled it beautifully. The illness made it impossible for Vanessa to pursue a career in the arts, as she planned to do. But Vanessa has been totally aware of her disease and the course it has set her on. I have never known anyone so brave and willing to accept what life has handed her the way she does. I am proud to report that she sings around Stamford with a wonderful group and volunteers in a soup kitchen. She is also very close to Caitlin, whose children she adores and showers with gifts and love. She has a beautiful life and often expresses how lucky she is.

CHAPTER 73

Real Life Out in the Field

· ·

A long with Columbia's rigorous course schedule, we were placed in the field for internships. From my days as a girl volunteering and entertaining in "old-folks' homes" (as we called them), I had miserable, haunting memories of the unpleasant odors and deep sadness on the faces of most of the elderly people there. I prayed for an internship anywhere but one of those places. Naturally, my first placement I got was at Parsonage Cottage, a senior-living facility in Greenwich.

The moment I set foot in the place, however, my whole view of these homes changed. Parsonage Cottage was clean, cheerful, and even elegant. The residents could choose from an array of activities. Also, it wasn't just rich people who got to live there; the State of Connecticut's Title 19 supplemented seniors in assisted living. When I learned about that, for one of the first times I actually felt proud to be a resident of Connecticut.

My position as a social worker entailed providing on-site individual counseling to residents and assisting with the application and reapplication process for entitlements. I looked forward to coming to work each day. The residents at Parsonage had a unique sparkle; they were bursting with stories to tell, and I was eager to hear them. I loved my work because I could see the immediate difference I was making. Moreover, merely being there affirmed for me the folly of going for results in life and not paying sufficient attention to the journey itself. In the end, everyone dies. The luckiest are those who make it to old age and, if they cannot live at home, can be in a place like Parsonage Cottage.

It was also my job to contact family members to arrange family meetings. Many of the family members were so thoroughly caught up in their lives they had little time to see their aging parents and relatives. I did the best I could to encourage them to make the effort.

After getting my degree, I was offered a temporary position at Nathaniel Witherell, the nursing home right next door to Parsonage Cottage, to take over for a staff member on maternity leave. This would be a tougher assignment. Nathaniel Witherell, more than Parsonage, felt like God's waiting room, the last step before the end. My position was the same, but these residents were infirm and needed a lot more help. The third floor was reserved for the Alzheimer residents. I noticed that with this particular group, it was the families who had the hardest time. The patients themselves were like children, curiously wandering around, discovering things, and living in a world of their own.

I tried hard in my work with the elderly there to shift their perspective from victim to survivor with strength and courage. When a woman named Mary was assigned to me, I discovered from her son during the intake process that she had worked all her life as a cook and housekeeper in some of the wealthiest homes in Greenwich. He also told me she had survived one son, while another had been battling a drug addiction for twenty years.

Mary had a sadness about her that broke my heart. The staff reported that she would barely eat, and when I asked her why, she told me she just didn't have an appetite. I started sitting with her during mealtimes and asked her questions about her life and the kinds of homes in which she'd worked. She began opening up about the parties she helped plan and the famous guests she'd waited on. As she talked, her eyes brightened. She relaxed and let me feed her a little. Over the months I spent getting to know Mary, I not only grew fond of her but also became impressed by her exquisite sense of style and prodigious knowledge of art and antiques. She could tell a fake painting from the real thing in a heartbeat. We had great chats together, and I told her I thought she was wonderful.

One day she looked at me intently and asked, "Do you really think I did okay?"

"Okay? You have had an extraordinary life!" I replied, meaning every word of it.

When I got to work the following morning, I learned that Mary had eaten a huge dinner the previous evening and that her general demeanor had completely changed. She was smiling and talking with the other residents. Soon after, however, she started having trouble breathing, and her body began to fail. The nurses called her family to come right over because it looked like the end, and indeed it was. Mary passed away that night with her family around her. The next day I received a call from her son to thank me for making his mother feel loved and validated at the end. I told him how grateful I was to have gotten to know such an extraordinary woman.

CHAPTER 74

Giving Back

....

One evening Bob shared with me that a business acquaintance of his had taken his own life. He was deeply shaken by the news. The two of them were the same age, and Bob was starting to feel a little panicky about life and purpose and whether what he was doing was of enough value. For Christmas Genevieve had given him Gary Fenchuk's *Timeless Wisdom*, and pulling it off the shelf that day, seeking inspiration, he found himself affected by the quote "We are all alike in our intentions, it is in our actions that we differ." I asked Bob how exactly he felt that pertained to him, and he said that considering our good fortune and the kinds of wealth we had access to, being in the financial community, we were in a position to do a lot of good in the world. I agreed and suggested something in the area of mental health, but Bob had a different idea.

Long before Bob entered into the financial arena, he'd been a teacher in his hometown on Long Island. During that time, numerous children confided in him that they were being abused at home. Unfortunately, at the time there was very little to be done. Frustrated, Bob had made a silent promise to himself that someday he would do something about it. When he read the quote, he was reminded of that old intention and couldn't get it out of his mind. So we decided that our mission would be the treatment and prevention of child abuse, and thus our charity was born.

The inaugural charity dinner took place in February 1998 at the Pierre Hotel in Manhattan. The charity was a genius move on Bob's part, as the hedge fund and the Wall Street community had recently been subject to some bad press, and all the top dogs were eager for a chance to show what good guys they were underneath. Neither Bob nor I knew much about nonprofits or how to best use our own money and the funds we raised, so I enlisted the dean of the Columbia School of Social Work to help us. With Columbia on our team, we were able to sift out the most legitimate programs in the city as our grant recipients.

When we arrived at the event, the first thing I found out was that Bob had seated himself front and center, and had me stuck at a different table. For the entertainment, Bob hired a doo-wop group. Never wanting to miss an opportunity to sing, he joined in for of his favorites, including an impassioned rendition of 'In the Still of the Night." When it came time for thank you speeches, Bob stood and acknowledged nearly everyone in attendance, except, of course, me. At later events, Bob would mention that it was me who had brought Columbia University on board. All that aside, it was the beginning of something wonderful. The charity would go on to raise millions of dollars for the treatment and prevention of child abuse worldwide.

CHAPTER 75

Singing at Lincoln Center

....

Getting my master's from Columbia was one of the most thrilling events of my life. After graduation, I put my degree to use working at Greenwich Social Services, and once I had accumulated enough supervised hours, I started my private practice.

I was a qualified therapist, but I found in practice what I'd always suspected to be true, which is that traditional therapy often kept patients in the drama of the story they couldn't change, rather than moving them through and past it. To combat that, I created a system that fused Science of Mind, The Sedona Method, life coaching, and some traditional therapy. I worked with clients on goals and releasing their wants around those goals. Some would challenge me, saying, "So if I release, I can have anything my heart desires? What if I want to be a ballerina but I have no experience?" I would explain to these clients that if they'd never taken a dance class, it was unlikely that being a ballerina was really their heart's true goal but rather something they had convinced themselves might be a *means* to the goal, for example: the accolades and appreciation ballerinas receive after performing. I would then help them release around their want for approval from themselves and others. To illustrate the point, I would turn it around on myself. "Let's imagine," I'd say, "that I make my goal to sing at Lincoln Center. I have no passion for singing, and I certainly have no talent for it, so why would I make that a goal? It must be because of something I imagine people who sing at Lincoln Center receive. I don't actually *want* to sing at Lincoln Center. So I can let that go." And I successfully used that example multiple times.

I was asked to be on the dean's advisory council and the development committee and I accepted. One day I received a call from Shelly, the

284

director of development for the School of Social Work. The dean was retiring and the board was planning a massive tribute celebration. Shelly was calling to tell me where I was supposed to meet the rest of the board to rehearse the number we'd be singing at the event. I had no idea what she was talking about and told her there must be some mistake because I didn't sing. "Oh, don't be silly, I heard you've got a beautiful voice!"

"What? From whom?"

"Your husband told me! I tried you a few days ago but you weren't at home. Bob and I had such a nice chat. He told me about your little hidden talent, and said you'd be a fabulous choice for the solo."

"Solo? I'm sorry. My husband doesn't know what he's talking about. Honestly, *I don't sing.*"

"He warned me that you might try to wiggle out of it!" Shelly laughed. "I'll see you Thursday."

"Wait!" I shouted, "I don't even know the song!"

"Oh! 'You're the Top,' by Cole Porter. Bob said you already had the sheet music. There's an intro at the beginning, that's the part you'll be singing by yourself. Looking forward to it, Kathalynn!"

"One more thing," I asked. "Where is the event?"

"Oh, Lincoln Center, of course!" And with that she hung up.

I called Bob and left an impassioned, incoherent message. He did not call back, but when he walked through the door that night he presented me with a Cole Porter songbook wrapped in a large red bow and wore a smile so big you would have thought he'd won the lottery. I'd been manipulated right into the tightest of corners. I opened the book and attempted to croak a few measures. Bob applauded and told me I sounded absolutely great. Then Genevieve emerges from her room and asked me to stop strangling frogs while she was trying to read. I threw the book at Bob and told him his joke wasn't funny; I wasn't going through with this, and he would have to sing in my place. He just laughed.

I called Shelly the following morning to tell her I was not going through with it, but before I could say a word she launched into how thrilled she was with the way the printed programs turned out, and I quickly switched gears to some neutral question about the party and hung up. I was distraught at the prospect of humiliating myself in front of my entire Columbia University circle—my classmates, my professors, even the president of the university. I was almost in tears when the words "I don't want to sing at Lincoln Center" escaped my lips for what was probably the hundredth time. Suddenly, I realized what I had done. Because the Law of Attraction did not recognize negations, all those times I had said the words "I don't want to sing at Lincoln Center" I was actually sending the message *sing at Lincoln Center* out to the universe. See how *wanting* really is the opposite of *having*? I wasn't wanting to sing at Lincoln Center, but I was *affirming* it. The universe, then, brought me exactly what it heard me ask for. And there was no getting out of it.

Excited as I was to be having this spiritual revelation, the fact remained that I could not carry a tune. The sound of my singing was upsetting me so much that I decided to give it a rest and just focus on learning the lyrics. I memorized the song by speaking the words aloud a few times, and then I thought, if I could just speak the words as if they were poetry, maybe I could communicate the message without forcing my musical ineptness on anyone's ears! That way I could sing at Lincoln Center without actually having to *sing* at Lincoln Center!

The night of the tribute, I performed the song with gusto. I spoke the lyrics the way I would a poem, and a group of advisory council members behind me joined in and sang the chorus. I don't think anyone even noticed that I didn't technically sing. Granted, no rep from Lincoln Center approached me with a music contract, but the president of the university gave me a high-five as I walked off the stage.

CHAPTER 76

Goodbye, Daddy

······························

In early winter 2001, my ninety-five-year-old father was acting crazy and accusing me and my Aunt Margie of all kinds of bizarre things. I was confused and didn't understand what was happening—I was a professional social worker and therapist and still could not figure out why my father was behaving so irrationally. Even though the truth was staring me right in the face, it never occurred to me that he had dementia.

I decided to try a past-life regression to see if there was something I could learn about my relationship with my father. I called Brian Weise in Florida, who wrote books on past lives, but his secretary told me that he was traveling and suggested that instead of waiting for him to return and coming all the way down there I might want to see someone in New York City. She gave me a list of recommendations. The name that jumped out for some reason Dr. Jas (pronounced Yahsh) Madison. I called his office and made an appointment.

As I walked into his reception room on East 36th Street, I was greeted by a pretty, upbeat woman named Lidia who I thought might be the doctor's wife or girlfriend. The doctor was ready for me, she said, so I continued through to his office.

"Dr. Madison, it's good to meet you. I'm Kathalynn."

"Please, call me Jas," he replied. He was an interesting, somewhat exotic-looking fellow with a cool but not too aloof vibe, and I liked him right away. We began our session and I told him about my father. He listened patiently. Then I told him how my stubborn husband was going to go to Maryland to try to convince my stubborn father that he needed some help. The doctor asked me why on earth I would send my salesman husband to do a job only a daughter should be doing. "Do you know how powerful you are?" he asked. I shook my head. "You are very powerful, it's time to stop giving all that power away to your husband. You should be the one to talk to your father."

After talking for an hour, he asked if I was ready to be regressed. I remember sitting in his big black chair and listening to his deep voice. And then a strange thing happened: I returned to a scene that had appeared to me earlier in life when I'd had another past-life regression, and one that I have often dreamt about since.

I was standing at a window, waiting for someone, my breathing constricted by the corset holding in my ribs. I felt the wind blowing the veil of my French hood against my face. I was worried as I looked down the dirt path out the window of our chateau, waiting for the boy I loved to come back from the war. All of a sudden two men appeared, my father and the young man he wanted me to marry. I became angry and rebellious and told them to leave me alone. My father shouted, "He's not coming back. He's most likely dead," and then they turned around and left. Shaking inside, I was filled with hatred for them both. Then I saw a dark-haired young man in a dirty military uniform walking up the path, noticeably struggling and limping. My heart racing, I ran from the window. A great sadness came over me as I relived all this, and soon I was sobbing. When the doctor could see that I couldn't go on any further, he woke me up.

As we discussed what I had seen, he suggested that the two men could have represented my father and Bob. We discussed why I became uneasy when they appeared. He said that perhaps they had power over me, making me feel as helpless then as I sometimes felt now. But in this life, the doctor noted, I had the power, and it was time I used it.

I left the office that day with a new confidence. I didn't make another appointment; I had gotten what I'd come for. After that session, I could manage my feelings around my father far more effectively, which gave me the energy and ability to better understand what was happening to him.

The night after the appointment, I had a dream in which my Uncle Pike, now dead, appeared to me as I sat on a chair in my parents' living room. "Pike," I said, "what are you doing here? I thought you'd died."

"I did," he replied. "I've come to get Joe."

I awoke, completely rattled, unable to shake myself loose from it for days.

Shortly after that dream, my father, stubborn old Joe that he was, tried to get his lawn mower up the stairs from the basement and fell, breaking six ribs. A neighbor called 911. Bob and I rushed down to Maryland to the hospital and found him weakening and in terrible pain. I wanted to bring him back to Connecticut with us, but the care he required made this impossible. With great regret we placed him in a veterans' home in the hope that he would get strong enough to make the move up north to us. Those hopes were not realized. My father became depressed, stopped eating, and died of failure to thrive on Tuesday, September 6, 2001, just before 9/11.

My Aunt Margie was with him when he died. When we arrived, just about an hour later, she told us that right before Daddy passed away, she saw a figure standing at the end of the bed who she recognized to be Pike. "I'm here to get Joe now," he had said. "It's time." And a few moments later, Daddy took his last breath. Pike, so close to Daddy in this life, had helped him pass into the next. This brought me some comfort.

The navy gave him a funeral a month or so later with full military honors at Arlington National Cemetery. Although standard practice was for the chaplain to perform the eulogy, I was granted permission to give it myself. It was a beautiful day in early October, but I couldn't help being affected by the sight of the large tarp over the Pentagon where the planes had hit, adding to the sad energy hovering over his resting place.

CHAPTER 77

Bert Parks Sings to Me . . . Finally

....

One day I was perusing the menu at C'est Si Bon, a French café in Greenwich where I often lunched, and I noticed that the man seated at the booth next to me was also alone and looked vaguely familiar. We locked eyes for a moment, and as soon as he smiled, I realized I was face to face with Bert Parks, the man who serenaded Miss America every year as she took her walk of victory.

"Mr. Parks!"

"Hello! What's your name?" he asked, extending his hand. He seemed pleasantly surprised at being recognized.

"I'm Kathalynn. I competed in pageants when I was younger, and it was always my dream that you would sing 'There She Is, Miss America' to me."

"No kidding! You look like you would have made a stunning Miss America. How about if I sang it for you now?" And then, keeping his voice at a volume just low enough not to disturb everyone in the restaurant, he started singing, "There she is, Miss America . . ." When he finished the song, a few patrons at nearby tables applauded. I sat there, moved and entranced and not the least bit self-conscious. My dream had come full circle. I was not eighteen and this wasn't Atlantic City, but for a moment, sitting right there in that café, I was Miss America.

CHAPTER 78

The Charity Circuit

....

Following the success of our charity, which quickly became a foundation, Bob and I quickly became fully immersed in New York's phil-
anthropic circles. Bob, who was doing increasingly well financially, was
committed, as was I, to supporting organizations he believed in, but he
also got a great deal of mileage from the prestige this conferred. Being a
big donor made him feel like a big man, especially if a tuxedo and celebrities were involved, and I was of course part of the package. This often
meant that shopping for, preparing for, and attending charity galas and
balls dominated our calendar. I did what I could behind the scenes, but
Bob mostly wanted me to dress up, show up, and shut up.

One year, at our annual charity dinner, Ed Cox, who was married to
Tricia Nixon, sat next to me. Bob was table hopping as usual, playing
"host with the most" while he entertained a bunch of people he seemed
to feel were his personal guests. Ed Cox and I had met briefly years
before, at one of the pre-parties for Nixon's inauguration. Despite his
best efforts at pretending to have remembered me, I could tell (with some
relief) that he did not recognize the insecure girl in the cheap gold dress
who had struggled to keep her falsies in place. This time, in the company
of a member of that prominent family, I felt far more at ease and not
remotely awkward. We ended up having a lively conversation about our
families' military histories and about Richard Nixon.

Poised as I had managed to be with the likes of Ed Cox, I could not
have been less mentally prepared when, at another similar event, I found
myself face to face with a true idol.

Back in the days of Stella Adler's acting class, we had all been
pretty much obsessed with Liv Ullmann, the Norwegian actress whose

movies (*The Emigrants, Cries and Whispers*) captivated us. As sensational onstage as she was on film—her Nora in *A Doll's House,* a role I'd dreamed of mastering, was definitive. She approached her work with an earthy realism while also maintaining that mysterious elegance of an international film star.

One day Bob had found himself seated on an airplane next to Jonathan Wiesner, chairman and executive director of the International Rescue Committee. The two of them bonded over their nonprofit ventures and he invited us to the next IRC dinner, at the Waldorf Astoria. As I approached my assigned table that night, I was stunned to spot Liv Ullmann herself, seated just one table over. She was still beautiful and dressed elegantly in black, her fair hair swept up. I summoned my courage and asked Jonathan to please introduce me. When we met, Ms. Ullmann took my extended hand into both of hers and looked straight into my eyes. I have zero recollection of what words may have been exchanged, but I do remember how gracious and present she was when I told her how much her work had meant to me.

Finding myself face to face with Liv Ullmann stirred up some deep emotion around my own abandoned dreams of performing, and I could not deny occasional pangs of regret. Yet there we were, Liv Ullmann and I, supporting the same cause we both believed in, both with equal reason to be there in our own right. We were sharing common ground.

That same night, as I was on my way to the ladies' room, still aglow from my encounter with Ms. Ullmann, I was stopped by an elderly man who extended his hand and asked me who I was. He introduced himself as Elie, and I told him my name and explained that my husband and I were here representing our foundation. He listened to me intently, as though completely fascinated with whatever I had to say. At first I didn't recognize him, but his expression, the way he carried himself, and the compassion emanating from him told me he was someone very special. It was then that I realized I was talking to Elie Wiesel.

At another IRC dinner, I was thrilled to hear that former president Bill Clinton would be showing up to say a few words; I was on the edge of my seat, but there was no sign of him during the meal. As we were finishing up dessert, however, I felt the energy shift in the room, and sure enough, over at one of the ballroom entrances was a tall, handsome, familiar-looking gray-haired man, and it was not simply because he was surrounded by secret service that you could tell it was unmistakably him. His presence was palpable, and his legendary charisma transmitted itself all the way across the room.

When Bill Clinton finished speaking, I knew I just *had* to meet him. Naturally, a crowd had instantaneously gathered around him, but I shamelessly squeezed my way through to get close. He spotted me, held out his hand, and for the moment my hand held his—space and time ceased to exist. As with Liv Ullman, I have no memory of what I actually said; I imagine it was something really clever and original like 'Great to meet you, Mr. President.' I do, though, remember how it felt when he smiled at me; because for that fraction of a moment, I was the only other person in the world.

CHAPTER 79

Le Cordon Bleu

....

By the summer of 2002, my children had become young adults. Caitlin had earned a master's degree in economics from Fordham and was happily engaged to the future father of her five children. Courtney was in law school, also at Fordham, and Vanessa was doing well. Genevieve had graduated from high school and was getting ready to leave for a semester abroad at the University of Stirling, in Scotland.

One night as Bob and I were having dinner on our patio, he kept complimenting my cooking, which I found odd because I considered myself a mediocre cook at best. He mentioned he was going to be traveling extensively over the fall and suggested I spend those few months in Paris taking a course at the Le Cordon Bleu. Odd as the proposition was (truly, I wasn't much of a cook), a trip to Paris did sound tempting. I took him up on the proposal, and in researching the school I discovered it also offered classes in London, which would work even better, considering I did not speak a word of French.

I applied and got into the program, which would start in September. Although I was aware of the Le Cordon Bleu's reputation as a serious cooking institution, my brain somehow did not compute that this so-called beginner class would consist of men and women who were wholly focused on becoming professional chefs. I just thought I'd show up, learn a few fun recipes to impress Bob and my kids with, and jet around Europe on weekends.

My first day in class was straight out of the movie *Private Benjamin*. Orders were barked at us sharply and indiscriminately, with the intention of beating us down. The assignment was soup, and I failed epically. People have since asked me how flunking soup is even possible, but I assure you, it *can* be done. When I called my daughters to share my tale of that hapless first day, they laughed and then rushed me off the phone to tell all their friends.

I'd like to say it got better from there, but it did not. Every morning we were expected to show up in full chef gear: traditional white double-breasted chef's jacket and that big white hat, the toque blanche. We'd observe a long demonstration followed by a short break for lunch, after which we were broken up into teams or "kitchens" to re-create what we had watched that morning. The master chefs were such purists when it came to how the food was prepared that there wasn't a single modern appliance in sight. Everything had to be cleaned, sliced, and mixed completely by hand. Even the chickens were brought to us with feathers intact for us to torch off, one by one.

The chefs in my kitchen, mostly women, were a lively and engaging international group who often went out for drinks after school; the only man in class was something of a playboy from the Netherlands. I was usually too wrung out after laboring for hours in a scorching hot kitchen to do more than return to my flat and crash, but occasionally I would join the party. One morning, after an especially late night with them, I was completely exhausted and probably should have taken the day off. One of our assignments that day was to make marzipan. When the master chef came by to examine my almond-paste creation—which, no surprise, looked nothing like it was supposed to—he said, "What is this?" In my delirium, I replied, "Menopause."

"What?" he demanded in his heavy French accent. "What is menopause?"

"You know, menopause! Vaginal dryness, hot flashes, and irritability." The entire group—mostly women of middle age—doubled over in laughter, but the master chef did not crack a smile.

"You Americans think you are funny," he scoffed.

"Well," I replied, recalling a favorite line from *A Fish Called Wanda*, "if it wasn't for us Americans, you'd be speaking German right now."

I learned how to make two bread puddings, one English and one French. Bob loved them both and liked to say that they cost him just about $25,000 but were worth every penny. Other than bread pudding, I am still a lousy cook.

CHAPTER 80

Brian Redux

....

During the course (which I did pass in the end, but only because the chef took pity on me, and under the condition that I never darken their door again), I spent the weekends traveling as much as possible. I have always loved exploring new places, especially on my own. One weekend, though, when Genevieve came down from Scotland, I bought the two of us tickets to a revival of *My Fair Lady* in the West End. During intermission in the ladies' lounge I spied a flier on the wall advertising an old-time rock 'n' roll concert coming to the London Palladium, with FEATURING BRIAN HYLAND in big bold letters. I shrieked so loud everyone turned around, but I didn't care. When Genevieve came rushing out of her stall, crying, "What?" I pointed to the poster and we both started jumping up and down.

The concert was slated for the Sunday night before my Cordon Bleu final exam, but I had already made plans for that weekend to fly to Strasbourg, France. (I was long past the point where studying would have made much of a difference.) I was relieved to see I was scheduled to land in London at five, and the concert wasn't till eight.

From Strasbourg, I wrote to Brian that I would be at the show Sunday night. I was hoping he'd remember me, but in case he didn't I threw in some details about how we'd met all those years ago. I brought the letter to the concierge of my hotel and asked that it please be faxed to the Palladium box office. I was so nervous that I asked him to proofread it out loud for me before sending it along. As he was reading it, he got so excited he called over the other girls behind the desk to tell them what I was about to do. When I left the hotel on Sunday, they all wished me good luck.

The plane was an hour and a half late leaving Strasbourg. When we were finally seated and ready to take off, I must have looked like a basket case, compulsively checking my watch, because the woman next to me asked if I was all right. I found myself explaining the whole situation to her, who then repeated it to the lady right across the aisle who'd caught a few tidbits and was dying to hear the rest. Before I knew it, the entire plane was in the loop. The stewardess brought me a free glass of wine, apologizing that it wasn't Champagne. When we finally landed in London, many of my fellow passengers applauded while I ran off the plane, and one even offered to pay for my taxi, which I politely declined. There was no time to stop at the flat and drop off my luggage, so I brought it along. I promised the cab driver there would be a huge tip if he got me to the Palladium for the show, and he sped away like a bat out of hell.

Arriving at the theater just in time for intermission, I handed my ticket to an usher, who told me Brian had requested I come to a private area offstage. I recognized Brian immediately. His hair, a little thinner than I remembered, was pulled back into a ponytail, but his eyes and smile were the same.

For the fifteen or so minutes we stood talking, time stood still. We made brief small talk, mostly about our kids. He pointed out his son, who was playing drums for him in the show. I told him I'd missed the first half and he said not to worry, he'd be returning for one more song at the end of the show. The bell rang signaling the end of intermission, and as I extended my hand to shake his before leaving for my seat, he leaned in instead and gave me a kiss.

Brian returned to the stage as promised and sang "You're Mine and We Belong Together." He was masterful on the guitar, and his voice rang out as smooth and clear as I'd remembered. Watching him up on the stage took me right back to that first night I'd seen him perform at the pageant. The years melted away, and instead of an aging man, all I saw was the boy I had fallen in love with forty years before. It brought a sweet closure for me; another perfect example of life coming full circle.

CHAPTER 81

Some Things Never Change

....

When I got back from London, Bob and I settled back into our routine. By now I had built a successful private practice out of our home that occupied some of my time, while Bob continued working in the city and staying out late most evenings. Once a week or so he'd make a concerted effort to be home for dinner. This was nothing new, of course, but with the last of our children officially out of the house, I began to feel his absence at night more acutely. We were a couple on the surface, coming together for appearances at charity dinners, business events, and holidays, but underneath, the connection was steadily weakening.

For my sixtieth birthday, Caitlin threw a beautiful party at a French bistro in Greenwich. Bob got there late because his early-morning meeting had interfered with his workout, which he felt compelled to fit in after work. When he finally did arrive, he made a star entrance, waving to everyone and welcoming them to the party. Then he made a beeline past me to the fortune teller who'd been hired as entertainment and monopolized her for remainder of the cocktail hour. When he finally stopped at my table to say hello (yes, we sat at separate tables), he discussed at length what greatness the fortune teller saw ahead for him in the music business. Throughout the dinner, several of our friends who'd come from afar gave toasts. Finally Bob stood up and launched into a discourse of love and appreciation for every person in the room—except me. He thanked them all for coming and plunged into personal anecdotes about various friends, but there was no mention of my birthday; it was as if the reason all these people had gathered there had just slipped his mind. After a while, guests started looking around awkwardly, not sure whether it was appropriate to continue their table conversation, because

Bob still had more to say. I was surprised, but I shouldn't have been. Bob was not inclined to acknowledge the role I played in his life or in any of our endeavors as a couple. Why would my birthday be any different?

My mind flashed back to a surprise birthday party I'd thrown Bob, back when I still lived at the Dakota. Bob was an avid Pac-Man player, so along with a catered buffet, I ordered a special Pac-Man cake, thinking he'd get a kick out of it. His friend, Voy also brought a cake—a small, flourless, homely mound that he insisted be placed on the table next to Pac-Man. When Bob walked in and we all shouted "Surprise!" he first hugged his mother, then individually thanked everyone but me. When it came time for dessert, Bob removed all the candles I had arranged on the cake and transferred them to Voy's. After he made his wish, he sliced up Voy's cake and passed the pieces around. My kids tried it, and finding it disgusting (which it was), coughed and spat it into their napkins. Furious with Bob, I brought the kids into the kitchen and gave them each a piece of the real cake. Watching them devour it, I felt a little better. At least *they* appreciated me.

One evening shortly after my sixtieth birthday, I asked Bob what his vision was for our relationship after he retired. He said, "I can't wait to go back to school for acting and directing and finally get my movie career off the ground. And of course between projects I'll record my album."

"And what if your album's a big smash hit? Are you going to tour all over the world with your band?" I asked, clearly joking. But my sarcasm went right over his head.

"Of course, but you know, there's a lot of downtime on the road, which means I'll finally have a chance to finish the self-help book I've been working on! You know I'm a Renaissance man."

"What about us, Bob? How do I fit into all of this?" This time I was serious.

"You'll be able to spend more time in Italy, you love Ischia (he was right about that, I did love Ischia). And there's no reason you can't go back to acting. Once a year we'll take a vacation together."

Evidently this man had a bucket list a mile long, and it did not include fixing his relationship with his wife. It was time for a change.

CHAPTER 82

The Thread Breaks

....

On the Wednesday before Thanksgiving 2009, Bob stood at the door of my home office complaining about his job. I could not help thinking about the other jobs he walked away from in the past for the same reasons. As I listened to him whining and blaming—he seemed to have learned nothing from his past failures and setbacks—it was evident that he was repeating the same mistakes, finding fault with others (always others), holding them accountable, and not taking responsibility himself. I had, in the past, tried to open conversations with him about how he might possibly have had some hand in how these events had played out, but he would have none of it, and by now I had just given up. As I looked at him, scrawny and underweight from his obsessive exercising, all I could think was how much I did not want to be in this marriage. Many times over the course of our relationship I'd considered walking away, but as long as there was a thread of hope that we could make it work, I was going to stay. We had history, we had a family, we had a shared spirituality, and for a time we'd had chemistry. But that was long gone, and something suddenly snapped inside of me.

I still had love for Bob. He was a basically good man and a good father who tolerated and generally supported my own separate quests. I didn't want to abandon the life we had built, or, if I was being honest, the comforts we enjoyed. Starting over as a divorcée wasn't what I'd envisioned for my sixties. But in that moment I felt the thread of hope break. We had precious little left together, and just as I had resolved some forty years before in Hollywood that I did not want to die under a palm tree, I now resolved that given the good years I might have left, I did not want to die under the figurative roof of this marriage.

Once the decision was made, my fear of the unknown began to dissolve. I was ready, and I knew that if I didn't leave now I probably never would, and I'd end up bitter and frustrated and very likely feeling just as lonely. But the holidays were approaching, so as I had once done with Brad, I opted to wait until the family could enjoy one more Christmas season together.

In early January, Bob was scheduled to be honored at a dinner at the 21 Club in Manhattan, so I decided to wait until after that event to tell him, so that he might enjoy the evening to its fullest.

If I had had any doubts about leaving Bob, that dinner dispelled them entirely. I gave him a generous toast, detailing his tremendous contribution to the treatment and prevention of child abuse. When it was his turn to speak, he stood, delivered a chilly, perfunctory "Thank you, Kathalynn," and then launched into thanks and praise to others for their support.

Once again, I felt dismissed and frozen out. I didn't need accolades, just a respectful acknowledgment as his partner, but I realized that this was my own road to insanity, doing the same thing over and over again, as they say, and expecting a different result. The man would never change, I knew that of course, but that night—that night I was done. Still, I couldn't let it go, and we fought the entire car ride home. He told me I'd had too much wine at the dinner and he was right, I had.

As soon as we got home, Bob went straight up to his office and closed the door. I took a moment to calm down and summoned what I could of my courage.

Could I do this? I asked myself. *Yes.* I climbed the stairs, knocked on his door, and walked in.

"Bob," I said, "I'm not going to do this anymore. I want a divorce."

"Great, Kathy." His tone was cold and flat. "I've already consulted an attorney. The way you've acted lately, I needed to get prepared. This is what you want, then have it, but you'd better know that I'm not leaving the house."

From that night on, Bob slept in Caitlin's old bedroom. I rarely saw him, and on the few occasions we'd pass each other in the hall, he'd look ahead stonily as though I were invisible.

At this point, we hadn't announced anything to our friends, so with our annual charity gala around the corner, I asked if he still wanted to go as a couple. He told me to fuck off. In any case, he said, the charity belonged entirely to him, and after the hand grenade I had thrown into our marriage, I was never to set foot anywhere near another event. I never did. I knew then that I was about to lose friends for being the big bad bitch leaving Bob, who among philanthropy circles was hailed as an angel. I would just have to accept it and move on.

To help me clear my head and focus my energy, I decided to head to Sedona for a retreat. The thought of that place brought up some of my best memories with Bob. Out of what was either nostalgia or some feeble attempt to save the marriage, or possibly both, I asked him if he'd consider going with me. "Hell no," he said, "Never in a million years. I hate your releasing bullshit."

Sedona welcomed me like an old friend, and the course was exactly what I needed. The trip gave me distance, a chance to do some serious releasing, and a safe place to confront my doubts and fears about my future. I also released on wanting to change Bob's attitude through this time. One morning while I was still there, he called me and said, "Kathy, I've thought it over, and you're right. I think it's time for us to move on and work this out in harmony. Let's tell the children." I thanked him and told him I would always love him. He said the same. What I did not tell him was that I'd already informed the children, all of whom understood, having had front-row seats to the unraveling of our marriage.

While in Sedona, I read Brian Weiss's *Only Love Is Real*, about past lives and soul mates. It touched something deep inside me. Having just finished the book, I walked to the small patio off the sitting room of my hotel and wondered if maybe in this lifetime I would not find my soul mate. Sadness ran through me as I contemplated this depressing possibility. And then something in me "let go," and I thought, *this is okay because in another life I will.* I was reconciled; I could live alone, and that was okay.

When I got back from Sedona, I went upstairs to Bob's office. He was away at his tango class—with, I'd later find out, the twenty-something theater student he had fallen in love with. Most of his things had been cleared out, with only the furniture left behind for the movers to take to his new apartment in the city he had rented without telling me. He was motivated to start a new life, and he no longer felt so strongly about staying in the house—that, and the assurances from a lawyer that by leaving our home he would not be liable for desertion. I walked through the house and started removing photos of us as a couple from their frames. Each one I held sparked its own sharp memory. As I passed from room to room, I was surrounded by the ghosts of our collective past. Suffused with sadness, I drew myself a hot bath, climbed in, and began to weep. I cried for three days.

I needed to talk with someone and get help through this time. As a therapist myself who had done heaps of spiritual work, I needed someone savvy enough to cut through the therapist tricks I knew all too well, and I imagined it wasn't going to be easy to find such a person. A major objective for me would be to uncover what it was that had caused me to marry Bob in the first place and then stay long after I knew it wasn't working. I'd spent twenty-some years trying to change a man who wasn't about to change. He'd thought that he was already perfect, of course, and who was I to continue to try to convince him otherwise?

I knew this much, anyway: I'd stayed stuck because I allowed my fears to rule me. I had abandoned a consistent spiritual practice and accepted a less than happy life in exchange for something I convinced myself was security. I used the kids as an excuse to keep me on the more comfortable path. I had no confidence in myself, my competence, or my looks, and no clue if or how I could do it alone. Bob, for all his faults and irritations and self-involvement, accepted me and wanted the marriage to continue. It was I who could not accept him for who he was. I needed to own up to it all and rediscover the girl who had sold out and given up her dreams. I needed to get right with myself.

Whom to call? I was coming up empty—until I remembered the man I'd seen once when my father was dying. I went to my desk and opened the drawer, and there, out of nowhere, appeared Dr. Jas Madison's card. It was an old card, and his number had probably changed, but I figured I'd try it anyway.

Much to my surprise, the doctor answered.

"Wow, it's you!" I said. "I thought I'd get a receptionist or an answering machine."

"Yes, it's me," he replied in that deep voice.

"Oh my God, I am so glad. I saw you about eight years ago. You helped me a lot. I don't know if you remember me."

He said he vaguely did.

As I told him what was happening in my life, Jas listened and said, "Just breathe and talk to me. I am here for you."

Sure that I was taking up too much of his time, I said I would just come in to his office.

"It's okay, just talk a little bit more. I have the time."

After talking for more than hour (which he never charged me for), I made an appointment for the next day.

CHAPTER 83

Therapy and Beyond

....

With keen anticipation I stepped into Grand Central Station on a chilly April afternoon. It had been years since I had seen Dr. Madison, who'd been so effective in helping me deal with my father's dementia, but I was ready to put myself back into his hands, and my expectations were as high. I entered his office expecting to be greeted by the same pretty blond, but instead I was met by the doctor himself. He welcomed me with a bow and a kiss on the hand. When he looked up into my eyes I remembered my first impression of him—dark and handsome in an off-beat, quirky way. He had a wild, rugged charm about him—the opposite of my more classically handsome soon-to-be-ex-husband, who lacked that powerful, enigmatic undertone emanating from the doc, who was, in a word, hot.

His office had moved down the street from where I'd seen him eight years earlier. The intriguing decor of the new space featured eastern religious art—tapestries and sculptures depicting versions of the Buddha, portraits and statues of Hindu gods, each of which had a story. Swords resembling the legendary Excalibur were mounted on the wall, reflecting his interest in medieval history. Was the sweet and pretty blond still working for him? I asked. No, he told me; that was his ex-wife, Lidia. She had remarried and moved to England.

I made myself comfortable in his cozy black chair and launched into my story. At one point, in a panic about my future, I blurted out, "Now I'll have to start all over. What the fuck have I done?"

"Start over? How old are you, forty-two, forty-three?" he asked with a laugh at what he thought was my exaggerated concern.

Now, I have never felt compelled to disclose my age to a man, but I figured if there was one place to be honest, it was in therapy.

"You have to be kidding," he said, when I told him.

"Nope, I wouldn't lie in that direction."

"I guess not," he said with a chuckle, "but how do you do it, look so young?"

Man, this guy knew just what to say.

"Genes, I guess," I replied. "How old are you?"

"I'm right behind you—fifty-three!"

I was able to open up to Jas from the start. He seemed to understand me well beyond a usual therapist who's paid to listen and give you feedback. Jas genuinely seemed to hang onto my every word. He didn't rush our session, and when I said I thought our time was up, he told me he had the time to carry on if I was okay with it. We continued that session for two more hours, with no charge for overtime.

I told him that Bob used to say I was like an angel with a devil's side, but it was clear to me that he was interested only in the angel and hated the devil. Jas, on the other hand, was interested in—and accepting of—every side, and although this was very much part of his job, I was so starved for this attentiveness and concern I was flooded with gratitude and relief. Instead of ignoring or admonishing my imperfections, he tried to understand me, and this gave me the validation that no one, least of all my husband, ever had.

With trust building and my receptivity growing, Jas led me to breakthroughs that would open up my life. In one conversation, he asked what my father had said to me on the way home from the Miss American Teenager finals. I told him we had ridden home in silence that night, as we did after most competitions. He gently suggested that perhaps my father's inability to be impressed by anything I (or anyone) did had contributed to my apathetic feelings about my own accomplishments and belief that I didn't have what it takes. The point wasn't to blame my father, but rather to adjust my own interpretation of his behavior and accept that his limitation was not a reflection of my own value or ability. I knew this intellectually, it was 'therapy 101!' But if this therapist was going to heal herself, she'd need another point of view.

In showing genuine interest in my stories and validating my points of view, Jas was only doing what any good therapist is supposed to do, but he seemed to be going above and beyond. It may have been a subtle seduction, a classic case of transference of my own feelings and desires onto him, but I began to fall under his power. I continued to show up every week and our sessions continued to extend well beyond the allotted hour.

Jas, who had a few theories about human nature, divided people into two categories: those who sought connection versus those who sought importance. According to his theory, my marriage had fallen apart because I was seeking connection with a man who wanted importance. For years I'd attempted to bring Bob around to my purpose, instead of seeking to understand his, and in so doing I'd pushed him away. Our priorities and intentions were fundamentally incompatible. When I began to figure this out, I felt a great sense of relief. What I couldn't see, of course, was that I was about to repeat the process all over again.

CHAPTER 84

The Swami, the Kiss, and . . .

. . . .

In one of our sessions I recounted a dream I'd had the night before:

Sitting across from a Hindu teacher I did not know, I was mesmerized by his long dark hair falling against the gold-embroidered white Nehru jacket. He had light brown eyes and luscious, dark pink lips. My eyes kept moving between those lips and the rich, dark tone of the backs of his hands against the pale pink of his nails. He spoke with a soft accent of experiences where time ceases and sounds and colors become vivid. I hung onto every word. My body was on fire except for the cooling beads of sweat running down my back. My mind relaxed as my body trembled. All I could think of was how badly I wanted to kiss those lips. "Kiss me, swami," I finally said. He leaned in and pulled me close. With our eyes locked, he kissed me. There was no space between us as I melted into his body. My senses were flooded with that ecstasy of oneness, that fragrance called love—and then I woke up.

"That's all?" Jas asked.

"Well, yeah, I woke up."

"But before you woke up, after the kiss . . . nothing?"

"Nope," I said, "nothing else happened."

"That was some kiss!"

"Yes, it was some kiss." I couldn't help thinking of the lines in a Rumi poem: "When soul rises into lips / You feel the kiss you have wanted."

What I didn't mention to my therapist was that the swami in my dream looked exactly like him. When I'd first met Jas, I'd assumed from

308

his coloring and the shape of his eyes that he was of Eastern Indian decent, and I guess that dictated my dream. It turned out that he was 100% Polish, however, and a self-proclaimed descendent of the great Genghis Khan. (How he managed to trace his direct lineage so precisely all the way back to the twelfth century I do not know. But he said it, so it must have been true.)

One day I brought pictures in of my family so Jas could put some faces to names. He got up from his chair and sat close to me on the couch. His body was touching mine so slightly that I couldn't quite tell if the proximity was intentional. I felt his body against my side as his torso expanded with each intake of breath and contracted with each exhale. As a mental health professional myself, I considered the possibility that this was 'transference,' and I was imposing an attraction and imagining all this. However, I couldn't believe it was as simple as all that. In addition, it seemed to be mutual. There was something in the air that both attracted and frightened me. These were not lines to be crossed, I told myself, and feeling as vulnerable as I did, I was not about to go there. Besides, how mortifying it would be if I was wrong about this—and how crazy of us both if I was right? Unsettled, I ended our session early with a lie about an appointment that had slipped my mind. Back out in the world, I could not shed the very real sense that something unusual and powerful was happening. Feeling confused and slightly disoriented, I considered where to go for some clarity, and figured the one place I could find it was, again, the safe haven of Sedona.

While I was there, I found myself thinking about Jas incessantly. Each time he floated into my brain I felt a gush of warm, loving energy course through me. I was walking through ridiculous pink clouds, and everything smelled like roses. I was falling into something that looked a lot like love—at a time when I least expected it. "Love planted a rose," Katharine Lee Bates wrote, "and the world turned sweet."

One morning while I was having breakfast, my phone made a funny sound, my first-ever text message coming through. "Thinking about you. Want you to know that I believe in you. Jas." I caught onto texting quickly after that. We spoke several times while I was in Sedona, and just the sound of his voice sent waves of electricity through my body. I could hardly keep my hands on the wheel of the car while driving. It was insane and wonderful. I felt more alive and joyful than I could ever remember.

The first thing I did when I got home was pay Jas a visit. He opened the door and we stood there for a moment, taking each other in. We both knew the relationship had shifted. I sat down on the couch opposite Jas' chair, and this time he pulled the chair close. When he was just inches away from my face he said, "Kathalynn, I know you thought about me a lot in Sedona."

"That's a little presumptuous, isn't it?" I asked, laughing nervously.

"Well, didn't you?" he persisted.

"Yes."

"What were you thinking about me?"

"Probably the same things you were thinking," I answered boldly, knowing from the severity of his gaze that the energy between us was far too intense to be one-sided.

"Look, I'm a man. I have feelings," he said somewhat cavalierly.

"What kind of feelings are you talking about?"

"Oh, come on, Kathalynn."

"Come on, what?"

"Any man would be attracted to you and . . ."

"And?"

"You happen to be just my type—blond hair, blue eyes, just the right height."

"Well, that's good to hear."

"Sure, except for the obvious thing: I'm your therapist, and even though we are also colleagues, there's the issue of professional integrity."

"I can get a new therapist, Jas."

"There's something else too."

Christ, I thought, *what now?*

"Although I am greatly attracted to you and feel tremendous positive energy flowing between us, I'm going to have children."

"You're going to . . . what?" I asked calmly.

"I'm going to have two children."

"When?" I asked, still calm. "And with whom?"

"I don't have that information," he replied.

"What are you talking about?" I asked. *Was he insane?*

"When my ex-wife couldn't conceive, I gave up on the idea of having kids. But in India I met with an astrologer, and he saw two children in my future."

"Do you actually want children, Jas? Or is this just something a psychic told you and now you think that you're supposed to follow through on it?"

"Of course I want them. I've always wanted them. I believe it's a man's duty to continue his line, especially one with my superior genetics."

"Superior *what*?" The conversation was getting weirder and weirder.

"You recall that I'm a direct descendent of Genghis Khan?"

"Okay," I said, standing up and starting to pace the room.

"Are you all right?" he asked.

"Yes," I lied, "I just need a moment to think about this."

My mind was racing. *He couldn't possibly be serious, could he?*

"Jas," I finally said. "Have you considered that maybe reproducing at your age isn't really what you want, but that what you're after is rather, I don't know, more of a *connection*? Maybe love?"

"Well, it's possible, sure, but—"

"Children are a huge responsibility."

"Yes."

At that moment, the buzzer sounded from downstairs.

"I'm sorry, Kathalynn, my client is outside; can we pick up this conversation later? I have a lot to think about, clearly."

"Sure, Jas," I said, not knowing what to make of the turn our visit had taken.

"I think this goes without saying, but I hope you'll understand that I'm not going to be able to see you professionally anymore," he added with a laugh.

"I do. And I hope you figure it out soon because I'm not gonna wait around for very long. As you said, I'm a hot commodity and could be snapped up walking from here to the elevator, for all you know!"

"I know." He smiled broadly, and then I left.

CHAPTER 85

The Sea of Love

·····························

The following weekend Jas was holding a seminar, and I signed
Genevieve and myself up for it. I wanted to support him, but I also
figured that since it looked like I was going to have a relationship with
this man, it might be a good idea for Genevieve to see him in action. The
turnout was small, and afterward the group went for coffee. I sat next to
Jas, and every time his leg brushed against mine under the table I could
feel it twitch and shake. I gently placed my hand on it to quell the shaking.
He dropped his hand under the table and placed it on top of mine, sending shockwaves of electricity up my arm.

As we were saying goodbye, he lifted my hand to his lips, kissed it,
and bowed.

Once we were out of earshot, Genevieve, my sarcastic one, said, "Who
does this guy think he is, Mr. Darcy?" I didn't get the reference. "Jane
Austen, Mom."

I tried to laugh it off, but she knew something was up. Over dinner
she started to press. "Okay, what's with the therapist?"

"All right!" I admitted. "I'm really attracted to him."

"And you think Dad's corny?"

"I don't care what you say! He's brilliant and sexy and cool!" I said,
laughing.

"If you say so," she said, rolling her eyes.

"I do!"

"Well, good for you. Time to start shopping for a new therapist."

The next day, Jas called asking if I was free to go out with him the
following weekend. I invited him to join me at my family's Fourth of July
celebration at the Millbrook Club, but he demurred. Actually, he said,

he'd been thinking more along the lines of an intimate dinner, just the two of us, maybe the next day. I accepted.

I drove my daughters crazy, bouncing off the walls like a giddy, love-struck teenager. I enlisted the help of my old Sedona friend Michael to help me "release" on Jas and let go of any expectations or need for approval, but in my state that was too much to ask.

On July 5, 2009, Jas took the Metro-North train to Connecticut and I met him at the Greenwich station. When he'd asked me what I suggested he wear, I'd told him I liked the pink shirt he'd had on that day in his office when I'd brought in the pictures of my family. He must have tuned out after I said "pink" because he showed up in khaki pants and a fla-mingo pink Hawaiian print shirt. The only thing missing was the ukulele. He looked ridiculous, yet somehow completely adorable.

I parked at the station and we walked hand in hand up Greenwich Avenue, venturing into a little park that I suppose had been there all along but hadn't noticed till that day. There was a small castle in the park. Jas and I sat on a bench and he told me about a castle in Poland he'd purchased, restored, and then sold. For the first time, he did most of the talking. I hung on every word.

We were just about to leave the park and walk to dinner when Jas turned to me, and taking my face in his hands, kissed me softly on the lips. The kiss brought me back to the time when kissing meant the world. For the first time, I felt like the princess I'd imagined myself to be all those years ago, standing next to an actual castle, and at last my prince had come. Then he looked at me and said, "My darling princess"—he actually called me his princess—"there is nothing more intimate than a deep, passionate kiss. Our lips and tongues are the ultimate portal to the human soul." He drew me close, and I could feel his heart beating in his chest. "There are many levels to kissing that most people never experi-ence, a mystical and physical magic to it."

It was corny as hell, even cornier than Bob had ever been, and I didn't care. I was so infatuated, every cheeseball word out of his mouth was its own poetry.

Reflecting on that day, and in particular, that kiss; I am reminded of another quote from my favorite poet, Rumi. "I would love to kiss you, the price of kissing is your life." I'd loved that quote for years, but until I kissed Jas that day I'd never really known what it meant.

After dinner, Jas and I went back to my house. After spending the day together, there was a build up of sexual tension that called for immediate remedy. I led him straight to the bedroom. "Aren't you going to give me a grand tour first?" he asked laughing.

"It's just a house, Jas! You've seen one, you've seen them all!"

Reaching the bedroom, Jas lost no time in getting undressed. To show off his class and good manners, he presented me with a bottle of Korbel. The old Kathalynn would have poured that cheap shit down the drain, but the new and improved, in-love Kathalynn guzzled that Korbel it like it was Dom Perignon. Then came the bag of tricks. Jas went over to the CD player (yes, I'm old, I still use CDs) and put on some Tibetan monk chorale meets techno fusion. He then pulled out a long, multicolored feather and began waving it rhythmically in time with the strange music. His dancing, I'll confess, left something to be desired, but there was something delightful, and definitely erotic about how freely he moved. Finally, he concluded his ceremonious gyrating and we moved to the bed. Not only did this man know what he was doing, but he had more stamina than a twenty-year-old. A student of the *Kama Sutra*, Jas came up with combination after combination, most of which I never knew existed. One practically had to be an acrobat to keep up! Finally, after several hours of passion and discovery, we fell asleep in each other's arms.

Eventually, morning came. I woke up to a welcomed feeling of something poking me from behind. Several hours later, after another exhilarating round, we finally came up for air. Jas got out of bed and walked over to the window. "You have a pool!" he shouted in delight.

"Yes!" I said, "Shit, I should have told you to bring swim trunks!"

"Swim trunks?" He laughed, "Please." He then yanked me out of bed, and dragged me, naked, downstairs and out to the pool. Together, we found more uses for that pool in one morning than I had discovered in over sixteen years of living there with Bob!

Nothing stopped that man. He told me that he was a Tantra master. Having no idea what that was, I ran out as soon as he left and bought a book on tantric sex, wanting to keep up with my ever-inventive partner.

I had been on a journey of self-realization and actualization spanning close to forty years. It wasn't until meeting Jas, however, that I began to feel myself on a primal, sensual level. I had worn a series of 'masks,' (as my EST trainers would have referred to them) over the course of my life. For years, I'd separated my sexuality from my identity. I had gone from being a smiley pageant contestant, a doe-eyed Hollywood starlet, a doctor's spouse, to most recently a 'Stepford wife.' For the first time, I didn't feel the need put on any mask at all. When it came to being with Jas, I was simply me.

In addition, I was finally able to wrap my head around what 'Cat On a Hot Tin Roof' was all about. The one thing that had been missing from my arsenal as an actress was sexuality. But with my appetite turned up to the max, I finally knew what it was to be a woman in heat. I could have played the living shit out of 'Maggie' that summer!

The somewhat embarrassing flipside to all this was that I became helpless over my addiction to Jas. Things like dignity, loyalty, and self-respect lost all power when pitted against my desire to be close to him. My children were, to put it mildly, horrified. Who was this spineless, love addict and what had she done with their mother?

For the next couple of months, I did little but live and breathe Jas Madison. On Friday afternoons, he'd hop on the commuter train at Grand Central and head to Old Greenwich. I'd meet him at the station and we would embark on a weekend of swimming *and screwing*, grilling *and screwing*, talking *and screwing* . . . you get the picture. Once in a while, he got stuck working late. On such evenings, he'd take a cab from the station and show up at my door in a cape—an actual cape—like the Maestro used to wear. He'd tell me he'd flown in from Manhattan like a sorcerer. I couldn't even see the dorkiness of it all, because to me, he *was* a sorcerer! He referred to me and himself as 'titans,' which literally meant, according to Greek mythology, descendants of primordial deities. Given the way I felt when he was around me, the nickname wasn't such a stretch.

I truly believed I'd hit the jackpot with Jas. I thought he was the *one*, so to speak. The only one who could love me unconditionally and repair my broken past. However, there were things about him, that even at my most obsessed, I couldn't totally overlook. For example, he was financially irresponsible and didn't have health insurance. His 'fuck it, I'm fine' attitude toward health insurance made me terrified for his safety. Not only that, Jas had some rather unorthodox views about sex and love and what it all meant. In other words, monogamy was a bit of a joke to him. I didn't know this, of course. After spending so much time together that first year, I assumed we were heading for some kind of stable future together. Considering my background of marriage or at the very least, sexually faithful relationships, it never occurred to me that Jas was pursuing other woman at the same time. After all, we were in love! *Right?* But increasingly there were times when Jas was unavailable, I thought because he was just busy with work.

Then, one evening, right before my first trip to India, Jas and I were having dinner with his childhood friend John and his wife Stacy. At one point Stacy, who had no filter, blurted out: "Jas," she said, "when are you going to handle your infidelity?"

Jas coolly looked at Stacy and said, "I have integrity."

"Your behavior does not reflect integrity," she replied.

The room became quiet. I broke the ice.

"Oh my darling Jas, you are not going to cheat on me while I'm in India, are you?"

His friends were dead quiet, awaiting his reply.

Jas looked at me, then at Stacy, and shook his head at her. A master at evasion, he swiftly changed the subject. We were on to a new topic before I realized he'd never even answered the question.

When it was time to leave on my trip, Jas took me to the airport and saw me off to India. We pledged to talk on the phone every other day while I was away, and he held to it.

CHAPTER 86

Poetry in Motion

. . . .

I returned in October, right in time for my birthday, and Jas was waiting for me at the airport, red roses in hand. When he saw me, he leaped over a rail, threw his arms around me, and kissed me passionately, stopping only to catch his breath and tell me how much he missed me. It seemed my absence had only, as the saying goes, made his heart grow fonder.

On my birthday, my children, Jas, and I gathered for dinner at a restaurant in Greenwich. After the meal, he stood up to read a poem he'd written for the occasion:

This is about our one and only kin
The extra super special Kathalynn
It's easy to see she is a goddess from Venus
Made a happy home on Mount Olympus
Despite that she is always on the run
She still shines on us like the sun
She never seems to miss a beat . . .
Because she has a lifelong lucky streak . . .
With mysterious powers of a shaman
She always succeeds in her plan
With her sweet gentle manner like a rose
She always gets personal and real close
Everyone will notice her beauty and charm
She will never do anyone any harm
She knows how to turn on the heat
Because she has a lifelong lucky streak

Everybody loves her for all she does with a twist
Because she's a great friend, mom, or therapist
So let's all wish her much more success
So we can all cherish the happiness
Kathalynn will always provide the best treat . . .
Because she has a lifelong lucky streak

My kids all looked down and gulped their drinks. By the second line, I saw Genevieve actually squirting wine out of her nose. Courtney, laughing as well, stood up and joined in on the refrain—raising his glass in mockery every time Jas said "lifelong lucky streak." Caitlin motioned for the server and ordered herself two more glasses of Cabernet, both of which she drained before the conclusion of Jas' performance. At the end, they whistled and applauded, each at some point throwing me a look as if to say *Seriously Mom?*

I was embarrassed, not so much by Jas—(despite his little show being admittedly dreadful) but by my children! Would it have killed them to be a little more gracious? Especially the girls—who knew full well how important this man was to me.

In any case, Jas did not seem to notice, living as he did in his own little bubble (not unlike his predecessor in that way). If he had picked up on their rudeness, it clearly didn't bother him too much. Jas had a way of letting things roll like water off a duck's back. He never seemed to take anything personally—I always admired that about him.

We spent Thanksgiving with Caitlin and her family, which I thought went well—her kids adorable, the food delicious as always, everyone in the spirit and getting along. When we returned to my house, Jas seemed distant and unhappy. Was something wrong? I asked him.

"You're all so established and wealthy," he muttered moodily. "Your children are successful, and who am I—just some guy making ends meet."

"What are you talking about, Jas? Why are you making this an issue?"

"Because it is an issue."

Thus began what was to become a recurring theme in our relationship—Jas' unease and resentment regarding my and my children's success. I was flabbergasted. I had thought this was one of the things about me that impressed him; I never imagined it would make him feel threatened or emasculated.

"I don't feel like a man around you," he'd say, "I could never take care of you like your ex-husbands. I'll never come close to their earning capacity." I did everything I could to show him it didn't matter, and that I loved him for *him*—but it was to no avail. He became obsessed with this; finding ways to work it into almost every interaction. I could not understand how after five months of this never having been an issue, it was suddenly such a big deal.

What I didn't know then, was that this complaint was just a convenient excuse with which Jas avoided commitment. He blamed circumstances for his needing to disconnect. He loved to tell me "it's complicated." But there was nothing complicated about it. Jas wasn't going to tell me that he wanted to be with other women because that would have broken my heart. Instead, he played the martyr—the poor, selfless man who would sacrifice his great love so that his beloved would be free to find a more appropriate match. I didn't understand fully what was going on then, but I knew something was seriously off.

CHAPTER 87

Ecstasy (If Only)

....

One Friday night in early December, Jas came for the weekend and brought with him some little white pills. He handed me one of them, I rolled it over in my palm and said, "I don't need any aspirin, Jas, my head is fine!"

"It's ecstasy, Kathalynn!" he said proudly.

"Ecstasy? As in drugs?"

"Yes, darling. Ecstasy as in drugs. I thought we could do them together!"

"Jas, you know I've never done drugs."

"All the more reason to try!" he said with a smile. I popped the pill and went upstairs to draw myself a bath. Nothing happened at first, but then at one point, I felt the water and my body sort of unite—as though this element was flowing through me, as me, and it was beautiful. Then I joined Jas in bed as we made love. The mattress, the blankets, everything, sort of mutated into a soft, enveloping cloud, floating aloft.

Jas looked into my eyes and began to speak. "My princess, my star," he said, "you are everything. You are talent, you are beauty, you are class! You are a movie-star, goddess, and sex-kitten rolled into one! You'd bring any man to his knees and I love you." I was blown away by this smattering of compliments, but before I could open my mouth to respond he added, "but it's still not enough. You are not enough."

"What?" I asked, not understanding.

"I want a house with a white picket fence and children laughing in the yard. I told you before that I'm going to have children. Why are you looking at me like this is a surprise?"

320

Exhausted from sex and from the conversation, with the ecstasy still working its magic in my system, I decided to let this go for now and drift off to sleep. The following morning, I went to work out and I couldn't stop hearing those words, *you're not enough*, echo through my mind. I was so confused. I flashed back to that night in the car with my dad, after I lost the Miss American Teenager America title. I loved my father and he loved me, but for some reason I always felt like I let him down. I wondered if this was my old demon, that 'I'm not enough' mantra I'd carried since childhood manifesting itself in the form of Jas Madison.

I decided to push what he'd said out of my thoughts. After all, I reasoned, it was probably just the drugs talking. All those things he said before about me being perfect—that's how he really felt. The holiday season was in full swing and I was busy decorating the house, buying gifts, and keeping up family traditions by taking my grandkids to Radio City and The Nutcracker. When Caitlin asked what plans Jas and I had for the holidays I found myself embarrassed and fumbling for something to say. The truth was, Jas and I had no plans. He had become increasingly distant. Most of the time he blamed work, but I knew something wasn't right.

The more red flags I saw, the tighter I closed my eyes. If I let myself see—really see—what was going on, I could not have gone on with the relationship. But I was so deeply in love, the thought of losing him seemed like a fate worse than death!

When Christmas approached, I hadn't seen Jas in nearly a month. I asked him what time he'd be arriving for Christmas Eve dinner and he told me he hadn't been planning on coming until the next day. Sensing my disappointment, he told me not to worry, he'd move some things around so he could be there. For Christmas, he bought me two tickets to the Alvin Ailey ballet and suggested I take Stacy, John's wife.

"Oh," I said, feeling hurt and confused, "you don't want to go with me?"

He forced a smile and said, "Oh! Yes, of course I do! I don't know why I said that." Then he kissed me, coldly on the cheek, and changed the subject.

CHAPTER 88

The Ball Drops on a New Year

·······························

Jas was ready to return to the city the day after Christmas when a huge snowstorm hit, making it impossible for him to leave. He made the best of being stuck with me, being useful around the house. He shoveled the driveway and hung two tapestries. We had a pleasant time, but as soon as the trains were running again, he wanted to get back. We agreed I would join him in the city for New Years' Eve—which turned out to be a disaster.

Because Jas had made no plans or reservations, we had to scramble to find a place that would take us for dinner, after which we headed to his cousin's annual party. In stark contrast to last year, when he proudly introduced me to his friends and stuck by my side like a man in love, Jas ditched me the moment we walked through the door. Within minutes, I spotted him dancing with (and drooling over) a young blond. The only time his hands left her hips was when they slid down to her ass, which was barely covered by her skimpy rhinestone encrusted dress. I could have really used a drink (or seven) but Jas and I had plans to spend the following day with his father and I'd vowed not to let myself be hungover. Sighing in resignation, I made a beeline for a tray of chocolate-chip cookies and systematically inhaled every last one.

Over the years, I had done my best to ward off the ravages of age and time; eating well (those cookies notwithstanding), exercising regularly, and even subjecting myself to a facelift (okay, two). But as good as I looked for a woman in her sixties—I was still, at the end of the day, a woman in my sixties. And there I was, alone at the snack table with a mouth full of cookies, glaring daggers at the twenty-year-old rhinestone tramp who had usurped my Jas. I could have really used a drink or seven—but Jas and I had plans to spend the following day with his father and I'd vowed not to let myself be all hungover. I was humiliated, my New Years' Eve ruined. Instead of dancing the night away in ecstasy, (the emotion, not the drug this time), I was wallowing in carbs and sugar.

Midnight rolled around and there was not a sign of Jas. A few minutes later he resurfaced to give me quick, passionless peck on the lips. In the cab, on the way home, almost nothing was said between us. Then suddenly, Jas pierced the silence by exclaiming, "I do everything for you! All I do is try to make you happy! It consumes me and I can't take it anymore! It's gone too far, I'm in too deep!"

"That's funny, Jas, I feel like it's the other way around."

"I can never live up to your standards, Kathalynn! You make me feel judged and inadequate. I'll never afford you! This all so fucked up!" When the driver pulled up to his building, he told me he was just too upset to make love and that I should go to sleep. Once in bed, he turned his back to me, inching as close to the far edge as he could without falling off.

The next morning, feeling a wreck from having tossed and turned all night, we headed to Long Island to visit his father as planned. On the ride out, he went on and on about the family he dreamed of having one day.

"Well, Jas," I said dryly, "Maybe I'll be your children's godmother."

"Now you're thinking! And we'll be lovers on the side!" Clearly my sarcasm eluded him, as my heart broke—because he meant it.

When we got back to Connecticut, it was well after midnight. Late as it was, Jas insisted we stay up, have a glass of wine, and talk.

"Kathalynn," he said, "I think we have become way too attached to each other."

"Is that a problem?" I asked, bewildered.

"It is for me," he replied coldly, "and I think it's time we take a break."

"A break?" I shrieked. "You mean as in break up?"

"How cruel the universe has been, to give me a gift that I cannot keep!"

"What gift?" I asked.

"You, Kathalynn! You are everything I've ever wanted in a woman, but you've come to me too late—twenty years too late!"

"Only twenty? If you're going to insult me, at least try to be accurate, Jas. You mean *thirty* years too late."

"It doesn't matter, Kathalynn, the point is you're too old! This whole thing just feels like a cruel cosmic joke on me."

"You're not making any sense, Jas. If there's someone else—please just tell me. Respect me that much."

"How can you ask me such a thing? Of course there's no one else! Do you want to read my texts?"

"No, Jas. I don't want to read anything, I just want this night to be over."

What a night. I'd gone from soulmate, to a gift he wanted to return to the store, to a cosmic joke. It was too much to take. I left my glass of wine, still half filled on the counter and went to bed. On my way, I passed the christmas tree, still alight and decorated. I'd have to take that down in the morning. Another year gone.

The following morning, I woke up with the dawn. Jas' weight on my bed like a weight on my heart, I couldn't breathe with him beside me. I forced him out of bed, shooing him down the stairs and out into the car. We rode in silence to the station. While parked below the platform, Jas began to sob, admitting his weakness as a man. He muttered some barely intelligible nonsense about how we were two masters of life—against the cruel world outside—whatever that meant. I had nothing to say. After what seemed like an eternity of sitting there, waiting, the southbound train arrived. He pecked me on the cheek and scurried up the stairs to catch it. The train departed toward Manhattan, taking my Jas, as well as my hopes and dreams with it.

Oh and by the way, of course there was somebody else.

CHAPTER 89

Loves Me, Loves Me Not

·····································

I resumed my life. I saw patients, worked out, got stronger, even trekked
to Queens to visit Arkady, my favorite spiritual healer. All this helped
me focus on what I could control. My divorce still in process, I prepared
to sell the house and return to my true home, Manhattan. The move was
as cleansing as it was practical. I sorted through my accumulated treasures, purging those which no longer served me.

I also used this time to release like mad. I forced myself to confront
the feelings of inadequacy that had driven me to attract a man like Jas.
He represented a mirroring of my internal fear of not being enough. With
that belief coloring the thoughts in my subconscious mind, it was no
wonder I drew into my life just the sort of man who'd confirm it. In addition, I'd been insecure about my age from the time I was a child. Most of
the time I just lied about it. Due to a combination of luck in the genetics
department and the fact that I spared no expense when it came to my
looks, I've never had trouble getting away with it. In fact, I'd always had
a sense I was born eight years too early. Was it a coincidence, then, Jas
being eight years my junior? I think not.

Jas wanted children, and for me that ship had sailed. It had sailed for
Jas too, of course, but in his mind at the time, he was virile. Fifty-four and
the world was still his oyster—all his best years ahead! He romanticized
fatherhood, having no experience of diapers and sleepless nights; and no
concept of the energy it would consume. Like Bob before him, he was
delusional.

Ironically, or perhaps predictably, the more I focused on releasing and
rebuilding my strength, the more Jas reached out to me on one pretense
or another. "Wasn't the latest snowstorm so beautiful and peaceful?"

he'd write, "but not so easy on the inside, when our desires and impulses take over and create their own madness!" He'd wax long and poetically about on my beauty, my brains, and my sensuality. But always with the caveat that it could never be. And when it came to light that he'd been engaging in romances with other women throughout the entire duration of our relationship, he blamed circumstance; reminding me that his need for a family of his own, combined with the misfortune of his inferior financial situation, made it necessary for him to keep options open, despite his desperate love for me.

What a crock.

PART V

New Worlds and Old: Finding Higher Ground

. . . .

Peace comes from Within.
Do not seek it Without.

—BUDDHA

CHAPTER 90

Regretting, Releasing, and Real Estate

....

Throughout the years my spiritual practice waxed and waned like the phases of the moon. When circumstances arose, triggering massive emotional reactions, I would often shelve my faith. Just when I needed it most, it would be in some neglected corner, collecting layers of dust. I'd see my sky become dark and the tide retreat. I knew the way out, but would not yield to the path of confrontation and work, even knowing that freedom was on the other side. Such was the case in my break-up with Jas. Why, one might wonder, wasn't my spiritual practice more helpful to me? Perhaps because the operative word in that question is *practice*. It had been some time since I'd honestly and sincerely checked in with myself; hence, I was spiritually *out* of practice. My efforts to 'release' on Jas were tainted, as my intention was always to change him, not myself, and thus I repeatedly violated the principle of what releasing is all about (poor Lester would be so disappointed, he'd be rolling over in his grave). But feeling, as I did, that his approval was as essential to me as the air I breathed, I simply *couldn't* let go. The intoxicating feeling of being in love, I attributed to him and him alone. I made him the source and sustenance of all my happiness.

Eventually and thankfully, however, no matter how far adrift I let myself go, I have always found my way back to Science of Mind and The Sedona Method. Every time I recommit to the path, my life and relationships improve, and I bask again in the light of a moon full and radiant.

My divorce became final in July. It was, as predicted, fraught with difficulty. I would receive eighteen percent alimony (which with Bob's now diminished earnings, was relatively modest). In addition, I kept the house, which Bob was willing to relinquish to me once he was happily settled into his new life in Greenwich Village. He got the lion's share of our one major investment. I put the house on the market and began to release.

Genevieve, now a writer and actress in her own right, wanted to use our house as the location for a film she had written and was going to star in. On the morning of the shoot, Ray, an actor in the project and friend of Genevieve's, complimented me on my lovely home. He asked me if it was true that I wanted to sell it. "Yes," I told him, "it's on the market." He then mentioned that he had a friend, Ed, who was married with a baby and looking to leave New York City for Connecticut. He suggested the two of us meet. What happened next was nothing short of kismet.

Ray's friend, Ed and his adorable wife, Ali fell madly in love with my house and wanted to make an offer on the spot, stopping short only because they did not yet have a buyer for their charming Upper East Side duplex. In a flash of genius, Ed suggested we trade theirs for mine! After some negotiations we made a deal that worked for both parties. We hired lawyers and did it all on the up and up with appropriate closing and purchasing on both ends. It was an inspired solution for both of us. At last, I would be back in New York where I belonged.

CHAPTER 91

Freedom in the City

....

I loved being back in my city—the streets I walked, the crowds I became part of, the staggering array of cultural offerings, the rich diversity at every turn—enchanted me. Moving on from the house in Connecticut and the baggage that came with it, especially the memories of the lonely years with Bob, freed me to reconnect with the single, pre-suburban woman I'd once been, and reclaim some of the joie de vivre I lost along the way.

Many of my Greenwich clients followed me to the city, and because most of my practice consisted of coaching with The Sedona Method, it could be done over the phone. This gave me purpose, certainly, but I knew there was something more to be mined from this phase of my life.

Jas and I did see each other from time to time, and it was during this interval that I was gradually, in stages—thanks to the inner work I was doing on myself and the healing miracles of time—able to forgive him, accept him as he was, and enjoy him without expectations or desperation to hang onto what was long gone. It didn't hurt that when Hurricane Sandy flooded his apartment and he stayed with me for several days I caught a glimpse of what life with him would be like 24/7: dining at 10:00 p.m., staying up into the wee hours, sleeping in till noon, switching on the TV (television during the daylight hours is a pet peeve of mine), having to navigate around clothing and belongings strewn carelessly about. I could see now how utterly impractical and disastrous marriage with him would be—not just because of his irritating habits or even his promiscuity but because, soul mates or not, our approaches to daily life were radically different. Mine included things like a sense of order, the joy of mornings, and the security of health insurance. We loved one another and still laughed a great deal together, but both of us could move on. I started dating other men. I was seeing life anew. I felt free and somehow lighter all around.

CHAPTER 92

The Promised Land

....

Mindful of the degree to which I had let much of my spiritual life languish, I sought reconnection to that part of myself through my travels.

Like India, Israel had intrigued me ever since I'd majored in world religions as an undergraduate. It also harkened back to my Jewish godmother, who, when I was a child, had plied me with doses of Yiddish and Bible stories along with her chicken soup. After Caitlin married an Israeli, making my grandchildren half Jewish, there was even one more reason to go. The problem was, I did not have the money for the trip.

I did have a beautiful three-carat diamond engagement ring I'd picked out when I was fifty years old, but once Bob and I were divorced, Caitlin noted that my wearing it might discourage potential suitors or give the wrong impression to the world at large, and she had a point. I decided to stow it in a safety deposit box for one of my daughters, but first I would have it cleaned.

Then I got a call from Roberto, my jeweler.

"Kathalynn, I have bad news. Your ring is cracked. Are you insured?"

"Yes, thank God," I told him.

When the company offered to replace the ring or pay me the value, I opted for the money, and the moment the check arrived I started planning my trip.

On my next visit to my spiritual healer, Arkady, an Orthodox Jew, I shared my intention to go to Israel. He was thrilled to hear this, and after explaining to him how I could afford it, he told me that for years the ring had protected me and was now giving me the gift that would change my life; it was destiny.

On an afternoon in June 2012, I landed in Tel Aviv. The moment we touched ground I felt a powerful surge of energy and excitement. Having studied the Old and New Testaments as well as the Qur'an, I was thrilled to be finally here, in the cradle of all three monotheistic religions. It seemed a culmination of years of studies and practice, almost a divine directive. I could not wait to plunge into all aspects of the Holy Land— the historical, the spiritual, the natural, the material.

Going straight to my surprisingly sleek and modern hotel, right across from the Mediterranean Sea, I was taken aback at the sight of the vibrant, sparkling cosmopolitan White City of '30s Bauhaus buildings. A broad promenade welcomed an active beach culture—volleyball, surfing, biking, the works. Jet-lagged yet too excited to stay put, I headed for the sea, slathered as usual in sunscreen on my fair skin and conditioner smeared all over my head to protect my hair.

The beach was lovely and filled with fit and beautiful people. Immediately after I jumped in the water, a wave took hold and I went under, and as I came up I felt arms around me that belonged to an exquisitely formed, magnificently handsome young man with black hair and turquoise eyes, the very definition of Adonis. *Oh my God*, I wondered. *Is this my personal 'welcome to the Holy Land' blessing?* As he held me while wave after wave came over us, he looked into my eyes. "I've been watching since you came onto the beach," he said smoothly, with an accent. "You are beautiful, and I want you."

Now, I'm no fool. I was in good condition for a woman of my age, but in my sixties I was no Aphrodite—especially coated with all that sunscreen—and adorable as he was, it was a bit late in the game for me to be taken in.

Extricating myself from his grip, I told him I was tired and needed to get out of the water and head back to my room. Might he join me? he asked. No, I said, I needed to rest. How about dinner? I refused, and when he wouldn't take no for an answer I agreed to meet him at the same time on the beach the following day.

The next morning, Ari, the guide who would be with me for the next two weeks, introduced me to this extraordinary city that so fully embraced the old and new. We wandered through streets of galleries and boutiques, stopping by the large, colorful Carmel Market, where a sharp aroma of exotic spices filled the air. We continued on to the vibrant outdoor Nachlat Binyamin arts-and-crafts market, where I found the delightful cafés and stalls simply enchanting.

I avoided the beach—and my persistent Adonis—until late afternoon, but once I was there I was prey to more circling young men seeking what I could only imagine was a sugar mommy. Seriously, I couldn't have a swim without being hit on. Finally, I told the girl at the hotel desk that I was having this problem. Her answer: "Welcome to the Middle East, Ms. blond-haired, blue-eyed woman. Deal with it!"

From Tel Aviv we drove to Haifa, my son-in-law's hometown, where from my hotel atop Mount Carmel I had a breathtaking view of the Mediterranean and the slopes leading to the Bahá'í Gardens and the Golden Dome Shrine.

I had decided, back in New York, that in Israel I'd buy myself a special piece of jewelry in place of my ring, as well as Christmas gifts for my daughters. Having traveled a bit, I knew better deals could be gotten with cash, especially American dollars, and so I'd left the States with a hefty $5,000 to cover all this. Yes, I know traveling with that kind of cash is stupid, and very soon I would learn just how stupid.

When I wandered into the jewelry shop in the hotel lobby, I found a beautiful gold necklace that was absolutely perfect. It was my last day in Haifa, and I had packed and checked out of my room. I had the envelope with the money in my zipped bag and took it out to pay the $1,000 for the piece. That's all I remember.

Ari joined me and we headed north for Tiberias, along the way stopping in a picturesque town where, I was told, the first Kabbalah center in the world was located, and where a powerful energy prevailed (and yes, Madonna had just visited the place). There in the charming artists' quarter near the center I spied, among unique jewelry and crafts, a necklace I knew would be perfect for Vanessa, and after negotiating a price I reached into my purse for the money, and—no envelope. Had I left it in my carry-on? We ran to the car and frantically searched every suitcase. Nothing. Had I been pickpocketed here in this village or back at the hotel? It didn't matter; the money was gone.

The drive to Tiberias was quiet. Ari, generous soul that he was, was greatly distressed on my behalf. I, however, felt no anger—only confusion. *This is the Holy Land!* I kept thinking. *Who gets robbed in the Holy Land?*

When we arrived, I changed into my bathing suit for a swim in the Sea of Galilee. I had to remind myself that this was the actual sea on which Jesus had walked. I'd read about these places in the Bible, of course, but now I was actually, physically there.

That evening, having dinner on the hotel patio, right on the sea, I sat alone, feeling sad as I thought about being pickpocketed and returning to my family empty-handed. At the table across from me, a man with compassionate-looking brown eyes was sitting with a small child and another older man. Upon noticing me, the man came over, and smiling warmly, picked up my plate of food and brought it to his table.

"Nobody should eat alone," he said. "You will join us!" Israelis, I was finding, seemed resolved to include this outsider. Then, after introducing me to his father and young son, out of nowhere he asked, "Why are you so sad?"

I shared what had happened and what was really bothering me. One reason I'd come to Israel was that I needed some more faith. Somewhere along the way, I had lost a lot of faith. I told him that being robbed had disappointed and disoriented me.

He looked at me and said, "Money? What is money? Nothing!" He grabbed my arm. "Do you have your arm?"

I nodded.

"Do you have your leg?"

I nodded.

He told me to look toward the sea, over which a magnificent full moon was hovering.

"Do you see that full moon?"

I nodded.

"Do you see the water?"

I nodded.

"Let me tell you something," he said. "Israel has so much light that it can be blinding, too much to take in all at once. The light is working on you and will continue to do so, and you will never be the same. You will make some huge changes in the next few years; be prepared. As far as the loss you had here, it was a lesson. The only important thing is your connection with the light. You have been too much with things, and that's not your real nature. You were not connected before you came here, and deep inside all you wanted was that connection—that is the faith you talk about. The light has connected you back. You have been blessed. Something will show you while you are here, I am certain of that."

This was a lot to take in. I never saw that man again, but his words will forever be with me.

The next day Ari took me to the Mount of the Beatitudes, site of the Sermon on the Mount. I got chills as I read the words of Jesus so familiar from Bible study because now I was where he'd actually given the sermon. Life-altering experiences were coming at me faster than I could process them. The man had been right; I was beginning to acknowledge that here there was so much light.

That light seemed to shine our way to our next stop, Jerusalem, where I had been waiting to go for what felt like forever. I spent the next few days putting myself completely into Ari's hands, knowing that once he left I would remain on my own for another week to explore the ancient city more fully. We floated in the unsinkable Dead Sea and stopped at Qumran, where the Dead Sea scrolls had been found. History came alive. In the Old City we strolled through the Muslim Quarter, Christian Quarter, Armenian Quarter, Jewish Quarter, and paused at the Western, or "Wailing" Wall, where I placed my little piece of white paper into the wall with my prayer request.

During our time together, Ari would occasionally mention that I was certain to have "my moment," when I would break down or have a great epiphany—everyone did, he said, even the most jaded celebrities and most hardened CEO's—but as in awe as I was of my surroundings and as grateful and even blessed as I felt I was to be there, I never broke down. I maintained an emotional distance I regretted but could do nothing about. *Was I even human?* I asked myself. "Somewhere the spirit will take hold of you," Ari assured me as we approached the Church of the Holy Sepulchre, in the Christian Quarter. "Many find it happens here."

In the church, beautiful and ornate, the place where Jesus was crucified and where his tomb lay, I retraced the path Jesus supposedly walked on the way to his death and took time at his tomb, and as much as I appreciated being there, still I felt nothing unusual. *Was I the most non-spiritual person alive? How in the world could I feel so little?*

Proceeding on to Bethlehem, now a Palestinian town just south of Jerusalem on the West Bank, Ari arranged to pass me over to a Palestinian guide at the border, who could not have been more accommodating, knowledgeable, funny, and eager to please. At the simple and lovely Church of the Nativity, where Jesus was said to be born, I knelt and meditated, feeling blessed and grateful. But nothing more.

Back in Jerusalem, as Ari and I said our goodbyes, he expressed some disappointed bewilderment over my not having had my "moment." In all his years as a guide, he told me, he had never met an American or European tourist who hadn't been moved to tears at some point or another. What could I say, I told him, feeling deficient and shallow. It wasn't like I could force it.

On my own the next day, I returned to the Church of the Holy Sepulchre in search of whatever it was that might tap some deeper response in me, but I left feeling no different than I had before. As I started back to the hotel, I gave my aching feet a break and sat on a bench. A woman next to me turned and asked what was wrong. My feet hurt, I said. "No, that's not what I mean," she replied. "You look unhappy. What's the problem?" I told her how strange I felt for not feeling more in this extraordinary place. "Darling," she said, "of course you feel nothing. You must go to Golgotha, 'the Place of the Skull.'"

I thanked her, headed out of the gate of the Old City, and tried to hail a cab, but when none appeared I started back to my hotel. Then I spied a gypsy cab stopped alongside the road—and by gypsy, I mean not only an unofficial cab but one driven by an actual Gypsy. I had been warned, of course, to avoid these people completely, but not being one to do what others told me, I popped my head inside the car window and asked the young driver if he could take me somewhere. Sure, he said, but he was waiting for his sister, who needed a ride home. That would not be a problem, I said. Sure enough, a minute later his sister appeared, wearing a long red skirt and lots of gold jewelry, just as she might have been costumed for a show. After dropping her off, he told me he was mine for the rest of the day.

We drove straight to Golgotha, where when walking in a little garden I met a young Muslim who told me I looked like an angel. Then a priest of some kind came to me and said he thought I need a prayer, and would I mind if he prayed for me. I accepted, and then he departed and returned with a lovely cotton prayer shawl and put it around my shoulders. "Please," he said, "accept my gift."

I wandered to the cliff, and there to my left, quite astonishingly, was the renowned skull in the stones. I got goosebumps. I had a vision of three crosses. This was the place where Jesus was crucified.

Sitting on a bench across from the rock that marked the burial place of Jesus, where he had risen from the grave, I felt a cool calm come over me. My mind-chatter stopped and I was relieved of all emotion. I felt no sensation rush down my spine, I saw no bright lights or colors, and I didn't shed one tear. All I felt was calm. I don't know how long I sat there in stillness. Time was irrelevant. When I finally did move, my first thought was *Don't try to figure this out.* No reasoning could explain this tranquility, this peace, what Philippians 4:7 calls "the peace of God that surpasses all understanding."

My Tiberius friend had been right; something in me was changed forever. I had indeed had my moment—not the moment I expected, full of tears and revelations, but something better. That gift of peace was within me now, and I never had to go anywhere to find it again.

The gypsy, whose name was Ben, became my guide for the rest of my time in Jerusalem, taking me to sights off the beaten track, some in Palestinian territory, where I always felt safe and welcome. After we said our goodbyes, I headed for Jordan, where yet another guide awaited, but to get there I had to cross over from Israel via the Allenby/King Hussein Bridge, which involved an Israeli representative waiting there with me while my passport and other papers were examined and reviewed, a tense and formal process right out of a movie.

My Jordanian guide took me to Mount Nebo, from where Moses first viewed the Promised Land. I could only imagine how that breathtaking view of the Jordan Valley and Dead Sea must have stirred him. We proceeded to the archeological "Rose City" of Petra, where on horseback we explored pink sandstone cliffs, soaring temples, treasury, elaborate royal tombs, burial chambers, and water channels—and I considered with some wonder the ancient civilization that had built it.

Each stop we made revealed yet another aspect and layer of what had come before us and informed what we had become. It was all alternately humbling and inspiring, as well as deeply spiritual, and I could see how, despite the realities of today's Middle East, the land and its history defied borders and politics.

It was time to return to Israel and then home. On our way, my guide stopped to point out Mount Sodom, from which rose a distinctive narrow mass pointing upward, in the shape of a woman. This was Lot's wife, he said, who had disobeyed God by looking back on the burning city she was fleeing from, and for that had been turned into a pillar of salt.

The lesson in this did not escape me. Never look back. Keep moving forward. A beautiful message on which to end my trip.

CHAPTER 93

Encore India

. . . .

My extraordinary experience in Israel and the depth it lent to my life only whetted my appetite for more of the same, and no place was calling to me louder than India.

This time I had no diamond ring with which to finance the journey. However, I did have an impressive collection of paintings, which were worth their weight in value. I'd began investing in art in my early twenties, as soon as I cashed my first few television commercial checks. Some of my favorite pieces were purchased with money left to me by my father, but the majority of them were spoils of my divorces from Bob and Mac. Having relocated from a massive estate in Connecticut to a comfortable but small apartment in New York, I had less need for wall ornaments such as these. Plus, I was spiritual now, and after my experience in Israel, I longed to free myself from the prison of belongings! (Okay, that's a joke.) The truth is, I didn't love the idea of selling my art, but adventure was calling and I needed the cash.

My destination this visit would be to the south where I would focus almost exclusively on yoga and meditation. I timed my trip perfectly and planned to arrive at the end of monsoon season, but the elements had not gotten the memo, and it poured for most of my trip. As the saying goes, 'We plan, God laughs...' Well, at least I got one spiritual lesson out of the way, right?

My guide knew I was eager to get to Pune, site of the once wild, old ashram of Rajneesh (aka Osho), which I heard had now been transformed into a magnificent international meditation resort. Having steered clear of it in its one-time, free-for-all heyday, I was curious to see it in its current incarnation. What I observed was a clean, beautiful, and tranquil retreat, accented with Buddhist and Zen elements, its ponds filled with koi fish and its huge swimming pool surrounded by trees and buddhas.

The atmosphere was serene, though the regulations were no joke. Osho, when alive, was terrified of the scourge that was HIV and AIDS. For this reason, all guests—even today, are required to submit to HIV and AIDS testing before entering the premises. Once there, everyone is outfitted in a maroon-colored robe, which signified oneness. These tasks dispatched, I joined a small international crowd in a large room where Dynamic Meditation was explained to us—a form of meditation I had explored some forty-five years before in New York. It was reassuring to see how the best of Osho's profound teachings had prevailed after all those crazy years. Still, it was enough to be a visitor and not a follower, and as planned I left after one day.

The highlight of this trip was in Cochin, where I meditated and did yoga twice a day with a master teacher who became my private mentor there. No distractions, no outside communication, plenty of rain. It was a challenge, and there were moments I thought I would go crazy, but it was also a great blessing. Meditation, the master explained, was all about awareness. Being an action-oriented person, I had always struggled a little with the concept of meditating. The reason for this, however, was that my preconceived understanding of what meditation was, exactly, was a little off. Nowhere in the rule book (that's a metaphor, by the way, there's no actual 'rule book') does it say that you have to sit cross-legged on a rock with your eyes closed to meditate. Anything can be a meditation, if it is done with awareness. Meditation is not to be used to escape the world, but rather, the opposite. Meditation is the practice of zeroing in on whatever is happening through and around you in the moment.

I shared with him my experience in Israel, where time had stood still and I had been immersed in an ocean of stillness and calm. It was a gift, he said, of having my mind stop for a few moments and actually be mindless. All that was left was awareness and my truest and most elemental nature, which was peace and calm, no more chaos or tension. But, I told him, I had *lost time* while I was in that peaceful state! Ah, he answered, but meditation went *beyond* time, time being only a construct of the mind. Mine had been a total experience of the present, without past or future; past and future were only in the mind. I had, without effort, been given a gift because we could not force these experiences.

The master teacher left me with these parting words: "Your mind is your servant, not your master. You have the ability to quiet it and direct it. When negative thoughts arise, and they will, you can let them go. When negative feelings arise, you can let them go. You are the master. Always remember this."

And of course I forget this sometimes, but not for long. His wisdom, like that of other great teachers in my life, has remained with me and informed my spiritual evolution. He provided me with a shift in perspective, for which I am eternally grateful.

CHAPTER 94

Taking Time, Taking Stock

·······························

The spiritual lessons gleaned while traveling brought me to a place of new understanding. From there, I was able to look at myself and my life with increased clarity and courage.

In 2012, Genevieve announced her intention to move to Los Angeles. She'd been out of school for six years and was beginning to make a name for herself in the New York City comedy scene but was feeling drawn to the West Coast. It had been a few years since I'd seen Garry Marshall, but I still had a number for him. I told her to give him a call, figuring maybe he'd take her out to lunch. Genevieve reported that it took about fifteen seconds for the two of them to become best friends. He invited her to audition for his theater's upcoming production of Neil Simon's *I Ought to Be in Pictures*. She booked the role. Genevieve would need a car for Los Angeles, so Bob drove her cross country in his old Subaru and then flew himself back, leaving her the car. Within a month, she totaled the sensible car and, using the insurance money, replaced it with an electric blue Sebring convertible, which she affectionately called "The Jesus Chrysler" (told you she was funny).

Sitting in the audience on Genevieve's opening night was one of my proudest moments as a parent—right up there with watching Vanessa graduate college with honors, Courtney get sworn in as a lawyer, and Caitlin achieve her master's and then marry the love of her life with whom she went on to have five fabulous children. Genevieve was sensational, and it warmed my heart to see her and Garry together. Their bond was truly remarkable, and I was reassured to know that my daughter had someone that upstanding and generous in her corner. As for finding myself in L.A. again, it was strangely invigorating for me to be back in the once-familiar town I had left behind and to see it with a new perspective.

Returning to New York, I wondered if I still had it in me to act— not necessarily as a career but as a conduit to help me understand and express whom I'd become in those ensuing years. Could I still put myself out there? I was honored to be accepted in an acting class taught by the brilliant Lyle Kessler, and I even did a short play, loosely based on the character of Mrs. Robinson from *The Graduate*. I played a character who seduced younger men on internet dating sites, by posing as her daughter. It was gratifying during this period to reconnect with the actress I once was, this time with no goal beyond exploring and creating in the present tense, with no concern for where it might "take" me professionally.

For the next few years, I visited Los Angeles with increasing frequency, enjoying quality time with some of my oldest and closest friends—Garry, Bill Cunningham, and Vicky, with whom I'd never lost touch. Although I'd been an East Coaster for nearly fifty years, the friends I'd held closest to my heart were all in California.

Meanwhile, things in New York were shifting in ways that were becoming less and less comfortable. The maintenance payments on my Manhattan co-op suddenly escalated at an alarming rate, and despite our friendship and new understanding, I was finding myself still vulnerable to Jas' yo-yo like behavior. I started to wonder if the universe was telling me something.

After three and a half years of living in the city, I was becoming restless, sensing I'd left something undone or abandoned. I kept thinking about my years in California and feeling that I needed to return. Now, Los Angeles, for all its hype—is polluted, the traffic is brutal, and at any moment, may fall into the Pacific Ocean. Why anyone would want to move there with all that in mind is beyond me. Especially considering the fact that I *love* Manhattan—I love everything about it! I felt safe, secure, and completely at home living there. I was thoroughly enjoying every one of its perks, which now included a community of actors I had grown to love. That being said, L.A. was calling me—and the call was relentless.

Determined to follow up on those feelings, and to the shock of many—including, at times, myself—I made a radical decision. I sold my co-op and packed up to relocate to Los Angeles, the place where dreams are made and sometimes even come true.

I had always looked for someone to fill me up—a prince to make me happy forever after, an enlightened being to help me heal and transform myself. By now I knew, through all the sadness and madness, that there was no prince or swami out there to rescue me. The swami is and has always been me. Wherever I am and wherever I go, the swami simultaneously surrounds me, watches over me, and resides within me. If I'd learned anything at all from the princes and frogs, swamis and stars, teachers and partners in and out of my life, it was that only by looking within, would I find that elusive acceptance of myself and trust that I would, in the end, be enough.

This time, on my journey flying west, I had much more with me than a Samsonite bag. Most of my life was behind me. I had been through two divorces, had four children, and was a grandmother of seven. I had become educated, even worldly. I had loved and lost. I was not the same girl who'd left Maryland forty-something years earlier.

The plane touched down and the captain's voice came over the intercom: "For those visiting, welcome to Los Angeles. It's a perfect day—clear skies, air quality good, and the temperature is eighty degrees. And for those of you who live here, welcome home."

Perhaps dying under a palm tree would not be so bad after all.

Acknowledgments

....

Special thanks to John Ryder, who encouraged me to write this book and offered support all the way.

Gratitude as well to my parents, Vanessa, Courtney, Caitlin, Kaylie, Shai, Aliana, Camille, Ireland, Boden, Jude, Margie Nolan, Garry Marshall, Jerry Belson, Bill Cunningham, Stella Adler, Bob McAndrews, Lyle Kessler, Eric Pace, Stuart Grayson, Michael Bernard Beckwith, Jay Scott Neale, James Mellon, Virginia Lloyd, Hale Dwoskin, Lester Levenson, Victoria Johnson, Hilde Gerst, Paul Harris, Ingrid McLachlan, Bethany Morgan, Arkady Yushuvayev, Richard Cohn, Susan Siefert, Lidia Ryder, Jeanne Delow, Karen Goldman, Eilhys England, Michael Kline, Michael Aronin, Steve Shur, and Sam Charney.

A special thank you to my Science of Mind friends, my Sedona Method friends, and my Gotham writers workshop teachers.

And appreciation to Kate Zentall, whose judgment, patience, expertise, and brilliance helped a struggling writer understand the art of a memoir.

Thank you to Jonathan Kirsch for his expertise and guidance and to Sara Stratton for her patience, dedication, and sense of humor that helped to bring this book to the world.

And a special thank you to Michi Turner, for her creativity, talent, and love.

The person I most want to thank is Genevieve Joy, who's been an inspiration with her patience, love, intelligence, talent, loyalty, and funny bone. She kept me truthful and authentic while encouraging me to dig deep into places I didn't want to revisit. Without her, I would still be rewriting the first section!

About the Author

....

KATHALYNN TURNER DAVIS is a life coach, psychotherapist, certified Sedona Method coach, high performance specialist and workshop leader, as well as an actress and writer.

Kathalynn has studied both Eastern and Western philosophies and teachings. She has traveled the globe to meet with many of the world-renowned teachers, swamis' avatars. In addition to her long psychotherapist and coaching practice, she has a body of work in film, television, and theater.

She is a graduate of Manhattanville College with a major in World Religion, as well as a masters (MSW) from Columbia University. Her life coaching certification is from New York University.

For more information, please visit Kathalynn's website: www.kathalynnturnerdavis.com.

To speak with Kathalynn directly, you may email her: kdavis9797@aol.com.